Mightier than the Sword

Alexander Tait

Published by Olida Publishing
www.olidapublishing.com

First printing: May 2014

Printed in the United Kingdom.

Cover Design: Paul and Joe Murdoch
Cover photograph: Paul Murdoch

ISBN: 978-1-907354-71-7
Other Titles by Alexander Tait...
Upon this Rock
ISBN: 978-1-907354-43-4
Whisky in the Jar
ISBN: 978-0-9558789-4-7
The Cup
ISBN: 978-1-907354-00-7

ACKNOWLEDGEMENTS

Publisher: Allan Sneddon and Editor: Ian Baillie
Some of the publications from which I took quotations,
information, or inspiration –
William Wallace: The King's Enemy by D.J. Gray
William Wallace by Andrew Fisher
The Acts and Deeds of Sir William Wallace by Blind Harry
The Wallace Book edited by Edward J. Cowan
The Book of Wallace by Rev. Dr. Charles Rogers
A History of Scotland by J. D. Mackie
Scotland: The Story of a Nation by Magnus Magnusson
Dumbarton Castle by I. M. M. MacPhail
Castle and Town of Dumbarton by Donald MacLeod
A Short History of Dumbartonshire by I. M. M. MacPhail
History of Dumbartonshire by John Irving
History of Dumbartonshire by Joseph Irving
Dumbarton Burgh Records: Joseph Irving
By the Rivers of Water by Iain Galbraith
Andrew Fletcher and the Treaty of Union by Paul H. Scott
       The Poems, Songs and Ballads of Robert Burns
Dirt & Deity: A Life of Robert Burns by Ian McIntyre
Memory & Identity: Personal Reflections by Pope John Paul II
A History of the English Speaking Peoples by Sir Winston Churchill
Salmond Against the Odds by David Torrance
"We in Scotland": Thatcherism in a Cold Climate
by David Torrance
The Sun
Glasgow Herald
Dumbarton Herald
Lennox Herald
Dumbarton and Vale of Leven Reporter

This book is dedicated in friendship to

David Campbell and Iain Johnston.

Introduction

The little man feared he had killed the giant. His stomach churned and he felt himself drenched in a cold sweat. Taken alive, they had said. He must be taken alive. It had been easy for them to say so – when they'd given him the little flask of the drug – to use enough to render the man helpless, but not to kill him. Well, just look at the size of him, lying there. All seven feet of him. Or so it seemed. He'd surely needed more to stupefy him than any normal man... than Kerlie there, for example. He glanced nervously at the other recumbent figure. So, he'd given the big man plenty. In a strong ale already fortified with whisky. They had no notion of how he'd had to screw up his courage to do it. Not that they cared, and, of course, he'd found himself between the devil and the deep blue sea – between the outlaw and the sheriff.

In the darkness and the silence – that terrible unnatural silence – he began to wonder if the soldiers really were out there. On the edge of hysteria he began to wonder if he'd run mad, if he'd imagined it all. Suddenly, lacerating these introspections like a dagger thrust, a deep, growling animal sound came from the giant. The little man's nerve broke. He scrambled up from his knees and bolted whimpering for the door.

They were there, all right. All sixty of them. Clad in chain-mail and armed to the teeth. They'd come on foot, so the outlaw wouldn't hear horses. From Saint Mungo's Cathedral and over the moor. Less than three miles as the August sun was setting over the Clyde.

The small man was roughly pushed aside as a dozen of them barged through the low doorway of the shepherd's hut. Three of them pounced on each of the big man's arms and legs in a manner which had been well practised. Kerlie had his throat cut almost casually. By the time their main captive recovered anything like consciousness they had him tightly bound, hands and feet, with a noose around his neck and half a dozen unsheathed swords inches from his face. When a kind of awareness came over him, his huge body jerked and strained ferociously against the ropes which bound him. Comprehension hit him like a bucket of freezing cold water. Automatically he twisted his head around looking for Kerlie. On seeing the prostrate figure on the earthen floor, he knew there was no hope. Eyes focussing on the points of those swords, he wordlessly accepted that it was all over. At last, it was all over.

He could not see the blood which had pumped from Kerlie's throat and he wondered if his friend was dead or alive. Realising they'd been drugged, he noticed that there was no sign of the little servant. The Judas.

He was now in a sitting position, his back against the rough logs of one of the walls of the hut. Long legs stretched out in front of him. The once-green tunic was soiled and ragged. The soles of the boots were almost worn through. The wild auburn hair and drooping moustaches had flecks of grey through them. The features were lined, skin sagging, dry and pasty. These last eight years had aged him prematurely. He was but thirty years old, yet looked twenty more. Only the eyes were still fiercely vital… and they gave his captors no mercy.

They were still afraid of him. Even though they had him helpless and at their mercy. The fear was palpable. It hung in the air like a foul smell. But there was more than fear. Most of these men felt shame. A shame which would cling to them all of their days. The bull-necked officer who led them was an exception. He was an ambitious man, and greedy. Orders were orders, and he intended to please his superiors. Never in all his years as a soldier had there come along a chance like this one to gain the favour of the men who mattered – all the way up to the King of England. He licked dry lips and removing the obviously unnecessary steel helmet, ran strong, fat fingers through the grey stubble of closely cropped hair. His cold blue eyes were pitiless but no match for those of the uncannily silent prisoner. He turned away and strode out into the evening air.

Around the hut, in a circle, stood four dozen of his men. Every one of them looking at him with an unspoken question. His curt nod was all the answer they needed, but there were no expressions of triumph. The officer turned and walked towards the little servant, who stood apart, head bowed.

"Go back to the cathedral. Report to the sheriff. Have them come now. You… you have done well."

The last words had been a matter of cynical policy. He despised the creature, but he was, after all, the sheriff's nephew, and civility, however insincere, cost nothing.

"Go now, and be swift."

James Stewart, known to his humiliation as "Jack Short", scurried onto the moor and began walking purposefully in the direction of the cathedral tower. Every so often he broke into a run. More than any attempt to make haste, it was a physical effort by which he vainly hoped to dispel the awful feelings of guilt which threatened to overwhelm him, for Jack Short felt more shame than any man there that night.

The officer watched him disappear into the dusk. There was a particular gesture the old soldier had in mind. A certain something which would enhance the sheriff's gratitude towards him and act as a reminder of this singular service. Not far from that lonely shepherd's hut there stood an old oak. In the undergrowth beside the tree, Jack Short had, as instructed, placed the outlaw's weapons when he'd first fallen into unconsciousness. There was a longbow, there were arrows, a dagger and, of course… the sword.

Watched by his men, the officer, using both hands, picked up that huge, heavy sword. His eyes followed the length of the wickedly sharp blade and he recalled some of the stories which men told about that weapon – terrible stories. Even to a hard and seasoned campaigner like himself, they were terrible stories.

It was not much more than an hour later when they heard the approaching riders. The giant, still closely guarded inside the hut, had yet to utter a word.

Jack Short was not with them. The sheriff was first to dismount. The ring of soldiers parted for him as, without so much as a glance at the officer, he strode urgently towards the hut. No matter. The arrogant knight could enjoy his moment of triumph. His flush of exhilaration and relief. Make his little speech to the outlaw – if he dared meet those eyes. Then would be the right moment for the officer to present the sword – a special symbolic gift for Sir John de Menteith, Sheriff and Keeper of Dumbarton Castle.

Church and Nation

*"Our native land is thus our heritage and it is also the whole
patrimony derived from that heritage. It refers to the land, the
territory, but more importantly, the concept of 'patria' includes the
values and the spiritual content that go to make up the culture of a
given nation."*
(Pope John Paul II)

I was nine years old. It was a Sunday morning. One of these
bracing spring days, with alternating blue skies and blustery
showers. I walked to the bottom of our street and crossed Bonhill
Bridge then turned northward. This was 1962. There weren't
many cars on the road and pedestrians were few and far between.
The long mile between the town of Alexandria and the village of
Jamestown in the Vale of Leven stretched alongside the river and
the derelict remains of buildings which had once been textile
factories.

Under a light raincoat I wore short-trousered Sunday best clothes
with highly polished brogue shoes. Around the halfway point I
passed a small, sordid red-brick building which was a gents public
toilet. It bore a sign reading "Stirling Road". A little further on,

across the street, to my right, stood Levenbank Terrace, where my father had been born and where my grandfather had died. Way ahead, I could see the steeple of Jamestown Parish Church – my destination, and I could hear the steady chime of the bell – a sacred sound I had known for as long as I could remember. Further on, forming the horizon to the north, was a gently rounded hill, *Ledrishmore*, the golden fields of which reminded me always of the "ploughman poet" – Robert Burns.

I reached the church and stopped there on the pavement by the gate. My attention focussed on a particular symbol which was painted on the wooden notice board there in front of the church. The Burning Bush – bright green leaves alight with little red and gold flames – and the silver and blue saltire of Saint Andrew, surrounded by a Latin motto – "*Nec Tamen Consumebatur*".

Years later I was to discover its meaning – *Yet it was not consumed*. That symbol, the centuries-old badge of the Church of Scotland, spoke to my soul. Instinctively I knew that it represented things important, things religious and historical. It evoked other words, the full meaning of which lay still beyond me, words like *Covenant* and *Reformation*. It was a symbol which had quiet dignity and power… and I loved it.

The doors of the church were not yet open. Boys and girls were beginning to arrive at the entrance of the adjacent church-hall. I ran over and went with them into the old building for one hour of Sunday School after which I'd join my parents, my grandmother and my aunt, seated on the family pew in the gallery of the Kirk.

Jamestown Parish Church was simply *the* House of God. I couldn't have told you then that it was just a modest village church which had been built by a Victorian industrialist to keep his workers on the straight and narrow. To my eye and to my mind the elegant dignity of that rosy-red soaring sandstone architecture was nothing less than magnificent. Not a mere annexe of Heaven, but rather it was my, almost literal, belief that God lived in a small dusty room high in that steeple. I visualised him, there, with his own divine hand, making people, in a pre-natal stage, as it were, with putty-like flesh taken from glass jars. From the wooden slatted windows of the bell-tower he looked down on the world and saw everything which happened in it.

My paternal grandmother was in her seventies, slim, erect, the personification of the dignified widow and very much a product of the Victorian Age in which she had been born. My father, in his forties, was of medium height and build. A handsome man with dark wavy hair and neatly trimmed moustache – strength, protection and authority – feeling the after effects of his Saturday night whisky. My aunt, his sister, also in her forties, an attractive spinster with the manner of a *memsahib*. My mother – three years younger than my father, good figure inclining to plumpness, dark brown curly hair, to my eye beautiful (when she wasn't annoyed with me) and with a certain snooty look adopted for the occasion. I was a red haired, small schoolboy, an only child and perhaps a little precocious.

There was a large congregation. The pews were filled. All ages were represented and everyone present wore their best clothes. In those days the church was revered perhaps more than any other institution. Its ministers and elders were accorded due respect. My grandfather had been an elder here.

There was, apart from anything else, a definite element of seeing and being seen. Men were bareheaded, women wore hats and "imperial mints" were soundlessly sucked. The focus of the internal architecture was the pulpit. High above the Communion Table, the font and the choir-stalls, the pulpit was surrounded by beautiful stained glass windows. Jesus with children, to the left, Jesus with the woman at the well, to the right; behind and above were the magnificent pipes of the organ reaching upward to the rose window which crowned all. Occupying the pulpit, wearing a simple black gown, was the Reverend J. Marshall Scoular, a relatively young man – in his early thirties perhaps. Very much an early 1960s minister, he probably told the first joke that had ever been uttered from that pulpit and he had the good looks of a character who might have appeared in an episode of *Perry Mason*. It was largely from this man and in this place, and from my parents, that I received Christianity. We sang hymns, prayed prayers, listened to Holy Scripture and heard sermons. Through the inexhaustible riches of the Bible I was regularly transported to the Holy Land of Old and New Testament times.

In that decade the United Kingdom was a Christian country. Most people were understood to have some degree of Christian belief. For myself, at that age, the teachings of my church were more or less scientific facts. Heaven and Hell were as real as America or the Soviet Union. The Bible was as factual as any school textbook. The Resurrection was as historically true as the Coronation of Queen Elizabeth the Second. At nine years old the adult world is rich with sophisticated mysteries, all the more so, therefore, the transcendent realms of theology and the spiritual. I had grasped, of course, the basic message of the Gospel (or so I thought), but there was much I heard in church which naturally lay beyond my understanding. All I needed to know, however, was that I was hearing the truth, as believed by my parents, by their parents before them, by all the adults around me and, as I assumed, by society at large. When the golden light of morning or of evening poured gently through these stained glass windows, I felt myself secure with my family and close to God.

*   *   *

It was Aunt Cathie who had the car. She was what was known in Scotland as a Health Visitor, which is to say she provided medical care for young children, and it was in this capacity that she had graduated from being a cyclist to being a motorist. She drove a little black Morris 1000 and I remember the registration number to this day (403 BGE). My father occupied the passenger seat, mother and I sat in the back. Gran had decided to stay at home that Sunday.

Half a mile out of Jamestown we passed Barrie's garage. The gold and red *Lion Rampant* flag which flew in the forecourt always set the tone for these trips as far as I was concerned. Leaving behind the post-industrial Vale of Leven the open fields of farming land stretched around us. Beyond the tiny village of Gartocharn a vista of Loch Lomond gifted itself to us in the north, then from Drymen we headed eastward towards the flat marshlands of Flanders Moss. Far off in the distance I could discern Stirling Castle high on its great grey rock. I had been taken there on several occasions and though it was now the headquarters of the Argyll and Sutherland Highlanders, its ancient buildings echoing the notes of bagpipes and bugles, I'd experienced an acute and potent sense of Scottish history in that fascinating seat of Stewart monarchs.

As we passed through the villages of Buchlyvie, Arnprior and Kippen, I sat quietly listening to the conversation of the adults. There was some discussion about a man who had been controversially found guilty of a murder in England and hanged. It had all been in the daily papers apparently. My father was trying to conceal his resentment at being a passenger while his sister did the driving. She hadn't long passed her test and he was keen to find fault. Sitting alongside me, my mother tensely attempted to soothe ruffled feathers with diplomatic interruptions. When we reached the end of that long stretch of road known as the Stirling Straights, and the castle loomed almost directly above us, rather than turning right into the town of Stirling, my aunt took a left then we crossed the River Forth and arrived at Causewayhead, where another impressive rocky hill, the Abbey Craig, formed the horizon and a great grey tower pointed towards the sky. The Wallace Monument.

In a car-park near the foot of the hill we all climbed out of the little black Morris. A footpath wound its way steeply up through the wooded slopes of the Abbey Craig, and as we walked I peered keenly among the trees and undergrowth quite convinced that the bones and the rusted weapons of ancient warriors could be found somewhere among the roots. At length we breathlessly reached the summit. Earlier the weather had turned cloudy, with a heavy shower of rain, but now the sun broke through and the blue sky and dripping leaves brought one of those moments of glorious springtime exhilaration.

I had been there before, but I still found the sight of those two hundred and twenty feet of sandstone reaching dizzily into the sky disturbingly awesome. There, up on a pedestal carved into the stone, stood an arresting bronze statue of the man himself.

William Wallace. In armour, chain-mail and helmet, the muscular and bearded hero raised his sword high with his right hand, while his left rested on the top of a shield. As I stood at the foot of this tower I could not help but feel an inexpressible correspondence with the steeple of Jamestown Parish Church.

My mother and aunt were laughing and only half-jokingly wondering aloud how they were going to manage to climb to the top. I noticed that my father had become quiet and sombre.

In the reception on the ground floor the adults bought tickets and I got hold of a free brochure. We then began to tackle the two hundred and forty-six steps of the stone spiral staircase, my father gruffly telling me to take care not to scuff the toes of my brogues. Beautiful stained glass windows radiated by spring sunlight reinforced for me the religious atmosphere. On the first landing there was a room in which one learned the story of the great Wallace, and there, in a large glass-lidded case lay the hero's huge two-handed sword. The sacred relic in the Holy of Holies. I gazed at it and tried to impress on myself the fact that William Wallace had actually held this thing in his hands, but somehow I just couldn't entirely make that leap of the imagination.

My rough understanding was that hundreds of years ago the English had invaded Scotland. This was self-evidently a bad thing. The English King Edward was arrogant and cruel, as were his soldiers, and they had no right to be here. Although most of Scotland's wealthy and powerful men had submitted to this indignity, the young Wallace was for having none of it. Over a short period he turned a small band of followers into a great army of common Scots folk who won an epic battle against the English at Stirling Bridge. It was because William Wallace had commanded his soldiers from up here on the Abbey Craig on that day that the monument had been built on this spot.

On our breathless way to the top of the tower, we passed through the "Hall of Heroes", where I was pleased to observe a marble bust of Robert Burns, for whom I had a great admiration thanks to my father's influence.

Finally we emerged into open air and bright sunlight at the crown of the monument. With the height of the hill added to that of the monument, we were some six hundred feet above the surrounding countryside. I was not entirely at ease with this and the parapet wall seemed just a little on the low side for my comfort. Even so, my father put his arm around me protectively, mother and aunt nervously counselling caution, and he steered me gently over to the wall. The views an all directions were breathtaking. Far below on the wide plain the River Forth flowed in great winding loops. Stirling town and castle were at no great distance, but on the distant western horizon we could see the mountains of the Highlands and, very much closer, to the east stretched the Ochil Hills. These steep hills were especially significant. My grandfather had been born in Alloa on the bank of the Forth, just beneath the Ochils, and his forefathers had come from the little Perthshire village of Blackford, over on the other side of the range. This was, then, very much the land of my kin.

Experiences such as these – formative encounters with religion and history – infused my soul with a potent sense of the interconnectedness of Church and Nation. I was to become increasingly preoccupied with this concept as I grew to manhood.

*   *   *

I was later to discover that this had been a day of two heroes. I had not known it at the time, but my father had a terror of heights.

*   *   *

Where Pappert Burn tumbled down off the hill and joined the swiftly-flowing River Leven, the clachan of Bonhill clustered around a little stone church. Around half a mile upstream was the Pool of Lynbren where a community of Cluniac monks from the Abbey of Paisley had been granted rights to fish the river for salmon, and not far from their nets the monks operated a ferry. At the end of the thirteenth century it was customary for the Church to provide accommodation for travellers. This was 1296. Accordingly the tall young man who sat brooding by the riverbank had been given basic board and lodging by the monks in the little ferry-house of Bonhill.

The parish church had been founded by one of the Earls of Lennox, and the stronghold of the present earl was situated strategically just two miles northward at Balloch, where the waters of Loch Lomond emptied themselves into the Leven on its swirling journey to Dumbarton Rock and the Firth of Clyde.

William Wallace sat by the ferry staring darkly and unseeing into those waters. He was sorely troubled and close to tears. There was not a day, not an hour, that he did not think of his father, that he did not long for the sight, the sound and even the very smell of him. He was experiencing the strange paradox of feeling his father's presence, his close and loving nearness, yet knowing that he would never hear his voice nor see his smile again this side of the grave. Since earliest childhood his every endeavour had been to please his father and to make him proud. Now there was this terrible emptiness, pointlessness... and burning hatred. He had thought that the act of vengeance might have brought some satisfaction, but it had not. He had not struck the fatal blow himself, had not even seen it done, so involved had he been otherwhere in yon melee. Boyd had done it for him. Wallace managed a hack at the Englishman, but Boyd had delivered the killing thrust. Then, when the fight was over, when the other English had fled leaving dead and wounded, there was just a corpse. A dead nothing which probably hadn't even known why it had died.

There, on the bare shoulder of Loudoun Hill, William Wallace had realised that this man, Fenwick, had been but an instrument of English barbarity, a symbol of the English mentality – their cold arrogance and that unquestioned assumption of superiority which seemed to be ingrained in them. They were a people who felt that every other race was beneath them, and Wallace burned with the knowledge that he'd spend the rest of his days hacking the bastards down to size.

Now he raised his eyes to the cold, grey sky above Strathleven and silently asked the Blessed Virgin how things had come to this.

*   *   *

There had been, it is written, a time of peace and plenty... relatively so. Peace, specifically, between Scotland and England, and prosperity by the standards of the day. The nation's burghs had flourished and foreign trade had been good. Exports included wool, timber, furs, beef and fish. The Church had become better

organised and increasingly effective in the life of the nation. The
Treaty of York in 1237 had implied English recognition of
Scotland's independence. Then in 1251 Alexander III of Scots
had married Margaret, daughter of Henry III of England,
enhancing the already friendly relations between the realms. In
1266 the Treaty of Perth had secured the Western Isles for
Scotland and put an end to recurring hostilities with Norway.
Occasional attempts by the English to assert "overlordship" over
Scotland had been resisted by diplomacy.

This happy state of affairs was shattered by a series of tragedies.
Over the span of a decade Alexander's English wife had died, as
had his two sons and his daughter. The Princess Margaret had
been married to King Erik II of Norway. On her death, her
daughter (Alexander's granddaughter), an infant remembered as
the "Maid of Norway", became the heir to Scotland's throne. The
prospect of a child queen unsettled Scottish nerves, but Alexander,
in October 1285, married Yolande de Dreux, a French
noblewoman, and it was widely hoped that he would father a
male heir.

One stormy might in the month of March 1286, Alexander
presided over a council in the castle of Edinburgh. Business over,
the company fell to feasting and drinking. At length the king,
possibly affected by wine and amorous desires, announced his
intention to return to his new wife, who awaited him in Kinghorn
in Fife. Scorning wise advice to remain safely within Edinburgh
castle's walls, Alexander insisted on taking the ferry over the Firth
of Forth, landing after a rough crossing at Inverkeithing on the
northern shore. He had an escort of horsemen, but in the
darkness and snowy squalls the king became detached from his
company. Horse and rider apparently strayed over the edge of a

cliff and in the morning Alexander's body was found on the shore. The king had a broken neck and Scotland had a three-year-old queen.

Six Guardians were appointed to govern the realm. The Scots regarded the prospect of a royal marriage between their new queen and an English prince positively as a step towards enduring friendship and peace between the two nations. Edward I of England, however, saw such a development as a means by which he would take over Scotland. Although the Treaty of Birgham in 1290 guaranteed the continuing independence of the Scottish realm and the Scottish Church, Edward was demanding control over all Scottish castles. He then announced that "he had it in his mind to bring under his dominion the king and the realm of Scotland, in the same manner that he had subdued the kingdom of Wales."

In September of 1290 the Maid of Norway set sail from that land for the port of Leith. There were heavy storms and the little queen, never having enjoyed robust health apparently, perished on the journey.

There was no clear and indisputable heir to the Scottish throne, but a number of men from the nation's leading families came forward to contend for it. Eventually there were no fewer than thirteen competitors for the crown, prominently Robert Bruce, Lord of Annandale – grandfather of the eventual Hero King – and John Balliol, Lord of Galloway. In spite of Edward of England's clearly stated intention to seize Scotland for himself, the guardians incredibly asked him to be overseer and arbiter in the matter of choosing the rightful King of Scots. Edward summoned the Scots leadership to his castle of Norham in May of 1291. He demanded that the Scots should accept him as "Lord Superior of Scotland". Naturally this provoked indignation, but each of the competitors submitted to it presumably because they hoped to gain favour with Edward. It should be noted that many of the Scottish nobles, in accordance with feudal requirement, routinely paid homage to Edward for their extensive lands in his realm.

In June the King of England toured Scotland, replacing Scottish officials with Englishmen of his choosing and demanding that all Scots should pay homage to him. Those who refused were arrested and detained. Eventually, in November of 1292, Edward presided over the appointment of John Balliol as the new king for Scotland. He was probably the rightful claimant, but it happened also that his personality suited Edward's purposes. To further emphasise his mastery, the English monarch forced Balliol to swear allegiance to him as his Lord Superior, and Scotland's Great Seal was destroyed, the fragments being placed in the English treasury.

Over the next couple of years, Edward tormented King John with a series of calculated insults and humiliations, eventually ordering him to muster a Scots army to assist the English in one of their interminable wars against the French. The Scots finally summoned the courage to defy Edward, and far from fighting the French they made an alliance with them. The English king was indignant. He raised an army of nearly thirty thousand men and headed north. The Scots prepared for war and moved against Carlisle. On the 30th of March 1296 Edward's army attacked Scotland's royal burgh of Berwick. The English massacred every man, woman and child they found in the town. It is said that the butchery continued for several days with Edward calling a halt only when he saw a woman being hacked to death while she was in the process of giving birth. The atrocities of Berwick set the tone for the unrestrained savageries of both sides in what was to become known as the Scottish Wars of Independence.

By the summer Scotland was a defeated and occupied nation. King John abdicated and was ritually humiliated before being imprisoned in the Tower of London. Edward stole or destroyed every object or document which had borne witness to or symbolised Scotland's nationhood. In August he held a "parliament" – in Berwick – at which every landholder, churchman and burgess in Scotland, who had not already done so, was required to place his name and seal on a document swearing allegiance to the King of England.

Sir Malcolm Wallace of Elderslie, was one of those who had refused to sign this "Ragman Roll". As a result he had been hunted down and killed by English military at Loudoun Hill in Ayrshire. The soldiers responsible had been commanded by the man Fenwick.

*   *   *

There was rather more to William Wallace receiving the hospitality of the Levenside monks than simply that it was the custom of the day. The young man had two uncles who were priests, one based near Cambuskenneth Abbey and the other not far from Dundee. Wallace, himself, had received his early education from the monks at Paisley Abbey, and arising from this he actually knew personally a couple of the brothers here in Bonhill Parish. It had even been suggested, some few years earlier, that he might become a priest himself and he had gone on to further schooling in Dundee, where he'd become competent in

Latin and French. Of course he was fluent in his native tongues of Scots and Gaelic.

The English had not been content to dominate the realm of Scotland, they had also made moves to take over the running of the Scottish Church. Not only had they long contended that the Scottish Church should come under the authority of the archbishopric of York, but Edward had replaced Scottish church officials with English ones. Accordingly, there were now no more determined opponents of English domination than Scots churchmen. Indeed Robert Wishart, Bishop of Glasgow, was destined to be one of the foremost leaders of the Scottish resistance.

Wispy flakes of snow from a heavy sky had started to fall into the Leven's swift current when Wallace heard the approach, from Lynbren Pool upstream, of two of his companions and one of the brothers. Their faces were as grave as his own.

"You should hear this, Will."

William Wallace was in his mid-twenties. An exceptionally tall young man, he had a lean, muscular and athletic build. He wore his thick auburn hair long, and his features, with down-curving moustaches, though now expressing a grim determination, were generally pleasing, except when he was roused and his cool blue eyes flashed a terrible anger.

The man who had spoken was Thomas Gray. Perhaps five years or so older than Wallace, Gray had been a parish priest in Liberton, near Edinburgh, until he had joined the rebel's company as a combatant and semi-official spiritual advisor.

"Word has come from Glasgow. They held some sort of council, and you have been declared an outlaw…"
To the surprise of his associates, the big man's face lightened. The eyes shone with an ironic twinkle and he raised his head skyward again, this time to laugh, to bellow, with an enjoyment of the situation which was entirely unfeigned.

"Outlaw? This has taken them long enough. What have I been to them this year past, then?"

"Aye, Will… Aye, but this is different, this is *official*, a bigger thing altogether. They've made a public proclamation. Anyone caught hiding you, communicating with you, aiding you or associating with you in any way, will be arrested and face the wrath of these English…"

The speaker this time was Brother Andrew, one of the Bonhill monks known to Wallace from his Paisley Abbey days.

"In the past they've regarded you as a brawler, a killer, yes, but a hot-head acting more or less alone, and always able to slip out of their net. But now… since Loudoun Hill and Cathcart – man, you've become a serious military threat. You lead a sizeable company of volunteers. You've robbed them of goods and gear. More than that, you've made them a laughing stock. Throughout the land men are hearing of the English being bested, and they are taking heart."

Another man spoke out. This was "Kerlie" – William Kerr – of an age with Wallace, dirty blond hair, teeth like a horse, and a bruiser devoted to his leader.

"He's right, Will. Percy can't let this pass. He'll really have to hunt you down now, or his own head will roll. Edward himself will hear of it and there'll be Hell to pay."

*   *   *

Wallace did, indeed, have form. There had been a time, when he was a student in Dundee, that he'd been walking in the market-place. Minding his own business, in as much as he was capable of such. A group of well-dressed, conspicuously armed and loudly arrogant young Englishmen had been pushing people around, helping themselves to goods without making payment, and generally indulging themselves in provocative behaviour. Of course, there had been good-looking young Scotswomen nearby, and these antics had been, in part at least, intended to impress them. Wallace with his height and bearing had not been long in coming to the attention of the bully-boys. It had been the Scotsman's habit to wear a Highland plaid at that time and the foremost of the English braggarts had made some derogatory comment about the garment in a voice deliberately pitched so that Wallace would hear and respond. Which he had. From beneath the plaid Wallace drew a dirk and murdered the man on the spot. Unfortunately, the dead youth turned out to be the son of one Selby, the English constable of Dundee. Wallace had been lucky to escape from the town alive. But he was to make a habit of such luck.

Some time later, when he'd been lying low in Riccarton in Ayrshire, he'd gone for a quiet day's fishing in the Irvine Water. At the time Sir Henry de Percy had been Warden of Galloway and Ayr and it happened that some of Percy's men came by and tried to take some of Wallace's catch from him. One thing had led to another and Wallace had killed three of them.

Then there had been a more serious affair. Another tangle in another market-place. This time it had been in Ayr. Some dispute had arisen with one of Percy's stewards. Yet again it had resulted in the official finding himself on the wrong end of Wallace's blade. This time, however, a large body of English soldiers had swarmed out of their garrison and the big Scotsman had been captured. Thrown into a foul dungeon, injured and then deliberately starved, Wallace had fallen into a state of unconsciousness which had been mistaken by his captors for death. His "corpse" had been dumped without ceremony, but supporters discreetly recovered him and he'd been almost miraculously nursed back to health.

Word of this had spread. Many saw this "resurrection" as a sign. Followers, longing to strike back in some way against the English occupiers, came to join the ever-growing band of Wallace's company, which now numbered around two hundred. They marked time deep in the Forest of Clydesdale awaiting developments and circumstances which would provide an opportunity to strike a further blow. Such news was not long in reaching them.

A convoy of wagons carrying supplies and treasures stolen from Scottish churches was on its way from Carlisle to Ayr. It was, they were informed, guarded by one hundred and eighty horsemen. Wallace held a council of war with his closest lieutenants, including Kerlie, Gray and a cousin of his own, Sir Robert Boyd (whose father had also been murdered for refusing to swear allegiance to Edward). An ambush was the obvious course of action, and, if wisely planned, they need hazard no more than fifty of their own company. Preparations had been well underway when further word reached them – the English officer commanding the convoy was none other than Fenwick, the man who had slain Wallace's father.

William Wallace was now a man possessed, but it was the cold and calculating devil of revenge which drove him. In the event, the ambush had gone largely according to plan. At the eastern end of the Irvine Valley, beneath the rocky outcrop of Loudoun Hill, there had been a gully in which the English had been effectively trapped and surprised. It had proved far less easy than he had hoped for Wallace to get to grips with the man Fenwick. In the noisy confusion of rearing horses and hand-to-hand combat, the Scots leader had been able only, with his long, two-handed sword, to inflict a severe wound on the English officer's leg. Thereafter, as Fenwick had lain bleeding and unconscious with shock, it had been Sir Robert Boyd who had butchered him with multiple stab wounds from his short-sword. By the end of the clash around a hundred of the English company had been killed, their surviving comrades-at-arms fleeing in disarray for Ayr.

From Loudoun Hill the rebels had returned to their base, deep in the Forest of Clydesdale, where their relatively few dead were buried with due reverence. After a suitable period of rest and healing for those who required it, the religious treasures had been securely concealed at a location, not too far from their headquarters and known only to Wallace's innermost circle. It had been agreed that it would be much more sensible to let the churchmen recover their own goods, rather than have the resistance men take needless risks transporting them through a land crawling with English soldiers. Will, accompanied only by

Kerlie and Gray, had proceeded, on foot and with great caution, north-westwards along the course of the Clyde towards Glasgow's great cathedral of St Mungo. Wallace sought guidance from Robert Wishart, Bishop of Glasgow.

On reaching that busy port, which had been thick with English military and English churchmen, after a great deal of surreptitious ducking and diving, in heavy disguise, and without actually gaining admittance to either the cathedral itself, or the nearby Bishop's Palace, they had received word, relayed through a chain of sympathetic Scots priests, that the Bishop was not presently in the town, but had gone north to Loch Lomondside, there to confer on matters allegedly ecclesiastic with the Earl of Lennox. Oddly though this had sounded, Wallace and his men had no reason to doubt it, and indeed they'd been hastened on their way with a dire warning that Percy had summoned English officers from far and wide to a meeting in the morrow which was, so the talk went, certain to concern Wallace and his recent outrages. Glasgow was no place for him and his.

*   *   *

So it had been another twenty weary miles, under cover of darkness, by the north bank of the widening River Clyde, wary of English patrols and giving the Royal Burgh of Dumbarton, with its English occupied castle, a wide berth, and on into Strathleven.

*   *   *

As the four men stood talking beside the Ferryhouse of Bonhill, a single horseman, wearing a surcoat in the red and white of Lennox, came riding at a canter along the riverbank from the north. This was the eagerly awaited messenger from Balloch Castle. He dismounted and strode briskly towards the company, bowing briefly to Brother Andrew, then addressing Wallace directly.

"His Lordship will be pleased if you will accept his hospitality..."

"Aye... We will be honoured so to do," replied Wallace almost abruptly and with a grave inclination of his head.

The messenger appeared embarrassed when he discovered that the three travellers were without mounts, and offered to have suitable beasts sent down for them forthwith. Wallace quickly eyed his companions with an unspoken question, then turned again to the horseman.

"There will be no need to trouble yourself on that account. It is but a short distance to the castle and the walk will clear our heads, for we have slept late this day."

The man looked distinctly doubtful. Evening was falling and the thickening snow was beginning to lie. He shrugged, raised a gauntleted hand in a swift gesture of parting, mounted without further ado and rode off.

Shortly thereafter Brother Andrew arranged for his three guests to be ferried over the river. There, on the eastern bank, they walked at a leisurely pace in the dusk through the reedy fields along Levenside.

*   *   *

Balloch Castle had been the seat of the Earls of Lennox since 1238. It was not large, but a good, solid stone structure, surrounded by a moat and situated in such a way as to control all of the small shipping between Loch Lomond and the River Leven. Indeed, the very name "Lennox" derived from the Gaelic *leamhnachd* or *Levenachs*, "the fields of the Leven" and *Levenax* was the Latin usage as it appeared in mediaeval charters.

It had been fully dark, with snow lying thick on the land, by the time Wallace, Kerlie and Gray had approached the stronghold. Eerily lit by flickering torches, its walls loomed high above them. They had, of course, been expected, and gained entry without difficulty, being led directly into the great hall which was brightly-lit with an abundance of torches and candles, and a welcome warmth came from one vast fireplace where a fierce blaze was fuelled by aromatic pine logs. Five men sat around the head of a long feasting-board. Foremost, naturally, was Malcolm, Earl of Lennox. Now in his mid-sixties, with a head of thick, silver hair, and fleshy, florid features, the aquiline nose and small, finely-shaped mouth suggested that he'd been a handsome man. Over an emerald tunic and belt of gold, he wore a plaid of striking tartan. The earls of Lennox were of Celtic ancestry and here, on the Highland Line, culture and language were Gaelic. At the sight of Wallace, he got to his feet and strode eagerly forward, hand outstretched and face beaming.

"From your height, young man, you must be William Wallace. It warms my heart to shake you by the hand. We have heard much of your doings, here at Balloch, and we... we approve!"

This effusive greeting from one of Scotland's earls surprised and embarrassed Will. He gripped the offered hand and mumbled introductions for Kerlie and Gray. Lennox acknowledged these politely and made his own introductions, the first being of Robert Wishart, Bishop of Glasgow, who had also left his seat to greet the newcomers.

"William and I are not strangers, my lord. We have met before, in the company of his uncles, worthy servants of Christ's Church in this land."

The bishop was of an age with Lennox, but better preserved, leaner and possessed of fine strong features with clear grey eyes. Dressed in official bishop's attire, lacking only the mitre – even his crosier lay propped against the chair he had vacated – he made an impressive figure.

"I understand you have come all this way from Glasgow to see myself."

The eyebrows were upraised quizzically. His gaze took in all three travellers.

The others present turned out to be stewards of the earl. The guests were bidden to table and they gratefully joined in the meal, being much in need of refreshment. It transpired that the bishop was here at Loch Lomond for the purpose of an investigation into the life, death and – in particular – the relics, of Saint Kessog. Apparently it was not clear whether Kessog had been a prince of Strathclyde, or whether he had come over from Ireland, but in 510 A.D. he had established himself on the island of Inchtavannach, near Luss, on Loch Lomond – the island of the monks' dwelling – bringing the light of Christianity to the people of these green forests, hills and glens. There in that magical setting

– a mere seven miles to the north of this castle of Balloch – Kessog had built up a community of monks and trained them for the work of evangelism. These labours having predated St. Columba's settlement on Iona by several decades.

From Loch Lomond, Saint Kessog and his monks had set out on missions to the Scots of Dalriada in the west, to the Picts of the north and east, and to the Britons in the south. He had been a brave man who'd lived in violent times. There had been, in his day, savage warfare between peoples and faiths. Kessog, though primarily a man of peace who had preached the God of Love, had nevertheless been trained in the use of arms, indeed – of particular interest to Wallace, himself a renowned bowman – Kessog was remembered as an archer. His had been an age in which the spiritual and martial forces of Christian peoples and those of older pagan religions had yet been pitted against each other in epic conflict, with much ebb and flow over the centuries. Saint Kessog had died a violent death about which there was some mystery. He had either been murdered (possibly by his adversaries the Druids at the time of their new year rituals) at Bandry Bay near Luss, or he been killed in battle around 540 A.D. The point was that Kessog had a become a bishop and was remembered as the special saint of Loch Lomond and the Lennox. But far more than this – Saint Kessog had been regarded as *Scotland's* patron saint before the adoption of Saint Andrew.

Luss had become a place of pilgrimage, and Robert Wishart was here at Loch Lomond specifically to seek out Kessog's Holy Bell. To the ancient Church the bell had symbolised the voice of God and the monastic communities of the Celtic Church had used special bells which were ritually blessed and greatly venerated. They were used for both practical and spiritual purposes – calling to prayer and worship, casting out of evil spirits, healing and celebration. The Bishop of Glasgow well knew these things, but he also knew the power of such a relic to inspire soldiers if it were carried before them in battle, invoking the support and protection of the saint in question. It was this purpose in particular which had brought him here.

Normally a bishop would, of course, have delegated a task of this sort to lesser clergy, but this business of Kessog's bell had given him an excuse to visit the earl and privately discuss matters political and military.

The following morning brought clear blue skies. Will and his companions stood awhile on the shore of Loch Lomond looking northward and appreciating the splendour of the scenery. Stretched before them, ruffled gently by a Spring breeze, were the waters of the loch, here at its broadest. In the distance Inchmurrin, southernmost of that lake's many islands, could be clearly seen, and all around the magnificent snow-clad hills, the head and shoulders of Ben Lomond further to the north dominating all. Will's eye was drawn naturally to the gentle contours of nearby Glen Finlas on the loch's western bank.

At no great distance from Balloch Castle there was a small chapel, and it was there, that morning, that Will was granted a private meeting with Wishart. Wallace's reasons for seeking an interview with Scotland's second most important churchman were, in fact, threefold. Firstly he wanted to acquaint the bishop with the secret location of the church treasures, so that arrangements might be made for the clergy to recover it. Secondly, Wishart being known as a zealous advocate of resistance against the English, Wallace sought his advice on how to proceed in that regard. How most effectively to deploy his forces. Thirdly, that young man sought spiritual guidance.

As far as the ecclesiastic treasure was concerned, Wishart expressed sincere delight and gratitude, while deploring the loss of life involved, assuring the younger man that he would, in due course, set in motion arrangements for recovery. The Church was the best informed institution in the land, so the bishop had a fair knowledge of the exploits of Wallace and his followers. His admiration was, however, tempered with caution.

"Word of these episodes, your doings, especially this of Loudoun Hill, has spread throughout the land. Not always, I suspect, with fullest accuracy, but a little exaggeration in such things is all to the good. The common folk are greatly encouraged when they hear of the English being humiliated, even when your victories have been small ones. It is no wonder that men from far and wide flock to you, William, but I fear there is a limit to what can be achieved by a band of men such as yours, however valiant and well-led."

Wallace nodded soberly. He had a fair notion of what was coming. Wishart continued.

"We will only rid our land of these English if we have well-armed and disciplined bodies of men led by the great landowning lords. The nobles who hold – or held – the important offices of state. I need not tell you, William, that our Scots lords have till now been overly concerned with self-interest – their lands in England and Edward's favour – to hazard all in the cause of Scotland's freedom. Too many of these men lack a sense of national belonging. They are Norman none too far back, most of them. Granted Scottish lands by David First, of blessed memory.

Married into our Celtic families, some of them. But they think of themselves as Norman lords before they regard themselves as Scots. Nearly all of them pledged allegiance to Edward as a matter of expediency, without a pang of conscience. I wept sore tears, William, when I heard of the fate of your brave father. Murdered for his refusal to bow down to them. With these others it has been all land and power, before king and country. They have no understanding of the concept of patriotism and little care for John Balliol, but if we are to lead a successful campaign against Edward, then it must be done in the name of our rightful King John. You may depend on our Scottish Church. As you know, the English have long sought to rule it from York or Canterbury, have been tugging at the sleeve of the Pope for his support in this. Now we have these English clergy supplanting our own priests. It is insufferable. Not to be tolerated. Why cannot the English ever be content with what is their own?"

Wallace had reasoned all of this out for himself. All of these opinions he shared, these bitter facts he had known, but it was needful that he heard Wishart confirm his conclusions. He tugged sombrely at one of his down-turning moustaches as the old bishop carried on.

"James the Steward, Lord of Renfrew, under whom you Wallaces hold your lands, he is true. He will lead and, given the proper circumstances, others might follow, in due season. But for you, you and your band?"

Wishart raised his eyes to the rafters of that little chapel, flaring his nostrils and sniffing thoughtfully.

"In the North – the Highlands – among our old Celtic Scots, that is where we must make our beginning. As you have doubtless heard, Sir Andrew Moray roars like a lion. There is a man we can depend on, William. Join with him. Take your men out of yon Lowland woods and go northwards to Moray. Together you and he may achieve much."

Wallace, set of features, nodded briefly, decisively.

It may be thought that a ruthless killer whose life was consumed with a lust for revenge would be unlikely to have much of a spiritual element to his nature, but people are more complicated than that. William Wallace, in fact, took his Christian faith very seriously. He had, as has been noted, been brought up in a family which had priests on paternal and maternal sides. Will had been educated by monks. The suggestion that he might become a priest himself had by no means been fanciful. He bowed his head thoughtfully before speaking. At length he met Wishart's eyes.

"Lord Bishop… I have thought of this… all this killing, this taking of lives. It has brought me no satisfaction. No relief. I find that I have even wept for some of those I have killed. Thinking of them as husbands, sons, fathers. Thinking of women and children with broken hearts… as mine was broken over my father. I have hated these English whom I have killed, hated them without knowing them… yet I have in other moments loathed myself for taking their lives."

He looked into the old bishop's features searchingly, almost beseechingly.

"How does this stand with the God of Love? Are we not taught to turn the other cheek? Are we not commanded 'Thou shall not kill'?"

The Bishop of Glasgow looked strangely at Wallace, long and hard, as though into his very soul. He compressed his lips, and after long consideration answered.

"It is well that you have felt so. That you have questioned thus. It speaks of a good heart. I, too, have wrestled with this, but Holy Scripture has other words to guide us. Did not the Ark of the Covenant go before the soldiers of Israel in battle? Sant Paul, in his letter to the Romans, speaks of the minister of God who will use the sword to execute wrath upon the evildoer. Did not our Lord, on the very night of the Last Supper, instruct his disciples to buy swords for their protection?"

He turned uncomfortably and looked absently out of one of the chapel's tiny windows. The sight of Loch Lomond granted him a moment of inspiration.

"Did we not speak, last night, of the blessed Saint Kessog, how he took bow and arrow against the armies of the pagans?"

A darker shadow fell over his features.

"We have a Christian duty to protect the weak and the innocent, and they are not always protected by mere words. But there is more to this, William. A greater evil than is commonly known. Edward of England makes much show of being a pious man, but he is a Plantagenet, descended from the Angevins who were come of pagans and steeped in witchcraft. Didn't Saint Bernard of

Clairvaux say of them that they came from the Devil? Men whisper that Edward is protected by Satan."

A look of horror distorted Wishart's face.

"Christ preserve us, think of Berwick, man! In Edward we are dealing with no merely human wickedness and cruelty, but with something truly diabolical, terrible forces of darkness. This king is the servant of Lucifer, and we must pray to God for the strength to vanquish him."

*   *   *

The year 1836 was a remarkable one for the Parish of Bonhill. The ferry which the monks from Paisley Abbey had operated in the 13th century had been taken over by the great textile works which made the Vale of Leven a highly populated community in the industrial age of the 19th century. For the bleaching, dyeing and printing of cloth, acre upon acre of textile factories had been built, densely-packed and with bristling chimney-stacks belching smoke, for several miles along both banks of the river. The chain-hauled ferry at Bonhill, which was used to transport workers to and from their places of employment, had been dangerous, lives having been lost – indeed, the minister, himself, had sustained serious injury in an accident at the ferry. However, a Road Act had been passed in 1834 which had given the local landowner, Admiral Smollett, the right to erect a bridge. Accordingly, in this year of 1836, work was underway in the construction of a fine suspension bridge.

Since the 12th century several little churches had stood on that spot where the burn had joined with the river. One had been built not long after the Jacobite Rebellion of 1745, only to be replaced some fifty years later by a building, which because of its location too close to the river became subject to flooding and structural weakness. In addition to this, however, by 1836 the population of the parish had increased to around four thousand souls, so a larger church had clearly been required.

The Reverend William Gregor had been presented to the Parish of Bonhill by the Duke of Montrose in the year 1808. Educated at Edinburgh University, Gregor was mildly eccentric, an accomplished scholar versed in classical and semitic languages, and an author. Tall and lean, he was a paternal, much-loved and respected parish minister. When the decision to build a new church had been made, the Reverend Gregor and his Kirk Session met with the heritors (the local gentry who would be required to fund it) and the eventual outcome had been a design by the Glasgow architect, John Baird. So now, in the Spring of the year in which Queen Victoria took the throne, the sounds of construction of the bridge and of the church, a mere few hundred yards apart, could be heard throughout the Vale.

Inevitably industry – and tourism – attracted the railway. Previously goods had been transported by horse-drawn carts or by gabbarts (sailing barges) which plied from Loch Lomond by the Leven, passing the church, to and from the Clyde ports with Highland trade. Timber, for example, was transported to Paisley by gabbart to be used to make bobbins for the thread which was manufactured there, and slate from the quarries of Luss was another cargo. The first railway line to run through the Vale of Leven was laid, between Bowling on the Clyde and Balloch at Loch Lomond, by the North British Railway Company, in 1850. Six years later a single-track line of the Forth & Clyde Junction

Railway Company linked Balloch with the Scottish Central
Railway at Stirling.

*   *   *

The Reverend Charles Rogers was a Church of Scotland minister
and chaplain to the garrison of Stirling Castle. In the year 1856 he
was approached by the proprietor of a Glasgow newspaper and
asked to be a public relations man for the concept of a monument
to commemorate the life and achievement of William Wallace.
The chaplain set up a committee which met in Stirling Council
Chambers on the 12th of May of that year. It was decided that a
great public meeting should be held in order to assess the demand,
as it were, for such an enterprise. Accordingly, under the
presidency of Lord Elgin, on the 24th of June, a vast crowd of
some thirteen thousand persons assembled in the King's Park and
its response, which reflected a great resurgence of Scottish
national feeling, was resoundingly positive. There were many,
however, who regarded the enterprise as an expression of anti-
English resentment. The *Times* curled its editorial lip and referred
to Wallace as being "the merest myth" and suggested that
Scotland had become a province rather than a nation. Those in
favour of the project, in their anxiety to celebrate nationhood
without defiling themselves with nationalism, rewrote history by
insisting in all seriousness that the victory of Wallace at the Battle
of Stirling Bridge had somehow made possible the eventual Union
between Scotland and England. Thereafter the promoters
organised fund-raising meetings in towns and cities throughout
the United Kingdom. At this time meetings were also being held
by expatriate Scots in Australia, the United States, Canada, and
the East and West Indies. The eventual result of all this was the
submission of a design for the proposed monument by Glasgow

architect, Mr John Thomas Rochead, which was enthusiastically accepted by the committee.

*   *   *

On Monday, June 24th 1861, Duncan Robertson was just four years old, but this was to be a day he'd remember for the rest of his life. At half-past five in the morning the three of them were dragged from their bed. Duncan, Isabella and wee Janet. The sky was black as night and rain lashed against the windows of their house at the top of Dumbarton's Church Street – as they were now calling the old Kirk Vennel. As his mother roughly scrubbed his face and brushed his carrot-red hair, Duncan began to fret in case the bad weather made the big folk call the whole thing off. Nine-year-old Isabella, tall, skinny and blonde, was his big sister, and wee Janet, nearly three now, was his cousin. As Agnes Robertson boiled the kettle she listened to her husband whistle as he polished his boots.

James Robertson, a forty-three-year-old stonemason from Glenfinlas in the Lochlomondside Parish of Luss, had learned his trade and lived here in the Royal Burgh of Dumbarton for some twenty-odd years. Unlike most who would be present, he had a professional interest in the event of the day. The tickets for the railway journey had cost him a small fortune, but he'd reckoned the expense would be justified, not just for the sake of the experience – and for the weans – but to show his neighbours that the Robertsons could swank with the best of them. He was handsome in a slightly portly way, with well-oiled black hair and luxuriant moustache. Today he would wear his Sunday best – black frock-coat and shiny top-hat.

By the time they finished their breakfast, the sky had lightened a little, the rain had eased and they could hear the first of the music. Today was a public holiday. Most of the shops and businesses were closed. At the corner of the High Street, just beyond the coal and timber yards, coming from Dumbarton Castle came the sound of the bands of Dumbarton and Bonhill. They were accompanying a procession which had come from Dumbarton Castle, and which was led by the town's magistrates and council along with the Master-Gunner of that ancient fortress. Behind those were representatives of the local lodge of the Freemasons, the Oddfellows, and the Dumbarton Artillery Corps. Even at this early hour the pavements were thronged with excited, cheering crowds, keen to contribute to the spirit of the occasion. By the time the parade had turned right into Church Street, James Robertson was standing among the crowd at the corner outside the United Presbyterian Church, with Duncan holding one hand and Isabella holding the other. A special train had been laid on to take them all the way to Stirling, and it was due to leave at seven o'clock. As they passed the College Bow at the entrance to the Burgh School, the rain became heavy again, but no-one seemed too bothered about that. Duncan was enthralled by the sight of those marching bandsmen, with their smart tunics and silver buttons, and his feet stamped to the stirring sound of their martial music. Opposite the Tannery were the County Buildings, outside which Duncan loved to see the big Russian Cannon which had, they said, been captured at Balaklava.

On they scurried along the wet pavement hemmed-in by the noisy crowd, past the College Park and St Patrick's Roman Catholic Church, until they all stood watching as the dignitaries, bandsmen, soldiers and sundry others on parade, filed impressively into the railway station.

Duncan reckoned there was no fathoming girls. Isabella had spent more time looking down at her own feet, admiring her new pair of button-up boots, than she had watching the procession.

It was the first time Duncan had been in the station, never mind on a railway train. The smells of coal and steam, the sounds of screeching metal and shrieking whistle, and the sight of that tall funnel, those huge wheels, the sheer power of all that iron and steel, all but overwhelmed the wee boy. Crammed into one of the little carriages, Duncan and Isabella had to stand in their damp clothing while their father, to maintain his dignity, sat equally uncomfortably beside an old lady who was dressed as though she were going to a funeral, and had the facial expression to match.

At the Vale of Leven more excited crowds piled into the already packed carriages. Out of the carriage window, Duncan's father pointed out the construction of Alexandria's new red sandstone Public Hall, down beside the suspension bridge. Even more passengers managed to press their way in at Balloch and then Jamestown. As the train puffed eastward via the stations of Drymen, Balfron, Buchlyvie, Kippen and Gargunnock, the rain ceased, and the sun shone out of a joyful blue sky. (At Balfron Duncan's father had relented. He stood, allowing Isabella to sit with Duncan on her knee. The old lady had won Isabella's heart by unexpectedly identifying the red tartan of her dress as Robertson.)

*   *   *

They kept arriving, on foot, by rail, by bus and by carriage, all through that morning until some eighty thousand souls had congregated in the King's Park of Stirling. The music of a multitude of bands – pipes, flutes and drums – enlivened the marching of seventeen companies of volunteers. Behind these there were numerous bodies representing a variety of the popular fraternities of the age. By three in the afternoon the multitude had reached the summit of the Abbey Craig.

It had been from this precise location, it was believed, that William Wallace had commanded the Scots army of common people, on that day in 1297, which had soundly defeated a more numerous and experienced English force. It had been a victory which gave the whole nation heart to carry on the war of independence.

With prayers from the Reverend Dr Arnot of Edinburgh, the foundation stone of the National Wallace Monument was laid. At a given signal there sounded a salute from the guns of Stirling Castle combined with the roar from eighty thousand throats. Several speakers spoke eloquently and with heartfelt sincerity on the themes of liberty and patriotism. Sheriff Glassford Bell, for example, spoke of those who had gathered on the day –

"To them no country is as dear as Scotland – no virtue more inherent than patriotism – no patriot through the ages more worthy of regard than Wallace."

While taking pains, like the other orators, to emphasize present friendship and partnership between the Scots and English, he struck a telling note when he said –

"…if either individual or national character be worth a farthing, it is not to be annihilated by any union."

A "time capsule" was buried with the foundation stone. It contained, among other items, the poetry of Robert Burns, the "Life of Wallace"... and a copy of the New Testament.

Oppression and Resistance

"From that time therefore there gathered to his side, like a swarm of bees, all those who were bitter in their outlook and oppressed by the burden of servitude under the intolerable rule of English domination, and he was made their leader." (Scotichronicon: Walter Bower)

One of my earliest childhood memories is the face of Robert Burns. My father was a member of the Alexandria Burns Club, and every year, after the annual Burns Supper, he brought home the programme for me. I recall being fascinated, even in my cot, by the head and shoulders portrait of the poet as it was printed in black ink on the cover of the booklet. At that age I was obviously too young to understand anything about the man or his work, but that image was the beginning of my lifelong appreciation of the national bard.

The Main Street Primary School in Alexandria had been built around 1850. A well established presence, directly opposite St Andrew's Church, I have mostly (but not entirely) happy memories of my time there. I suppose we must have been taught some Scottish history in the Main Street, but I have no clear recollection of it. There was one cold grey November afternoon, though, when, as I remember, we were each given the enjoyable and satisfying task of painting the St Andrew's Cross, Scotland's national flag, onto a square piece of wood about the size of a hymnbook. I ran home that dreich day, all the way down Bridge Street, desperate to show this rough icon to my mother. By the warm, comforting light of a table lamp, I lay on the living-room carpet, beside the old coal fire, glorying in the sky-blue and white of that ancient symbol. Saint Andrew – Scotland's patron saint – another association between Christianity and nationhood.

One day, when I'd have been seven or maybe eight, my father and I were walking along the Main Street, between the top of Church Street and the Albert Hotel. I don't know what prompted me to enquire, but I asked him if Robert Burns had ever been a soldier. He thought for a moment, then replied,

"Some men fight with a pen."

I never pass that spot to this day without recalling those words – which, curiously, I instinctively understood, even at that age – and here I am now, I suppose, in my clumsy way trying to fight with my pen. As it happened, though I didn't know it at that time, Burns had ridden past that very spot on his way to visit the monument which had been dedicated to Tobias Smollett, the Scottish novelist.

I was brought up, during the nineteen-fifties and sixties, in what was a particularly British Scotland. I think this was in large part because most of those of my parents' generation had lived through, and participated in, the Second World War. This had obviously been a defining experience and, not unreasonably, most Scots were left with a sense that we, the British, had all been in it together, and separately we would never have been able to defeat the evils of Fascism. Even so, there were Scots-English tensions which surfaced from time to time in expected and less expected ways. International football was one, usually good-natured, example, but I can, with the advantage of hindsight, think of another. Again it is a matter of a place invoking a memory.

We didn't have a telephone at home until I was twenty-six years old. At the time of which I speak, if some emergency arose which necessitated the use of a telephone, one of my parents was required to walk or run the couple of hundred yards over the Station Brae and under the railway-bridge to the public telephone box which was situated beside the town's old Post Office. The building is now used as a dental surgery and in the space which had been occupied by the phone box there is now a large plastic bin. Even so, when I pass this spot, as I do most days, I recall the comical occasion when I breathlessly and tonelessly sang down the line to my aunt a song which had at that time been made popular by a Scottish singer called Andy Stewart. The song was called *Tunes of Glory*, and it had come from the theme music which had been written for a 1960 British film.

A couple of times most weeks I was taken to "the pictures" by my parents. There were two cinemas in Alexandria – *The Strand*, in Bank Street, and *The Public Hall*, in Bridge Square. I think it was in the former that I saw, around the age of eight or nine, that film – *Tunes of Glory*. Starring Alec Guinness as Acting Colonel Jock Sinclair, and John Mills as Colonel Basil Barrow, the film was based on a novel by Scottish writer James Kennaway. In essence the story was about a power struggle. Set, as we understood, in Stirling Castle (although there were a couple of external shots of the castle, it turned out not to have been filmed there), the drama concerned the garrison of a Highland regiment not long after the war. Jock, an enlisted Glaswegian, had been promoted during active service in the North African desert campaign. Basil Barrow, who'd been captured by the Japanese and imprisoned for the duration, arrived at the castle to take over command. A spry little English gentleman (Oxford and Sandhurst), he was regarded by the top brass as an infinitely more suitable commanding officer than Jock. The impression I took away from that film was that, broadly speaking, all those who'd remained loyal to Jock – the goodies – had been down-to-earth Scots, and those who'd sided with Barrow – the baddies – had been snooty English (or English-sounding). The message seemed to be that the English were patently superior – more clever, more civilized, simply natural officer material. Whereas the less articulate, coarse and occasionally brutal Scots could aspire to no better than non-commissioned status. I cite this film because, as I have suggested, it seems to me to have given expression to the Scots – English tensions which existed in the post-war era. There will be those who will say that I have confused class with nationality, but that would be, at best, a half-truth. My impression may have been simplistic or even mistaken. It may not have been what the author or director had intended to convey, but it was an impression which was reinforced a thousand-fold and in divers ways over many years. It was, and it obviously remains, an impression shared by many Scots. In *Tunes of Glory* Alec Guinness's character, Jock, had been decorated for gallantry and was adored by his men. Significantly, however, before the film had got into its stride, almost as soon as Jock had opened his mouth with that Glasgow accent, I remember my father commenting quietly to my mother that such a man could never in reality have been made a colonel.

That I can recall, I received no education whatever in Scottish history in my secondary school, the Vale of Leven Academy, between the years 1964 and 1970. The only references that remain with me were some fashionably cynical comments made by a young Art teacher about James VI never washing and Scots nobles not caring about their peasants – the implication being, presumably, that the monarchs of other realms were, in those days, meticulous about personal hygiene, and that foreign barons were much concerned with the social welfare of their serfs.

It was the year Harold Wilson came to power, Mods and Rockers were running amuck in English seaside resorts, and the African states of Malawi and Zimbabwe gained independence from Britain. When I was eleven years old our family moved from Bridge Street to McColl Avenue. The Bridge Street house was an old property which my parents rented from a company of local landlords. In many ways it was a fine home, but it had none of the modern conveniences, and the outside toilet was hard going in the winter months. Our name had been on the council waiting list for some time when we were given what was then known as an "electric flat" in Tullichewan, on the western side of the valley. My mother, in particular was thrilled, not only for practical reasons, but because she considered the old house to have been unlucky. This because it had been burgled twice for the contents of the gas meter, and she had been attacked by bag-snatchers on the pavement outside our front door. The new flat had an electric cooker, a refrigerator, a washing machine and, most remarkably, under-floor heating. It was part of a housing project which was systematically replacing the existing aluminium prefabricated houses which were all around us in Tullichewan. These had been a temporary measure to address the post-war housing shortage.

Directly across the street from our flat there was a row of newly built terraced houses. I quickly became friendly with a boy of my own age whose family lived in one of those houses. Stuart was the middle one of three brothers. One day, as I walked down the path leading from our flat, I looked up and saw, in the bedroom window of Stuart's elder brother, a large poster. It bore a symbol I'd never seen before. It was like the Saint Andrew's Cross, but with the bottom two arms, as it were, joined together in a deep loop. This turned out to be the logo of the Scottish National Party, and the poster read "Independence Now".

*   *   *

In mediaeval times, as now, it was no rare thing for a beautiful woman to catch the eye of a young man in church. She was perhaps half-a-dozen years older than Will. Tall, for a woman, she had hair of a shade almost identical to Wallace's own, but straight, parted in the middle and flowing like silk over her shoulders. Her pale face glowed in the morning sunlight which illuminated finely-chiselled features, blood-red lips and deep green eyes. Her simple saffron gown clung to a figure which, though slender, lacked nothing in womanly form.

"Who is *she*?"

There were other women in that little congregation of Saint Kentigern's Church by Lanark, but Kerlie well knew she to whom his leader had referred.

"Ah...", with a knowing leer, "Yon is the Lady Mirren Braidfoot, the heiress of Lamington. It's said that Heselrig murdered both her father and her brother..."

"Merciful Jesus," Wallace ground his teeth and clenched his fists. "Is there no end to the evil of these bastards?"

"Unsuitable talk for God's House, Will." Kerlie spoke with not a little irony, but Wallace lowered his voice.

"Where does she bide? Is she under protection?"

"She has a house in Lanark town, but only servants with her. Word is that she pays tribute to Heselrig in order that she may be left unmolested."

Wallace barely suppressed another outburst. Sir William Heselrig was the English Sheriff of Lanark.

Mirren Braidfoot noticed Will briefly at the end of the Mass. Their eyes met for an instant. Her expression betrayed nothing, his everything. It was much later that they spoke.

One evening, on a hillside in the outskirts of Lanark, they sat in silence. Some strange atmospheric phenomenon had caused the sun to turn red. When they made love for the first time, at the height of their passion a thunderstorm broke.

*   *   *

When Wallace, Gray and Kerlie had left Balloch Castle, they'd gathered men of the Lennox and taken them eastward, over the marshy wilderness of Flanders Moss, in the direction of Stirling. Some half-dozen miles from that burgh, the English had established a small garrison in the old peel-tower of Gargunnock.

With his company of around fifty men, Wallace had found the place poorly guarded and vulnerable to unexpected assault. Will had literally torn the door down with his bare hands and the result of the ensuing encounter had been twenty-two English dead, with Wallace's men briefly in possession of the tower. Yet again word of this little victory was carried the length and breadth of the land.

On leaving Gargunnock, before the considerably larger English force based in Stirling Castle had come to terms with the news and ventured out in pursuit, Will's company had headed northward through Menteith, crossing the River Earn and going to ground in Methven Wood. This particular lair was some five miles to the north-west of Perth. With seven members of his company, Will had discreetly entered the town, strolling casually, eyes and ears open. They'd learned that the English commander here was a certain Sir Gerard Heron, his second-in-command being Sir John Butler, son of Sir James Butler of Kinclaven. In one of the town's drinking dens, indiscreet English soldiers had let it slip that Sir James would shortly be leading a convoy from St John's Town of Perth to Kinclaven Castle. For William Wallace and his men, opportunity clearly beckoned.

Accordingly, in a thickly-wooded little glen by the River Tay, they'd carried out a successful ambush which had ended with their temporary possession of Kinclaven. Sixty English cavalry had been killed and around a dozen Scots.

After spending a few days within Kinclaven's walls, the resistance men had set fire to the castle and returned to Methven Wood. Young Butler had sallied out of Perth at the head of a thousand men, determined to avenge the death of his father. The majority of these soldiers had encircled the wood with two hundred plunging in after the Scots. What had ensued was essentially an unequal archery contest in which Wallace lost more men and sustained an arrow wound to his neck. Although young Butler was slain, as a fighting unit, the Scots had effectively been trapped, so it had become a case of scatter and every man for himself.

On a stolen horse, and closely pursued by English riders, Wallace made it to the village of Blackford in Strathallan. There he'd obtained a fresh mount and managed to traverse the Ochil Hills. Miraculously, given his state of exhaustion and loss of blood, he'd somehow swum the River Forth and found refuge with a sympathetic widow woman in the Tor Wood, near Stirling. As far as the world was concerned, William Wallace was missing presumed dead.

At nearby Dunipace, Wallace's priestly uncle received word of his nephew's circumstances. Discreetly he provided some quality horses and gear for Will and a group of his companions who had caught up with him in the Tor Wood. When Will had been restored to full health, they then made their way to Dundaff, the seat of Sir John the Graham. The Graham's son, young Sir John, had revealed himself as an admirer and staunch supporter of Wallace and his achievements.

At this time Lochmaben Castle, the seat of Robert Bruce, Earl of Carrick, had been held for Edward by an English garrison, and Wallace had determined to capture it. As it happened, though, he was attending Mass in a nearby church when Clifford, a nephew of the Lord Percy, and some associates, chanced to observe the quality of the horses tethered outside the church. Being of the opinion that mere Scots had no right to such fine mounts, they had entertained themselves by hacking off the animals' tails. Wallace and his company, hearing the disturbance, emerged from the church and set about the offenders, slaying some fifteen. The commander of the garrison, on receiving word of this, rode out at the head of a company, but by that time Wallace had picked up reinforcements led by Sir John Graham. By subterfuge they'd managed to gain entry to Lochmaben Castle, and as unwitting English straggled back into the fortress, they'd been summarily dispatched and the castle was now securely returned to Scottish possession.

When William Wallace had emerged from the Tor Wood after being written off as dead, this second apparent "resurrection" caused an even greater sensation throughout Scotland than had the previous one. Taking full advantage of the national mood, something of a recruitment drive had been undertaken, and from having been a company of some few hundreds, Wallace's resistance force began to take on the magnitude of a proper army. Recruits almost exclusively from the "lower orders" of Scottish society – common folk and minor gentry – had flocked in to become a national army.

It was a strange time to talk of marriage.

"No... No, I will not!"

Wallace's features stiffened. His heart appeared to stop and he found himself speechless. Mirren took advantage of his silence.

"Would you be prepared to give all of this up?

His eyes widened in shock. Disguised, somewhat ironically in the circumstances, in the habit of one of the Paisley monks, he was visiting her in her house in the town of Lanark.

"Could you tear yourself away from all this of fighting and leading and... being the great man?"

He opened his mouth, but before he could form words she went on.

"It is a wonder it hasn't turned your head, all the horror of it. Spilling men's guts out of their bodies, their brains out of their skulls, hacking the limbs from them. Seeing boys who were once babes in their mother's arms being turned into piles of rotting meat..."

"Mirren, lass, this is war. If killing is the price of Scotland's freedom, then it must be paid. These English – none of them need have died, had they but remained in their own land and at peace with us. Would you have Scotsmen bow and grovel to such as these?"

Her eyes flashed bitter defiance.

"Do not Scotsmen bow and grovel to their own great lords? Do they not break their backs in their own fields so that the earls and mighty ones may live off the best while they, their wives and bairns, get by on the crumbs? Do they not go where they are told and do as they are told and fight when they are told and die when they are told?"

"But, lass..."

"Would it be so terrible if we just obeyed their laws and lived our lives? They are all Normans anyhow. These lords are neither English nor Scots. They care for no land other than the land they own. And what is this of being a Scot, or being an Englishman? Is it not but some notion in the heads of foolish men – some accident of birth, to be born in this glen or yonder dale?"

Wallace could scarce believe his ears. He'd believed that he knew this woman.

"But I thought you… approved. I thought you valued freedom as much as any…"

"I have seen the maimed – men blinded, men without hands, without legs, men so deformed they frighten the bairns, men gone mad. What is *freedom* to them?" There were tears running down that beautiful face.

"If there *must* be killing, leave it to others. Leave it to yon Andrew Moray, or John Graham, or… or James the Steward. What of all your precious captains? Leave it to them. Let them get on with it. You have given them their army, is that not enough?"

"But… but it is *me* that men follow. For some reason – more curse than blessing – I seem to give them courage, put fire in their hearts. I… inspire them, they tell me."

"You! Aye, that's what it boils down to in the end, isn't it? The great William Wallace, leader of men!"

"No, Will. A thousand times no. What kind of father would you make? When you are not butchering men you are hiding in forests. Gone, disappeared for months on end. How long until you too are thrown into some hole in the ground?"

Her fists were clenched, the knuckles white. Her teeth were bared.

"Unless you can convince me that you will lay down that sword and never pick it up again. I will hear no more talk of marriage."

*   *   *

The word reached him at Sir John Graham's castle of Dundaff by the Hills of Fintry. Heselrig the Sheriff intended to marry Mirren to his son. There was no time to rally any large body of men. Almost within minutes of hearing this news, Wallace and Graham galloped out of the peel-tower at the head of just a couple of dozen men. They rode like demons southward, skirting Glasgow and on to Lanark. In the centre of the town they found themselves confronted by a company of apparently prepared English soldiers led by a certain Sir Robert Thorn. A clash of arms ensued, but filing through the narrow surrounding wynds came two hundred more English, directed by Heselrig himself. It had been a trap.

Fortunately for the Scots, the physical restrictions of the town's geography prevented the Sheriff from bringing the full weight of his force to bear. Slashing and gouging ferociously, Wallace and Graham hacked their way through the streets eventually gaining entrance to Mirren's house, and, climbing through a back window into the orchard, made good their escape to the densely-wooded Cartland Crags outside the town.

A handful of Wallace's men were slain in the fight, more were taken prisoner. Fifty English were killed.

Mirren had absolutely refused to flee with Will. She would remain, she insisted, and delay the English with talk and misdirection. In the circumstances, it was neither practical nor desirable for the two men to drag her away by brute force.

*   *   *

A fierce blaze, well-stocked with good, dry logs, was crackling in the large stone hearth of Mirren's kitchen. Two English soldiers, still wearing chain-mail and helmets, held her down, while others bound her with cruel efficiency to a finely-carved wooden chair. Her servants, who had no information to give, were murdered in front of her – as a demonstration of Heselrig's seriousness – their butchered corpses left lying in full view.

"Time, my Lady, is just what we are short of. The more we chaffer, the further away this bandit may run."

Heselrig was short, fat and swarthy. Richly dressed and wearing a chain of office, he twirled his little black moustache in a gesture which verged on the comic.

"The usual methods of persuasion can take rather longer than circumstances permit."

She sat like stone, lips compressed, staring with all her concentration at a crucifix which hung on the wall behind him. Heselrig wagged his head in a gesture of command, and his men began to tear tapestries from the walls, piling them, along with dry logs, around the chair.

"Now... you will tell me this instant where the man Wallace is to be found, or you will burn alive."

Mirren might not have heard him. The soldiers looked on dispassionately. The silence lengthened to minutes. He looked at her with a cold, diabolical fury, slapped her viciously in the face, drawing blood and knocking out teeth. Without taking his eyes from her beautiful, ruined face, he thrust out a hand and was given a burning torch of pinewood. Almost casually he first set alight the hem of her long dress, and then standing back a pace, stretched out his arm to set that long, auburn hair ablaze.

*   *   *

The old woman, crooked and unsightly, had escaped the attentions of the sheriff's soldiers, and she alone knew where Wallace and the others were heading. The Highland crone, Shona, who had been Mirren's nurse in childhood and had been devoted to her ever since, had managed to hide in an outhouse in the orchard, from which place she had heard the raised voices of Heselrig and his henchmen. And then there had been the horror of the flames and that terrible screaming. She'd been all but deranged with grief, but she knew that if she broke from cover in order to fly to Mirren's aid, she would have been cut down in an instant.

Now, weeping and stumbling through the woods of Cartland Crags in the darkness, she sought William Wallace.

At first it seemed as though the big man wasn't going to believe it, as all around him men were stunned into horrified silence. Then, in the flickering light of a small fire, his features contorted into such an expression of shocked realisation that the old woman fell back cowering. Suddenly he turned and strode quickly away from the company into the dark reaches of the woodland. From a distance his men heard the sound of terrible retching. Time passed slowly and he was gone for so long that some began to fear he had done himself some mischief, but not one of them dared to approach him.

An eternity passed. He returned to them. Stepped into the firelight. Calm – unnaturally so. Quietly, icily, he began to give orders.

There were three groups of four men, led respectively by Graham, Auchinleck of Gillbank, and Wallace himself. The last place the English garrison expected to find William Wallace that night was in the streets of Lanark. In fact most of the sheriff's men had ridden out hours before in speculative pursuit of the "bandit". The remaining English soldiers were far from vigilant, leaving both town and castle but poorly guarded. The three groups threaded their way, from different points of the compass, through the dark wynds and alleys of the old market town, converging at length, undetected, under the walls of the castle itself. The guards were awakened by the sounds of crashing timbers and shrieking hinges. Wallace had personally kicked down the badly neglected door of the main entrance.

Resistance in the courtyard was negligible and dealt with swiftly and easily. Shona, the ancient retainer, had been able to advise as to the location of Heselrig's personal quarters and Wallace wasted no time in leaping up the winding stone stairway to the sheriff's bedroom. Again, the door proved no effective barrier to one of Wallace's strength and determination. Heselrig leapt from his bed and in his panic upset a well-filled chamber-pot. The identity and purpose of his assailant was horrifically clear to him and in a voice shrill with terror he screamed to his now-dead guards for help.

Wallace had intended to give Heselrig precisely the same death as that which the sheriff had dealt out to Mirren, but in the moment of immediate personal confrontation he lost objectivity and an animal self took over. He raised his huge two-handed sword and began by hacking off Heselrig's head...

By the time he was finished – and it took him considerable time – Wallace was covered from head to foot with blood. The floor was awash with it and the walls were horribly spattered with it. Apart from the severed head, hands and feet, there was nothing in that mound of steaming intestines, shattered bone, and butchered flesh which was recognisably human.

Lanark Castle was, of course, put to the torch, and two hundred and forty Englishmen were killed that night.

It was the murder of the Sheriff of Lanark which finally brought William Wallace to the personal attention of Edward Plantagenet.

*   *   *

The Reverend John Alison was, in a manner of speaking, the spiritual descendant of the Paisley monks who'd ministered to the folk of Bonhill Parish in the days of William Wallace. In fact, as it happened, he'd come to the Vale of Leven from the mid parish of

Paisley some eight years previously. He was a small, bearded and intense man who did not enjoy good health. The winter months tended to bring with them chest complaints. Fortunately this was summer – Sunday, the fifteenth of August, in the year 1869, to be precise – and the minister was in fine fettle. Which was just as well, because this was going to be a big day.

A couple of years earlier, Bonhill Kirk had had a membership roll numbering one thousand and fifty souls. However, the Vale's prospering textile industry continued to give rise to an increase in the population. Originally a hamlet consisting of little more than a single row of cottages, Damhead, in the north of the parish, was now known as Jamestown. The Levenbank Works and the Milton Works, both owned by Archibald Orr Ewing, had swollen the population of the village, and two rows of sandstone terraced houses had been built to accommodate the workers and their families. Accordingly the Bonhill Kirk roll had increased by some five hundred. Put simply, the church had no longer been big enough. The Kirk Session had met with the local landed gentry (the heritors), and put it to them that an additional place of worship was required for the folk of Jamestown, and the outcome was the setting up of a fund-raising committee. In due course the architects Messrs. Clarke and Bell had submitted a design which had been accepted by the Jamestown Church Committee on the 2nd of September 1867. A couple of years later, building was completed and Archibald Orr Ewing had presented the new kirk with a fine bell of twelve hundredweights.

The clear notes of that bell reached the ears of the Reverend Alison that fine August Sunday morning, as his carriage was driven up the Jamestown Road in order that he might conduct the first service in the new church.

* * *

The following morning, the Monday, some seven meandering miles down-river from Jamestown, an excited group of children gathered on the battlements of Dumbarton Castle.

One of the important principles of the Scottish Reformation of the sixteenth century was that every child, of no matter which class or circumstances, should receive an education. Provision of schools, however, had not always been easy. Now, in the latter half of the nineteenth century, Dumbarton had its new Academy in the Burgh Hall, at the top of Church Street, a handful of small private schools, the Free Church School and St Patrick's School. Even so, with the considerable increase in population, as a result of the town's thriving shipbuilding industry, many children were having to walk daily to and from schools in the village of Renton and Dalmonach at Bonhill, several miles distant. Curiously, though, there was a little school on Dumbarton Rock.

Throughout the course of that century various regiments had had units of infantrymen stationed at the castle, and, ten years past, one hundred men of the Edinburgh City Militia had garrisoned the Rock. It was during those years that the school had been established to provide education for the sons and daughters of serving soldiers. Latterly, though, the garrison had been drastically depleted. Eighteen artillerymen had served at the castle in 1867, but now there were but seven left, and they acted more as guides to visitors than as proper soldiers. Nevertheless, the school remained, and a class of a dozen pupils, made up of offspring of the artillerymen and some children from the Burgh.

The schoolmaster, Gunner Thomas James Irwin, was a most interesting man. In his mid-thirties, he was tall, dark and handsome. He had piercing blue eyes, a long aquiline nose, strong, cleanly-shaven chin with luxuriant whiskers. He was never sure if he was Scots or Irish, having been born in Ireland to a Scottish father. Thomas had joined the Royal Artillery and been posted to Leith Fort, near Edinburgh. As a bombardier, he was transferred to Dumbarton Castle in 1866, and, well-educated man as he was, had been schoolmaster here for the past two years. His dozen pupils were congregated in the Duke of York's Battery, in front of the big barracks, peering with fascination down onto the Leven shipyard of Messrs. Scott & Linton. On that fine, clear morning, their young senses were filled with the sights, sounds and smells of that veritable hive of industry. Hammering, sawing, singing ropes, shouting men. Fathers and uncles of some of the children were among those workers. The vessel which held their particular attention was no ordinary ship. Two hundred and ten feet long, with a beam of thirty-six feet, this ship was being constructed entirely of teak, a wood so expensive that it was rumoured around the town that the company was on the verge of bankruptcy – not that the children thought of that side of things.

The ship, which had been designed by Mr Hercules Linton, was months behind schedule, hence the frantic activity. Intended for the China route and the lucrative tea trade, this craft was what was known in the trade as a "clipper". Inspired by the poetry of Robert Burns, it would be named after the beautiful young witch from his famous "Tam o' Shanter" – the *Cutty Sark*.

Transcending the clamour of the shipyard below, from behind the barracks building, came the clear notes of Gunner Irwin's brass hand-bell, summoning the scholars to their labours. The long, two-storey building which housed the class-room nestled deep in the cleft of that twin-peaked rock of basalt which towered high over the confluence of the rivers Leven and Clyde. This particular building had been used to accommodate French prisoners during the Napoleonic Wars, but it now housed the Master Gunner's quarters and the Armoury. The little school occupied the northern room on the upper level.

Duncan Robertson, now twelve years old, sat in the front row of desks. He was a particularly promising pupil, without being in any way a favourite of the master. Isabella, his big sister, now seventeen, was of working age, but Wee Janet, his ten year-old cousin, sat alongside him. As a stonemason of excellent reputation, Duncan's father, James, had on a number of occasions undertaken work on the fortifications and buildings of the Rock. It had been as a result of the influence arising from this that he'd been able to get Duncan and Janet enrolled in the Castle School.

Lessons were just about to commence – dull and deadly arithmetic, which Duncan loathed – when the door of the school-room swung open and a colourful figure entered.

In his early forties and now inclining to plumpness, Master Gunner Thomas Wiggins, unlike the schoolmaster, wore full uniform at all times. Looking splendid in his blue tunic with brass buttons and gold epaulettes, he looked even more theatrical than usual this morning, for tucked under his arm was what appeared to be a copy of the *Dumbarton Herald*, and held in both hands was the most treasured object in Dumbarton Castle. The schoolmaster smiled indulgently behind his dark whiskers.

His superior was another fascinating individual. Thomas Wiggins was unequivocally Irish. Born in County Armagh, he had enlisted in the Royal Artillery in 1847. Serving in the Crimean War and in China, he'd become quite a man of the world. In the kindest possible way it might be said that he gave way to occasional pomposity, but he had the affection and respect of his men. His ginger moustache bristling, he strode to the centre of the room, in front of the three rows of scholars. Gunner Irwin politely stood aside for him.

The priceless item which Master Gunner Wiggins held in his outstretched hands was a large sword. To be exact, it was a double-handed weapon of five feet, six inches in length, including the handle. Weighing six pounds, it had a down-curling hilt, with a complex guard. For some reason, as yet undisclosed, the Master Gunner had brought it this morning from its securely-locked mahogany case in the Arsenal. Duncan Robertson had first seen this revered relic from a distance on that unforgettable day on the summit of the Abbey Craig, on the occasion of the laying of the foundation stone of the Wallace Monument, these eight years previously. Then, brought from Dumbarton especially for the occasion, it had been raised aloft by the previous Master Gunner – Mr Murdoch, flanked by two sergeants of the Dumbarton Artillery. At the sight of it now, Duncan's eyes widened and his nostrils flared with a keen interest. For the other children, this was the first time they'd set eyes on it.

With great care the tightly uniformed officer leant the sword, point upward, in a corner of the room. From under his arm he took the newspaper, turning its pages evidently looking for some specific item. Having found it, his eyes lit up and he addressed his audience in a voice which retained its attractive Irish lilt.

"Gunner Irwin, Boys and Girls…"

He beamed good naturedly around the faces of his listeners.

"…I see from today's *Herald* that next month, at long last, our magnificent National Monument to the Great Patriot, Sir William Wallace, is to be officially opened."

Little eyes glowed. They'd all heard about the Wallace Monument.
"Now I know that you've all heard many a tale of your national hero, but I wonder if this would not be a most apt time for you to learn the full facts about William Wallace and this great sword of his, which has been held securely in this castle of Dumbarton for over five hundred years."

He turned with a mischievous twinkle in his eye to the quietly respectful Irwin.

"Now, this is not an order, you understand, Gunner Irwin. I have no wish to upset your excellent curriculum, but might you be kind enough, over the next week or so, to find the time to instruct these good young people on the inspiring history of that great Scotsman and this magnificent symbol of their nation's freedom?"

The Master Gunner knew his man, for Thomas James Irwin was a keen historian who would relish the task.

"What a splendid notion, Sir. I will do that very thing. You may depend upon it!"

Fire and Sword

"Wallace had behind him the spirit of a race as stern and as resolute as any bred among men. He added military gifts of a high order. Out of an unorganised mass of valiant fighting men he forged, in spite of cruel poverty, and primitive administration, a stubborn, indomitable army, ready to fight at any odds and mock defeat." (Sir Winston Churchill: A History of the English Speaking Peoples).

I was coming to terms with a new home in a new neighbourhood. I was adapting to a new school and new friends. In a sense, I've often felt that, although I was only eleven, these changes marked the beginning of the end of my childhood. There was a different atmosphere around both the new house and the new school. Bridge Street had been a quarter of a mile of red sandstone houses which had stood for over a hundred years, and about which there had been familiarity and a warm sense of deeply-rooted community. The flat in McColl Avenue was a sterile concrete block, one of several surrounded by a building site and the condemned prefabs. It was too early for any sense of community to have developed. Similarly, the Main Street Primary School had been old and architecturally interesting. My mother and her parents had been taught there. It was a small community. The Vale of Leven Academy, on the other hand, had been recently built and incorporated all of the characterless, lego-like architectural banality which was so symbolic of the Sixties. The secondary school was larger in every way – more teachers, more pupils (many of whom were almost adult) and more threatening. Perhaps worst of all – it was my introduction to cynicism dressed up as wisdom.

1964 was also the year of a General Election. Until the McKinlays had introduced the concept of Scottish independence to me, I'd never thought of it in anything other than an historical context. I think I subconsciously entertained a vague notion that it would mean going back to a land of horses and carts and thatched roofs. The notion of Scotland being independent in the present, or in the future, was invigorating and challenging. At that time the Vale of Leven branch of the Scottish National Party was not so much run on a shoestring as hanging by a thread. Its handful of members seemed to me to consist mostly of idealistic young men, in their late teens or early twenties, and a few pensioners. With a schoolboy's enthusiasm, I quickly became involved. One of the few middle-aged activists was a man who had a joiner's business. One day half-a-dozen of us piled into the back of the joiner's van and twenty minutes later I found myself handing out leaflets to bemused strangers on the streets of Helensburgh.

The branch had no official premises, but during that election campaign use was made of a derelict flat which was adjacent to one of the town's less popular fish and chip shops. I recall an occasion when, with another schoolboy and an old man, I was minding the fort in this place and we heard a loud voice booming in the street outside. We ran out onto the pavement to be greeted by the sight of Patrick Telfer-Smollett, the Conservative candidate, standing on the back of a Land Rover, posing in a very patrician manner to streets which were empty, apart from ourselves. We felt more or less obliged to shout some half-hearted derision at him, but foolish urchins could hardly compete with the amplified tones of a toff's election agent.

One of the more imaginative teachers in the academy came up with the idea that my class should stage a mock election. The daughter of a bank manager stood as the Conservative, I don't remember who represented Labour, but I volunteered to be the Scottish National Party candidate. We were given a week to prepare. For the occasion, my mother made me a beautiful rosette in the colours of the party – yellow silk and black velvet. I suppose I probably put forward the same arguments as the actual candidate – that Scotland, contrary to Unionist propaganda, was actually a rich country (he singled out our whisky exports as an especially convincing asset), that under London governments our local factories continued to close, and that each year, within the Union, Scotland lost thousands of its people through emigration.

When the moment came for me to stand in front of my twenty-odd classmates and put these points in the form of a speech, I was crippled with self-consciousness. What made matters worse was that I knew there was among them a "friend" who had warned me that he intended to embarrass me in some way as yet undisclosed. The ordeal of public speaking over, the teacher invited questions. My friend, who happened to be an English boy, put up his hand and, almost puce and visibly perspiring with his own shyness, asked – "What does the SNP candidate think of restrictive practices?"

I could have struck him. Of course, I had no idea what restrictive practices were. Nor was I aware that they were utterly irrelevant in the context of the debate, but I floundered, looked incompetent... and was laughed at by the class. He sat back gloating.

Labour won, as was inevitable with the pupils naturally taking their opinions, consciously or otherwise, from their working-class parents. Afterwards, a girl approached me. I had known her all through primary school, but she was one of those girls who'd matured quickly. She was attractive, way out of my league, but I fancied her a lot. She intended it in a kindly way, I'm sure, but she tapped the side of her head with her index finger and quietly asked –

"Do you really think we Scots have got it up here to run our own country?"

It was my first experience of the Scottish inferiority complex.

Incidentally, during the weeks of the campaign, the island of Malta gained independence from Britain. In the West Dunbartonshire constituency, the Scottish Nationalist lost his deposit.

My own conversion to the cause of Scottish independence resulted in bafflement and, it has to be said, embarrassment to my parents. They were Labour voters, as had been their parents before them. It was the general understanding that the Labour Party best supported the interests of the working-class, and I appeared to be letting the side down. "Appeared" was the operative word, because my new-found political allegiance was something I was, as it were, shouting from the rooftops, so there was a fair element of "What will people think?" The SNP poster I'd insisted on sticking up on my bedroom window, the party badge I habitually wore, my general wearing of my heart on my sleeve, made them decidedly uneasy. To be fair to them, they were careful to respect my feelings and give me space to express those feelings, but they most profoundly hoped that I was just "going through a phase". Two events have remained with me.

My father was a keen golfer, and I spent many a happy evening with him on the course of the Vale of Leven Golf Club. On one occasion, at the time in question, we were in the clubhouse after my father's round of golf. In the crowd of members my father spotted an elderly man whom he knew to have been a significant figure over the years in the Labour Party. He took me over and made a point of introducing me to this man.

"Jimmy, this is my son, Billy – you know him. He's got his head full of this Scottish independence stuff. We don't seem to be able to talk him out of it. You know your politics. See if you can get through to him."

The old party hack treated me to an infuriatingly patronising smirk.

"You know, son, I'm in my sixties now, but when I was a young fellow, I had ideas that I'm ashamed of now. What you'll find is, that when you're that bit older, you'll look back and be ashamed of all these SNP ideas. Wait till you've seen a bit of Life…"

That was his best effort, this distillation of his years of political experience. I'm now in my sixties, by the way.

The other thing was surely a desperate resort. My Uncle Duncan, my mother's brother, who had felt the need to emigrate to Canada in the early Fifties, was enlisted in the family campaign to bring me to my senses. He was actually prevailed upon to write me a letter (an unheard of departure) in which he tried to talk me out of supporting Scottish independence. His argument – predictably for a man who'd been at Dunkirk and in the Arctic Convoys – was that "we" had all stood together during the War. We'd needed the English then, so it made sense to be governed from London. Foolishly, I sent a reply. I argued that "we" had also needed the Americans, but nobody was saying that we should be run from Washington. Wisely, my Uncle Duncan did not prolong the exchange.

It wasn't until many years later that I learned that this notion that the Scottish population, almost unanimously, felt grateful to the English for looking after us, was a Myth.

The Scots National League, which called for independence, was formed in 1921. Seven years later it combined with the Glasgow University Scottish Nationalist Association to form the National Party of Scotland. The Scottish National Party was founded in 1934, winning its first Westminster seat at a by-election in 1945, when Robert McIntyre represented Motherwell for a short time. But surely these organisations represented the views of only a tiny fraction of the Scottish people? In fact, in that same decade the Scottish Covenant Association called for a devolved parliament, and between 1949 and 1950 over two million Scots signed the covenant in support of this measure. It was totally disregarded by Westminster.

*　　　*　　　*

William Wallace had drawn to himself hundreds of men from the lower strata of Scottish mediaeval society. These men had fought bravely and with effect, but the English were not going to be expelled from Scotland by ambushes, skirmishes and night raids. There would have to be full scale pitched battles, and these must involve the country's ruling class – the great lords who had hitherto shown little inclination to serve any cause beyond their individual narrow interests. Some of them continued to hold out hopes for grabbing the crown. Most were concerned for their vast English properties – hence their willingness to swear allegiance to Edward. Few were prepared to take risks or be led by the likes of Wallace.

The slaying of the Sheriff of Lanark, however, somehow acted as a catalyst finally bringing at least some of the aristocracy over to the cause of resistance. Robert Wishart, Bishop of Glasgow, had, of course, long been committed to opposing English domination, as had James the Steward. Now, however, they were prepared to step out of the shadows and openly declare their support for Wallace.

There had occurred two other barbaric atrocities. The English Justiciar of Ayr, responding to indications of increasing resistance, ordered the Scots gentry of the county to attend a Justice-Ayres – a supposed conference which had seemed an irritating but relatively harmless summons. The gathering assembled in a huge barn which was being used as a barracks by soldiers of the occupation. Those attending had been required to do so unarmed.

In the event they were overpowered on arrival and hanged en masse. Three hundred and sixty Scots had been thus treacherously murdered. Their naked bodies were displayed in public, supposedly to discourage acts of rebellion. Included among the victims was Sir Ronald Crawford, uncle of William Wallace.

The nephew had responded in a manner which should have been all too predictable. Raising some three hundred of his men, he had descended on these barracks under cover of darkness and with much-practised stealth. The garrison had been complacent and stupefied by drunken celebration. Wallace, acting now in cold blood and remembering the unspeakable horror of Mirren's death, had given orders for the doors to be barricaded and the barracks set alight. Quickly that wooden structure had become an inferno. Any Englishman managing to escape the flames had been hacked down by the swords and axes of surrounding Scots. The sound of screaming men being burned alive and the stench of their roasting flesh remained as a recurring and life-long torment in the memory of many of those who had been involved.

The Abbey of Scone, situated just outside Saint John's Town of Perth, was regarded by the Scots as their most sacred place. They believed themselves to be descended from an Egyptian princess of biblical times called Scota. According to the legend, she had fled Egypt, eventually reaching Ireland, and bringing with her "Jacob's Pillow" – the stone upon which Jacob was understood to have rested his head when he dreamt of the ladder which reached up into heaven (the stone having been brought to Egypt by the prophet Jeremiah).

"I am the Lord God of Abraham thy father, and the God of Isaac: the land whereon thou liest, to thee will I give it, and to thy seed."

Inspired by these words spoken by God to Jacob, according to the book of Genesis, the Scots of Ireland used the stone in their king-making ceremonies, in the belief that wherever the stone was kept, there would they reign.

It was further understood that, around 500AD, Scots from the north of Ireland had settled in Argyll, naming their colony *Dalriada*. The first ruler of this kingdom, Fergus, brought the stone with him. In the ninth century the Scots and Picts united, becoming the kingdom of *Alba*, and Kenneth mac Alpin moved the Scots capital from Dunadd to Scone, which had been a Pictish centre of power. So it had happened that all of Scotland's Celtic kings had been inaugurated sitting on what had become known as the Stone of Scone, or the Stone of Destiny. This, of course, was the sacred national treasure which had been so sacrilegiously stolen by King Edward, and Scone itself was now in English hands.

The Bishop of Glasgow, acutely conscious of the symbolic significance of this, requested William Wallace to attempt, by force of arms, to bring the Abbey back into Scottish possession. Wallace had by this time managed to take the bishop's earlier advice and entered into a military partnership with Sir Andrew Moray, the knight who had been so effectively leading revolt in the Highlands. So with Moray and Sir William Douglas, at the head of some four hundred cavalry, Will headed determinedly in the direction of Scone, armour-clad and sweating in the heat of summer.

The English official who occupied the abbey was Justiciar Sir William Ormsby, a particularly loathed individual, on account of his general cruelty and the fact that he had been especially active in the pursuit, apprehension and execution of Scots who had refused to take an oath of allegiance to the King of England.

On reaching his old sanctuary of Methven Wood, Wallace's mounted force lay low until nightfall, enjoying the relief of cooler air and savouring the scents of the forest. The capture of the abbey, in the misty dawn, had proved in the event a relatively easy accomplishment. Bitterly disappointing, though, was the fact that Ormsby, apparently and mysteriously forewarned in the very nick of time, had managed to absent himself and avoid being captured. Locked fast in one of the abbey's cellars the Scots discovered a vast hoard of treasures which Ormsby's soldiers had stolen from numerous Scots castles, lairdly houses and churches. The English clergy, who had supplanted Scottish churchmen, were ordered to remove themselves from Scone and from Scotland. Those who were courageous or foolish enough to attempt defiance were killed out of hand.

Particularly frustrating had been the failure to capture the hated Ormsby, especially given that a recent and very similar raid on the Bishop's Castle of Glasgow had equally failed to apprehend Bishop Anthony Bek, one of Edward's most zealous lieutenants.

At the beginning of July 1297, James the Steward, supported by Robert Wishart, Bishop of Glasgow, assembled a Scottish army outside the seaport of Irvine in North Ayrshire. The host included Sir William Douglas and the young Earl of Carrick – Robert Bruce.

Edward was, of course, fully informed of developments in the northern realm, but he was preoccupied with preparations for a war with France. Irritated by the news of insolent acts of rebellion in various quarters of Scotland, he commanded that an army attend to these disturbances of his peace – as he put it. So it was that Sir Henry Percy and Sir Robert Clifford, accompanied and advised by Hugh Cressingham, Edward's appointed Treasurer for Scotland, led a force of some forty thousand trained soldiers northwards to confront the impertinent nobles of this irksome nation. The two armies camped some distance apart, all glistening steel and brightly coloured heraldry in the summer sun, with spectacular views of the Firth of Clyde and distant Argyll.

There was something of a convention that, when the upper echelons of mediaeval society were involved, in accordance with notions of chivalry, opposing leaders would engage in conference prior to battle to negotiate and seek to come to terms in order that actual conflict might be rendered unnecessary. So it was then that, in the baking heat of that July, the great ones of the Scots and English armies sat around a table exchanging hypocritical civilities and engaging in double-talk. As the talking went on, day after day, William Wallace was raising more men.

The news reached him in his headquarters, deep in the forest of Selkirk.

"Surrendered?"

Those fierce eyes flashed with a mixture of anger and disbelief.

"Surrendered?" The repeated word was delivered in a harsh and strident bark.

On the receiving end of Wallace's furious incredulity was the messenger, John Blair.

The pair had known each other since Will's student days in Dundee. Blair was a Benedictine monk who was chaplain and devoted friend to the huge resistance leader. He was very much of the church militant, in that he had stood shoulder to shoulder with Wallace in many a melee, wielding sword and dagger with the best of them. They presently stood in the middle of one of the many large clearings in the forest which had long been places of sanctuary to the hardcore of Will's band of followers. The greater part of his now much enlarged army had been dispersed among their home districts, to be summoned swiftly as and when the need arose for their willing services.

"Blessed Virgin… twenty thousand men-at-arms led by the so-called nobles of this realm *surrendered* without a blow, you tell me?"

"There was much parley… Day upon day of it. Percy and Clifford looking down their English noses at us, and Cressingham silent, goggle-eyed like some vast toad."

Blair, hitching his monastic habit, seated himself unbidden on a fallen bough. There was no ceremony between these two.

"But you know how it is with our great lords, Will. None would accept another's right to lead. The English could see this and they played on it. James the Steward had the right, if any man, but he is a thinker, a talker, he lacks the power to impose his personality and will on other men."

Around them a circle of avid listeners stood at a respectful distance. These included Thomas Gray, Kerlie, Sir Robert Boyd, Edward Little, one of Wallace's nephews, Adam Wallace of Riccarton, one of his cousins, and one known as Jack Short who had become one of Will's most devoted personal servants.

"I could see that Cressingham had the brains. He worked Clifford and Percy like a puppet master, behind the scenes telling them what to say and when. Flattering young Bruce, threatening the Steward, warning the Douglas…"

Wallace unconsciously flicked a buzzing fly from his auburn head.

"Flattery, threats, warnings… what of swords and spears man? What of battle-axes, bows and twenty thousand Scots eager to cleanse their land of these arrogant English?"

This brought a low growl of approval from the gathering. Blair frowned uncomfortably.

"Well you know, Will, the twenty thousand had no say in the matter. As ever it was the dozen or so great lords who mattered in this. Most of them with a sight more in common with Percy and Clifford, aye and Edward himself, than with the men in the field."

Wallace's scowl of impatience signalled that Blair had better come to the point.

"It began to be obvious that our lords were overawed by the confidence and style of the Englishmen, who spoke as though they had already won the battle. The Bishop, Wishart, I think would have stood up to them, but Bruce and the Steward and the others, they... well, they began to talk like beaten men. Asking for favours... almost for mercy. Wheedling for assurances. If they surrendered could they keep their estates? Would they be left at liberty?"

Wallace, towering above the seated monk, looked as though he were about to explode. Angry voices were raised around them, which he silenced with one swift gesture.

"Go on."

Blair looked down at the grass around his feet.

"On the seventh of the month they put their seals to a formal surrender. All of them except the Douglas. They agreed to the handing over of hostages as security for their... their good behaviour. And they renewed their pledges of loyalty to Edward... begging his pardon."

There was a long and tense silence which was broken only by the droning of insects and the distant cooing of a wood pigeon. Wallace spoke in a quiet, icy tone which even his closest friends had learned to fear.

"Pardon? Young Bruce begged pardon? The Steward? The Bishop? What of Douglas?"

"These others, yes, but not the Douglas. He refused the terms. They have imprisoned him in Berwick Castle."

The very mention of the word "Berwick", on top of all this talk of surrender, pardon and loyalty to Edward, was too much for the company. Howls of anger, indignation and affront broke out. Wallace let it die down before he spoke again.

"So now we know. They have shown all Scotland, these great ones, what they are made of. They are not fit to wipe the arses of the men they were supposed to lead. You Adam, you Kerlie, you Robert…"

He stabbed a pointing finger at each man as he addressed him.

"You have more nobility under your toenails than these traitor filth."

He leant on his longbow and ran fingers through his shaggy hair.

"It's up to us then. Those of us here and those who will follow us. The common men, the humble men, the landless men without pretension, greed or ambition, other than to gain the dignity of freedom. Men with neither rank nor gold. Men with nothing to lose but their lives and their loved ones. Men bearing the only title worth having in this land today – Scotsman!"

A roar of acclaim rang through the forest. Eyes shone and hearts swelled, with a lump coming to many a throat. Blair had risen to his feet. Wallace looked at him steadily.

"John. Will you lead us in prayer?"

*   *   *

At twelve years old Duncan Robertson had reached the age of doubt.

With a final avuncular smile, Master Gunner Wiggins left the school-room, taking his newspaper and the unwieldy sword with him. The Master bent and placed his hands, palms downwards on the surface of his desk, pursed his lips in an expression of pretended thought, and announced to Duncan's profound relief –

"Well, boys and girls. Why leave till tomorrow what we might usefully make a start on today?"

He looked around the little room, from face to face, as though the question had not been rhetorical.

"Very well. Just leave your desks and follow me in an orderly manner."

There was a barely suppressed ripple of excitement, for Duncan was not the only pupil to dislike arithmetic. In single file the dozen of them descended the steps with care and came out of the "French Prison" into the sunlight of the Barrack Square. Passing the Well, they processed onto the stone stairway which was cut deep into the cleft of that mighty Rock. It was as they neared the high Portcullis Arch that Duncan's nascent scepticism began to make itself felt. To the side of the steep stairway there were certain large blocks of the basalt of which the entire Rock was composed. It was not unknown for the artillery men, in their capacity as guides, to assure naïve visitors that upon one of these very slabs no less a personage than Her Majesty Queen Victoria had placed her royal behind in order to rest during her visit to the castle some twenty years earlier. On mentioning this to his parents, Duncan had been assured that on no account would the queen have done anything so undignified. This had made the boy wary of some of the other yarns employed by the soldiers in order to coax "gratuities" from tourists. There was, for example the sundial which stood outside the Officers' Quarters. It was routinely described as having been especially commissioned by Mary Queen of Scots. Tosh, his father had said – and he should know – it was no older than the time of King George. Then, above the Portcullis Arch itself, there was a stairway which the guides called "Jacob's Ladder" and spun a lot of silly blasphemous tales about, and all for the odd sixpence. Well, all this had introduced Duncan to the unsettling idea that he could not always believe what grown-ups told him.

Beyond the Portcullis Arch they reached the Officers' Guardroom, by this time speculating keenly about where Gunner Irwin was taking them, and why. As they walked in the shadow of the little tunnel which led under the first storey of the guardroom, Wee Janet clutched Duncan's hand. This made him a little self-conscious, in the manner of a twelve-year-old boy who naturally felt vastly senior to a ten-year-old girl. As they all emerged from the tunnel, Gunner Irwin instructed them to arrange themselves on the steps and on the grassy verge in such a way that they could look upward facing the old guardroom building. It was an interesting edifice as to structure and location. Built prior to the Reformation, in the sixteenth century, it had been described as the chamber between the rocks. This was most accurate, for it was sited so as to straddle the passage which ran through the very heart of that ancient fortress, and it acted as a defensive barrier between the western "White Tower Crag" and the eastern "Beak", these being the names given to the two lofty summits of the Rock. Tradition held that William Wallace had been imprisoned in an earlier building which had been located here.

Gunner Irwin's role as schoolmaster was somewhat resented by certain others of the artillerymen of the castle. Too mean-minded to acknowledge the man's learning and intellectual capability, they felt he had got above himself and imagined that he looked down his nose at them. A couple of them were idly hanging about at no great distance, staring with a suggestion of mockery, but rather than be put off, Irwin took satisfaction from adding a certain aplomb to his manner. Thrusting one hand behind the tail of his black frock-coat, he boomed importantly.

"Children, with regard to the story of our great national hero, I propose to begin, not at the commencement, but at the completion, or rather, *nearly* at the completion."

So saying, with an assumed pomposity, he pointed dramatically to the top, right-hand corner of the building. There, high above them, at the bottom of the crow-step gabling, but a yard from where the masonry joined the living rock, there leered down at them a hideous face carved in stone. Great, fleshy lips were parted, left hand clawing at the corner of the mouth, exposing grinning teeth in a sinister expression which could be interpreted according to the intuition of the individual viewer. Some thought mockery, some inclined to guilt or torment.

"Boys and girls, who can tell me the name of that man?"

The lounging artillerymen smirked complacently.

The children all knew, but inevitably it was Anne McCaffray who shouted out the answer – daughter of one of the guides, and habitually top of the class, to Duncan's chagrin.

"Fause Menteith, Sir."

"You tell him, hen." The aside came from some unseen and disrespectful commentator on the lower terrace, and the schoolmaster ignored it with dignity.

"Quite so, Anne. Well done."

He sniffed, flicked his black whiskers with an index finger and continued.

"Fause Menteith – or rather *False* Menteith. False because of betrayal. It is said, children, that this carving represents Sir John de Menteith – a Scotsman, mark you – the Sheriff of Dumbarton and Keeper of this castle who, in the year 1305, through treachery and deceit, affected the capture of Sir William Wallace and handed him over to King Edward of England."

The Master paused for dramatic effect.

"According to tradition, on this very spot…"

He did not, however, have the fullest attention of one of his pupils. Duncan had heard all of this before. Most of them had. His thoughts ran on another matter. A related question which had been troubling him for some time. The guides were decent enough men. Their idleness wasn't their own fault. Given the opportunity they would probably have made fine soldiers, but circumstances had reduced them to this business of buttering up visitors to the castle. They had their charm and were generally kindly men, but their present demeanour, added to Duncan's recollections of their habitual, if perhaps harmless, deceptions, had caused the boy to brood over this other, and to him more important, doubt. He waited until Gunner Irwin came to another pause in his delivery, and then calling on every reserve of his courage he falteringly spoke out.

"Sir... Sir, the Sword? Master Gunner Wiggins said it has been here, here in the castle, Sir, for more than... than five hundred years."

All eyes were on him. His face burned with embarrassment and nervousness. The expressions of the guides had become serious.

"Is it... can it really be... is it truly the sword of William Wallace?"

A little girl sniggered. Overhead seagulls screeched unnoticed.

The Master licked his lips thoughtfully. He looked unusually perplexed. He darted a glance at the guides. They looked on intently as the silence lengthened. How was he going to handle this?

Gains and Losses

"What are the aims of the SNP?" (journalist)

"Total world domination." (Donald Stewart MP)

I left school, aged seventeen, in the summer of 1970. In my reference the Rector wrote that I was honest and pleasant, but that my examination results had been disappointing. Damned with faint praise, I believe the expression is, but probably a fair appraisal.

My first job was seasonal. I was Assistant Purser on the paddle steamer *Maid of the Loch*, which provided pleasure cruises on Loch Lomond. I didn't fully appreciate it at the time, but it was a wonderful job. The loch is twenty-four miles long and, with its islands and surrounding mountains, it affords some of the most magnificent scenery in Europe. On most days there were three cruises, so the scenery was constantly changing. On the steamer I worked with some fascinating people. The deckhands – or "seamen", as they preferred to be called – were from the Hebrides, and spoke Gaelic among themselves. The engine-room and catering staff were local Lowlanders. Most interestingly, people from all over the world came to see Loch Lomond. Every day I encountered people of different nationalities and cultures. Being but twenty miles and a forty-five minute train journey from Glasgow, we also had many working-class passengers from that great city. Each week there was an evening "showboat", which featured live music and occasional violence. It was all a tremendous learning experience for a naïve seventeen-year-old. Obviously I have many memories of that season, but there is one I'd like to record.

I'm sitting cross-legged on the roof of the bridge as the *Maid* sails southward, pounding through the chain of little islands that run along the Highland Line. My long hair is streaming in the wind as the Lowlands open out in the distance before me. Passengers and crew are eyeing my youthful arrogance askance, as the Rolling Stones belt out *Jumpin' Jack Flash* over the ship's speakers – echoing off the mountainsides. A little moment of unforgettable exhilaration.

I started my first real job that winter. One cold, dark morning I got the train from Balloch to Dumbarton Central, walked across the town's "Common", up Round Riding Road, and into the glass and concrete, angular sterility of the Garshake headquarters of Dunbartonshire County Council. There I was shown to a desk in the Rates Section of the Finance Department. Thank God I didn't know it then, but it was the first day of my thirty-six year sentence as a local authority tax collector… and I was lucky to get it.

Britain was still using pounds, shillings and pence. We had little or no computerization. That year the United States lunar mission,

Apollo 13, famously had to be rescued. The New English Bible was first published and Aleksandr Solzhenitsyn won the Nobel Prize for Literature.

There had been a General Election during my time on the steamer, but I had been too young to vote and I think I must have been too distracted by life on the boat to have had much interest in the political world. I was concerned with flamboyant clothes, the music of the Incredible String Band and, of course, girls. As it happened, Harold Wilson's Labour government was knocked out by the Conservatives led by Edward Heath, and Donald Stewart, standing for the Western Isles, won a seat for the Scottish National Party.

At the beginning of the Sixties the Nationalists had been regarded as harmless, even amusing, eccentrics. The electorate needed little persuading that a vote for the SNP was a "wasted vote". During that decade, however, the party had grown in membership and improved its organization greatly. In 1967 Winnie Ewing won the Hamilton seat in a by-election, putting the party on the map. The following year Edward Heath promised to establish a Scottish Assembly if his party came to power, and shortly after that a canny Labour government had set up the Kilbrandon Commission to consider devolved powers for the Scots.

*   *   *

Tonga, an archipelago in the Pacific Ocean, gained independence from Britain that year.

*   *   *

At this stage I had no active interest in Scottish history... but that was to change. Right next to Balloch railway station there was a John Menzies shop which was stocked with a wide range of paperbacks. One day I picked up a copy of "*A History of Scotland*" by J.D.Mackie. My eye had been caught by the cover, which showed a wonderfully ragged Saint Andrew's flag fluttering above a loch which closely resembled Loch Lomond. Shortly after that, from Langland's newsagent's in Dumbarton, I bought a copy of *A Short History of Dumbartonshire* by I.M.M. MacPhail. Over the following few weeks, I devoured both volumes.

From Mackie's work I began to gain an understanding of those mysterious words I remembered from childhood – *Reformation...* *Covenant... Jacobite...* and, of course, much else besides.

From MacPhail's book I learned how the national had related to the local.

These two works stimulated an appetite for my nation's history which would become a great hunger. A lifetime of reading lay ahead of me.

I have before me, as I write, my first Scottish National Party membership card. It is dated 11th March 1974, and was issued by George Mackay, Chairman of the Old Kilpatrick branch. Why the Old Kilpatrick branch rather than the Vale of Leven, where I lived, or Dumbarton, where I worked? Well, the approach to membership had been a long and gradual one. The outcome was, I believe, inevitable, but the moment of decision happened spontaneously. George Mackay was one of the accountants with Dunbartonshire County Council. A big man, then in his forties, he was treasurer of the local government trade union, and one of the very few nationalists I knew in my workplace. It was in conversation with George that I finally reached the decision to join the SNP.

The office in which I worked at that time accommodated a dozen desks. Most of them were occupied by rent collectors. These were working-class folk with the same background as my parents. The men were all ex-servicemen who had fought in the Second World War. To a man they believed in the Union with England and I think they all, but one, voted for the Labour Party. There was a very real "generation gap" in the office, and I considered people of their age to be dull and lacking in vision. Their opposition to Scottish Independence was, I felt, frustrating and depressing.

At this point it should perhaps be mentioned that, around the age of twelve or thirteen, I'd rebelled against being sent to church and my parents saw that forcing the issue would have been counter productive. I found self-justification very easy, because then, as now, there was no shortage of popular literature which undermined Christianity, and society's opinion formers – academic people and the media – seemed to be very condescending to Faith and the Church.

The office Tory was an elder of Jamestown Parish Church. He knew my family and had known my grandfather. Because of who he was and what he was, and because I liked him, I felt uneasy and unsure of myself when he'd quietly and respectfully told me that he thought my nationalist views were mistaken.

It think is worth quoting from that 1974 card the Aims of the party I joined –

(a) Self-Government for Scotland: that is, the restoration of Scottish National Sovereignty by the establishment of a democratic Scottish Government, within the Commonwealth of Nations, freely elected by the Scottish people, and whose authority will be limited only by such agreements as will be freely entered into with other nations or states for the purpose of furthering international co-operation and world peace.

(b) The furtherance of all Scottish interests.

The 11th of March was just after a General Election which, on the back of a hung parliament, had seen Harold Wilson return to 10 Downing Street.

I remember sitting with my cronies in a candlelit *Tudor Lounge* of the Tullichewan Hotel in Balloch, drinking bottled beer because there was no electricity for the lighting or the draught beer pumps. The United Kingdom was in a rare old state. There was an energy crisis. Miners and electricity workers had taken industrial action, so the Conservative government had introduced a "Three Day Week", which in effect meant that non-essential businesses were supplied with only enough power for three days out of seven. Throughout the length and breadth of Great Britain people were plunged into the winter darkness of regular power cuts. This had been the background to that General Election.

In the West Dunbartonshire Constituency Ian Campbell attempted to hold the seat for Labour. He was challenged by Moira Carse of the Conservative Party and Alex Murray of the SNP. With a friend, I responded to an advert in a local paper which welcomed "offers of assistance" with the Nationalist's campaign. We found ourselves, one grey Saturday afternoon, in the election offices at number 3 Wallace Street, Dumbarton, folding leaflets and discussing policies with the election agent, Willie Dick.

I'm reminded of an amusing story from, I think, that same election. The friend – who can remain nameless – and I, were leafleting door-to-door in Drymen Road, Balloch. I was working my way downhill along the left side of that tree-lined brae, and he was delivering to the opposite side. At about half-way, I heard a raised and rather refined voice –

"I say… I say… Young man… You there!"

The minister's wife had come out of the Manse and was chasing my fellow leafleter down the street. It transpired that a Conservative Party worker had been delivering his own leaflets just two or three doors ahead of my friend. The lady of the Manse had observed that my colleague was removing any Tory leaflets which were sticking out of the letterboxes, prior to inserting the SNP literature. I distinctly recall the phrase she used –
"Don't you think that's rather *sharp practice*?"

It was a rhetorical question, of course, but I couldn't have agreed with her more. I crossed the street to join the pair and try to defuse the situation. At that point she was saying –

"Just give me my Conservative leaflet and I'll say no more about it."

She was puce with indignation, and I felt that, in the circumstances, he would be getting off lightly.

"Go on… give her the leaflet, " I urged. But he just looked at me like a stuffed sheep, making absolutely no attempt to placate the woman. Eventually she marched off muttering threats about contacting the authorities.

Exasperated, I asked –

"Why didn't you just give her her leaflet?"

He swallowed stupidly, went slightly pink, cleared his throat and answered –

"Well… as I was taking out the Tory leaflets, I was sticking them up my jumper, and I knew if I tried to take just hers out, then all the rest would have fallen out too… It would have been embarrassing."

Indeed.

Ian Campbell held the seat for Labour with 16,247 votes. Alex Murray, a farmer from the Loch Lomondside Parish of Luss, came third with 11,144. The Scottish National Party, however, increased its number of MPs to seven and its share of the Scottish vote to 22 percent. Now a force to be reckoned with. Not funny any more.

*   *   *

On the 23rd of July in the year 1297, Hugo de Cressingham, the man appointed Treasurer of Scotland by Edward Plantagenet, sent his king a letter which described the political situation in that unruly realm –

"By far the greater part of your counties in the realm of Scotland are still unprovided with keepers, as well by death, sieges or imprisonment, and some have given up their bailiwicks and others neither will nor dare return, and in some counties the Scots have established and placed bailiffs and ministers, so that no county is in proper order excepting Berwick and Roxburgh, and this only lately."

In other words, so successful had the resistance efforts of Wallace in the south, and Moray in the north, been – in spite of the capitulation of the nation's "ruling-class" – that the English were losing their grip on the land. English, or collaborating, officials had in so many places been killed, imprisoned, or forced to flee, that those who remained feared for their lives. Meanwhile Scots were beginning to recover these positions and resume control of government, at least at local levels. Cressingham knew that William Wallace and a large element of his force were to be found somewhere within the wild and extensive Selkirk Forest. The Treasurer had a large English army stationed at Roxburgh and he counselled that it should move to hunt down and destroy the resistance, but Percy and Clifford would have none of this. They insisted on waiting for reinforcements.

John de Warenne, Earl of Surrey, had been placed in overall command of Edward's armies in Scotland. He was elderly and in no hurry to force a confrontation. He sat with his army at Berwick.

The arrow thudded viciously into the trunk of an oak after having missed a startled deer by a hairsbreadth. Hunting was one of the more useful ways of passing the time, here in the deeply secluded woodland. Half-a-dozen hitherto invisible archers emerged from the undergrowth. They had learned, whenever possible, to wear the colours of the foliage. Hunting was carried out usually with relatively short bows. Wallace was one of the few who possessed a longbow, and it was used in battle.

"D'ye think they'll come into the forest, Will?"

It was Sir Robert Boyd who asked the question.

"Well… they couldn't bring their cavalry in. They'd have to split infantry into small groups. Even if they had guides, it's a big forest. Too big for them to surround. We'd have every advantage. We could ambush them, cut them off from each other. No… No, I think they'll have sense enough to stay out."

"Maybe we should attack them, then. Percy and Clifford at Roxburgh. They'd least expect it."

Kerlie was always for attack, no matter the odds.

"No. There are far too many of them. Roxburgh would be too well defended for us to prevail with the numbers we have here in these woods."

"Then what, Will? Would you have us sit idle until they move around us and retake the towns and castles we've cleared of them?"

Plain talking from Blair the churchman.

"No, John. Well you know that men don't sit idle with me. We will move back north. I think it's time we renewed our acquaintance with Moray."

This was received with shrewd nods and grim smiles. Edward Little removed his arrow from the oak and rubbed dark earth into the white wood which had been exposed by the torn bark. By the dawn their camp was deserted.

All the way, they gathered men. Through the forest. Through the Lothians and the Lennox. It was rumoured throughout the realm that Edward intended to coerce ordinary Scotsmen into serving in his war against the French. This had the effect of fanning the flames of resistance. They crossed the River Forth by Flanders Moss, bypassing Stirling, and carried on to the north-east in the direction of Saint John's Town of Perth. Of the thousands of men who had flocked to Wallace's banner on the way from the Forest of Selkirk, two were to prove especially significant. William Sinclair, the young Dean of Dunkeld Cathedral, and Sir John Ramsay of Auchterhouse. These two, and Sir John Graham, aided Wallace in his assault on Perth.

The town's defensive wall was understood to be insufficiently high to be of itself effective, but there were surrounding ditches which had to somehow be dealt with. Using timber from the district's abundant woodland, and ingeniously floating the logs down the River Tay, siege engines were constructed and brought strategically to bear. Wallace's thousand men were able to fill in the ditches with earth and rubble, thus gaining access to the walls. Fighting was savage, with the English defenders giving a good account of themselves, raining down every available kind of missile on the attackers. Eventually sheer force of numbers prevailed and the Scots poured over the walls in several places. Fierce hand-to-hand combat ensued with, again, the English acquitting themselves valorously, but they had to contend with Wallace's men to fore and townsmen behind them who, with makeshift arms, were taking the opportunity to hit back at their oppressors. The outcome was inevitable. Perth was back in Scottish hands. Appointing a new sheriff, Wallace headed his army in the direction of Cupar. Reaching the Cistercian Abbey there, they were disappointed to be informed that the English-appointed abbot had abandoned his charge, fleeing from the wrath of the liberators.

Dunnottar Castle was spectacularly situated on a cliff-top looking over the North Sea, just to the south of Stonehaven. As Wallace's army – a Saint Andrew's Saltire flying proudly before them – had swept wreaking vengeance through the country, thousands of retreating English soldiers had sought the security of its supposedly impregnable walls, but in the event many of them found themselves trapped in a nearby church.

"In the name of our Merciful Lord, no, Will."

Dean Sinclair actually dropped onto his knees in front of the giant warrior. The assembled Scots force looked on for the most part uncomfortably.

The churchman continued to implore, wringing his hands. He was a soldier himself, but this was beyond human wickedness.

"It is consecrated – the House of God – it would be most dire sacrilege."

There was some silent nodding, but more growls of dissent. Seagulls screeched mockingly and the waves washed rhythmically on the rocky shoreline. Wallace knew the mood of his men but, beyond that, any trace of compassion or human sympathy, had long since died in his breast. Since the murder of Mirren he had become simply an agent of cold, heartless, and cruel revenge.

Ignoring the entreaties of the kneeling Sinclair, he raised an iron-gauntleted fist in signal and the church was duly, and it is to be feared – enthusiastically – set alight. It was the Barns of Ayr all over again. The emblem of Saint Andrew was shamed that day.

From Dunnottar a large force of light cavalry was dispatched to Aberdeen with maximum speed. That seaport was also a destination for fleeing English military. When the Scots cavalry descended on them, far from taking up effective defensive positions, Edward's soldiers were fully occupied with the business of loading booty onto numerous ships in the town's harbour. As a result of this lack of vigilance it was a relatively easy matter for Scottish arms to prevail. Cargoes were recovered, the ships were put to the torch and sunk, and it is recorded that English clergy, women and children were allowed to leave the town unharmed.

Created a Royal Burgh by David the First of Scots in the twelfth century, Stirling, with its massive fortress rock, had ever been of the greatest strategic importance. Situated, as it was, at the lowest fording or bridging point of the River Forth, it was effectively the gate through which armies must pass between Highland and Lowland Scotland. At this time, in July of 1297, Stirling Castle was one of the few strongholds of note still in English hands – a situation which could not be tolerated. Accordingly, William Wallace, now sharing command of the army of Scots liberation with Sir Andrew Moray, marshalled their considerable forces and headed southwards – to Stirling.

At this same time, John de Warenne, Earl of Surrey, having been forced to accept the bitter reality that, to all intents and purposes, Scotland north of the Forth had been repossessed by the Scots, was finally stirred to action. He had no choice but to join with Percy and Clifford and advance northwards – to Stirling.

The scene was thus set at last for the grand scale pitched battle the result of which would determine Scotland's future.

*   *   *

When young Duncan Robertson asked Gunner Irwin, in front of pupils and guards, if the sword displayed at Dumbarton Castle was truly that of William Wallace, the schoolmaster found himself on the horns of a dilemma. He had always stressed to these children the importance of telling the truth. Now he was confronted with a very difficult choice. He could tell them a convenient lie. He could dissemble, try to evade the question – or he could tell Duncan and the others the uncomfortable truth. These listening artillerymen, the guides, as a matter of routine, policy, and to some extent civic pride, informed visitors to Dumbarton Castle that the ancient weapon was the veritable Sword of William Wallace. No ifs or buts. All these children believed it was the Sword of William Wallace, as did the folk of Dumbarton Burgh.

During that long, silent and tense pause, Irwin weighed in his mind certain pro and cons, rights and wrongs, then finally reaching a decision he spoke.

"Duncan, your question takes me by surprise. The story of the sword is a long and interesting one. I don't have time to tell it now, but I promise, you and I will speak about this when time permits. In the meantime, I think we should all return to the school-room… and our Arithmetic."

This was greeted with scowls of disappointment from the pupils and suspicious looks from the guards. Duncan seemed pleased.

Perhaps England's most celebrated soldier – Arthur Wellesley was an Irishman. Born in Dublin in 1769, to aristocratic parents, he was sent to Eton, then, aged eighteen, he joined the British Army. He served with distinction in the Netherlands and in India. During the Napoleonic Wars, in the Peninsular campaign, he was made a Field-Marshall. Though he was twice a Tory Prime Minister, he was most famous for winning the Battle of Waterloo. He was, of course, the Duke of Wellington.

In 1818, during the government of Lord Liverpool, Wellesley was appointed Master-General of the Ordnance. Responsibilities of this office included artillery and related engineering, fortifications, transport and military supplies, among other less obvious matters. The Ordnance was headquartered in the Tower of London. In November of 1821 the Duke of Wellington, in his capacity of Master-General, received a letter from a Dr Samuel Rush Meyrick.

Meyrick was born in 1783, the son of an artilleryman who was also a Fellow of the Society of Antiquities. Samuel inherited his father's interest in antiques, becoming something of a collector himself. He was educated at Queens College, Oxford, gaining a

Bachelor of Arts in 1804 and, some years later, a Doctorate of Civil Law, practising as an advocate in ecclesiastical and admiralty courts. In 1803 he had eloped to Wales with a young woman called Mary Parry. Samuel's parents had considered her to be socially inferior and, arising from the resulting ill feeling, Samuel found himself cut out of his father's will.

However, like his father before him, Meyrick was elected a Fellow of the Society of Antiquities, the "Meyrick Collection" receiving considerable regard. He had the field very much to himself when, in 1824, his rather onerously titled three volume publication *"A Critical Inquiry into Ancient Armour as it existed in Europe, Particularly in England, from the Norman Conquest to the Reign of King Charles II"* gained him something of a reputation as an authority.

In his portrait, executed by Henry Perronet Briggs, some years later, Meyrick with noble brow, long face, aristocratic nose and fashionable side-whiskers, is a darkly handsome man. He poses (perhaps with a trace of smugness) with a plume resting above an item of armour and a sword hilt. The arrangement has been said to symbolise the phrase – *"The pen is mightier than the sword".*

It was no doubt in anticipation of the recognition to come that Meyrick, three years prior to publication, had written to the Duke of Wellington expressing his concern regarding the condition of the ancient armour then in the Tower of London. He offered his suggestions as to lighting, layout of rooms and various related matters – and he questioned the historical accuracy of some of the items then being displayed.

The year after *"A Critical Inquiry..."* was published, the "Wallace Sword" was sent from Dumbarton Castle to the Tower of London to be repaired, and at this time the duke submitted that ancient weapon to Meyrick for his considered opinion. The learned Doctor pronounced that "the two-handed sword, shown at Dumbarton Castle as that of Wallace" was comparable with another weapon which was connected with the Earldom of Chester, and from the reign of Edward IV. This particular sword was understood to have been one carried in state by Edward V when he was invested as Prince of Wales. It had been dated to 1475.

In other words, if Meyrick was right, the weapon from Dumbarton could not have been the sword of William Wallace... and a report to that effect was sent to the castle.

It was fortunate, in the circumstances, that Duncan struggled with long-division, for it gave Gunner Irwin a plausible excuse to keep him in the school-room after the other pupils had been dismissed, thus affording an opportunity to discuss this unfortunate matter of the "Wallace Sword" with the boy in privacy.

"So now you know, Duncan."

The schoolmaster gravely folded the old report and returned it to the bottom of a strong wooden chest which was reinforced with iron bands. He placed the key carefully into the deep pocket of his frockcoat.

"I've told you this, Duncan, because you are an intelligent boy. I think you will make something of yourself in this world, and I believe you're ready to learn that everything is not as it seems in Life."

Duncan returned his gaze with respectful attention and not a little pleasure on receiving this praise. Gunner Irwin continued.

"But this means that I must depend on your discretion. Do you know what I mean by that?"

Duncan knew perfectly well. His parents were articulate people and one benefit gained from listening to the sermons of the minister of the town's Kirk was that the boy had picked up a rich vocabulary.

"I've to tell no-one, Sir."

Irwin grimaced and wagged his head to one side, as though to say – "That's about the size of it."

Duncan looked uncomfortable.

"Does the Master Gunner not know about it?"

Irwin grinned wryly.

"Oh yes, he knows fine well, but he refuses to believe it. The sword seems to mean a great deal to him… as it does to the town in general."

"What about the soldiers, Sir?"

It amused Irwin to hear his "comrades-in-arms" dignified with such a title.

"I'm not at all sure if *they* care." Which was unfair to them.

"Are you very disappointed, Duncan?"

Duncan gave the schoolmaster what he interpreted as a brave smile.

"No, Sir. Not disappointed. Not at all."

It was a strange thing, but though he'd had doubts about the weapon, now that he'd been told the story of the "expert's" dismissal of it, he was filled with a conviction that it must be authentic – the very sword which had been held in the hands of William Wallace. A strange thing.

Victory and Veneration

It is curious how certain events can make connections which lead on to unlooked for developments in our lives.

It was the year in which a young student of St Andrews University joined the Scottish National Party. His name was Alex Salmond.

One quiet afternoon in 1973 the peace of the rent collectors' office in the headquarters of Dunbartonshire County Council was shattered by a particular telephone call. It was around two in the afternoon. Most of the collectors were out at their offices in the various little communities of the county, but one or two were in the HQ office which they shared with my own little team of Rates Rebate staff. The shocking news was that the old collector – the one who had been a church elder with my grandfather – had been attacked and robbed at knifepoint in the rent office out at Duntocher, near Clydebank.

When he was escorted back to HQ he actually had a sticking plaster covering a slight facial cut which the attacker had inflicted in order to intimidate and show that he'd meant business.

I do not recall how much money the thief had gotten away with, but one result of the occurrence was that from that time onwards no collector was permitted to perform his or her duties unaccompanied. A number of lads in their late teens or early twenties were borrowed from the finance department and deputised, so to speak, to travel in the private cars and taxis which took the collectors to their assorted outposts, there, by their very presence, to hopefully deter further robberies.

I was one of the chosen. Aged twenty at that time, I couldn't have punched my way out of a paper bag, as they say. The whole arrangement was absurdly amateur.

However, it was when in the town of Kirkintilloch one day in this capacity that I found myself at lunchtime in a shop browsing through a stand of paperbacks. I was by then keenly interested in history, but had not been drawn in any way to historical novels. Even so, I picked up a title by a popular author of such works – *The Black Douglas* by Nigel Tranter. The information on the back cover told me that this was a 15th century story about the House of Douglas and William the 8th Earl involved in a feud with the royal Stewarts.

I suppose it caught me in just the right mood. On impulse I bought it and it is not an exaggeration to say that that moment changed my life. Having read the work, I became a devoted fan of Tranter. Actually, in the beginning I mistook him for another writer – Ian Grimble, a historian who'd had a series on television and accordingly I credited Tranter with great authority in the detail of history (with entire justification, as it turned out). Over the years I have read over fifty of his books (many of them several times over) being entertained and greatly informed, but most profoundly having my sense of Scottish nationhood constantly nourished by his work. More than these things, though, Tranter gave me the enriching pleasure (or the convincing illusion) of sharing the lives of the characters he so wonderfully portrayed.

The year 1974 had me utterly absorbed in what is now known as his *MacGregor Trilogy* – three books about Rob Roy, his nephew, Gregor of Glengyle, the MacGregor clan and their part in the Jacobite uprisings of the 18th century.

It was a year of great political activity, for there was a second General Election, held in the month of October. My contribution, at local level, was still mostly door-to-door leafleting. I religiously read and distributed copies of the *Scots Independent*, the unofficial newspaper of the Scottish National Party, so I was well-versed in all the political and economic arguments for Scottish self determination. Also I talked... though admittedly most of my talking was done in the pub. I have mentioned the *Tudor Lounge* – I recall walking down from my house in Tullichewan during those times – long hair, fringed boots, denim bomber jacket with imitation fur collar, nationalist badge and a MacGregor tartan scarf. The scarf being an affectation which had, of course, been inspired by Tranter's novels. That was the routine – the day spent in the finance department, the evenings delivering leaflets, and the last few hours of the day (closing time ten o'clock) talking a good fight. I was physically in the year 1974, but in spirit I was in 1707 drawing a metaphorical sword with the Jacobites against the hated Union of the Parliaments. After the last pint of Tennents lager I used to walk out of the door of that lounge and look northwards through the darkness of night and visualise the men of Clan Gregor huddled in their clachans of Inversnaid and Glengyle, quaffing drams and plotting against the House of Hanover. Such comparison was, of course, the romantic, almost offensive, folly of a young man. Even then I knew it was so... but it sustained me. Romance in a different sense of the word – there was a certain beautiful girl, whom I'd known since my schooldays, who one evening, while passing our table, gently tugged the long hair which hung over my shoulders. When I looked up, surprised, she smiled and said – "I like your badge." She was one of us, and these words of hers bound me to the cause as mere patriotism could never have done... but that is another story.

Most of my friends who sat around that table were fellow nationalists and we were, in our own era, fervently hoping to put an end to that Union by the ballot-box. During the campaign Winnie Ewing, Nationalist MP for Moray and Nairn, addressed a public meeting in the Vale of Leven Academy. She told those present that –

"The only language that Westminster understands is the ballot-box, and I think that, certainly before I am very much older, I am going to step through the door of a Scottish Parliament."

Again, Alex Murray, the Luss farmer, was the Nationalist candidate for West Dunbartonshire. He was confident. He felt, as did many of us, that there was something in the air. By then "Scotland's Oil" (the oil reserves in what was understood to be the Scottish sector of the North Sea) was a major card in the SNP hand. Murray spoke of a "war on poverty" and assured voters that Scotland was also rich in water, timber, agriculture and fishing.

Ian Campbell held the seat for Labour, however, with 15,511 votes to the SNP's 13,697. Nationally, Harold Wilson also won for Labour, now with a majority of three seats, but the Scottish Nationalists increased their number of MPs to eleven, capturing 30 percent of the Scottish vote.

That week Neil Armstrong, famously the first man to walk on the moon, visited the General Time factory in the Vale of Leven.

*   *   *

It was an English sentry on the battlements of Stirling Castle who saw them first. Initially as a dirty brown cloud, then as a dark smudge stretched along the horizon. Then sunlight caught on polished armour and the sharpened points of spears. An army approaching slowly over the wide lowland plain. His own army – far off and long awaited.

There was talk of fifty thousand men. That and a thousand cavalry. Hence the dirty brown cloud, he supposed.

The Scots generals– Wallace and de Moray – saw them too, of course, from the Abbey Craig. They had received accurate intelligence as to the numbers and rate of approach of the enemy. Far from being dismayed by the extent to which they were outnumbered, the two leaders felt only impatience to get to grips with this English host.

Wallace had been fully occupied with the siege of Dundee Castle when the word had reached him of the English advance. Priorities being obvious, he and Moray led the bulk of their force southward, leaving Alexander Scrymgeour to direct siege operations at Dundee.

Andrew de Moray belonged to a prosperous Celtic family which possessed lands throughout the realm of Scotland. His father was Sir Andrew Moray of Petty and his uncle was Sir William Moray. All three had been captured at the disastrous Battle of Dunbar, with young Andrew being imprisoned in Chester Castle. He had managed to escape, however, and returned to Scotland, and there, in due course, Andrew had embarked on his highly successful campaign of resistance to English occupation.

He was of average height and slim. Not of obvious physical strength, he stooped slightly, but had intelligence and determination written on his features. The dark beard was neatly trimmed and his clothes were richer than those of Wallace. Differences of rank and background between these two men were as nothing compared with the militant patriotism which had bonded them together. As they looked down across the plain which stretched some two miles to the great rock of Stirling Castle, it was breathtakingly apparent to them that the English multitude, spread out so vastly and so colourfully behind the meandering River Forth, outnumbered their own force, which was secreted behind them among the steeply sloping woodland, by fully five to one.

It was not yet noon, but that morning in early September was already heavy with a humid, oppressive heat which made men sweat under their armour – if they were lucky enough to possess any. The sky was pale gold with a mist which sulkily refused to lift and open out to clear blue. The atmosphere was tinged with a sense of unreality. Surrounded by their various loyal lieutenants, Wallace and Moray focussed eyes and minds on a single feature of that rich and fascinating panorama. The bridge...

Edward of England had ordered the mobilisation of this army for one simple reason. It was to advance into the Highlands of Scotland, engage with those Scots who had taken up arms against his overlordship – and crush them once and for all. In order to enter these Highlands, Edward's army must first cross the Forth – and they must do so here... by Stirling Bridge.

Prior to combat, lengthy periods of inactivity, of waiting, are hard-going. They fray the nerves, leaving men's imagination to run riot. Horrors can be mentally anticipated – fates worse than death – unspeakable injuries, maimings, torture following capture... The Scots spread throughout the woods of the Abbey Craig waited long, agonising hours that day, fuming and fretting as their leaders sat on horseback staring down endlessly at the milling English multitude and that wooden bridge. Birds twittered, leaves rustled and stomachs rumbled. The mist had finally lifted, giving way to the pale blue sky of early evening, when a party of some dozen riders could be discerned crossing the bridge under a flag of truce. Also raised above these horsemen were banners – the gold, white and blue of Stewart, and the red roses of Lennox.

This was going to be another Irvine, or so the English assumed. They considered themselves superior in every way. Obviously, they were numerically superior. They were superior in terms of military leadership, skills, equipment, training, discipline and experience. Theirs was a professional army of battle-hardened veterans – used to victory. Beyond this, however, was that unquestioned sense of inbred superiority which was so much a part of their being. These Scots were a mere rabble of peasants led by a bandit chief. The Steward and Lennox were sent to communicate Warenne's terms of surrender to the Scots.

Naturally they would see the futility of opposing this English force in arms, and, as at Irvine, clutch at the chance of coming out of this folly with their lives.

Looking down at the approaching party, Wallace and Moray exchanged sour looks. Around and behind them men growled mixed expressions of curiosity and contempt. After brief discussion, it was decided the wiser course for representatives of the Scots leadership to go down and meet the deputation at the foot of the Abbey Craig.

Left to his immediate personal inclination, Wallace would have refused to exchange speech with these people. He had come to despise them. The Steward and Lennox had been bold enough in the beginning to encourage Wallace in acts of resistance. To lead many a good man to a premature and violent death. But as soon as these great lords had been threatened with the loss of lands and position they had bowed and grovelled to English Edward, and now they were shameless enough to be his lackeys in this message bearing errand. Wallace realised, however, that more lives, many more lives – a nation's future, indeed – might hang on the words which were to be spoken here below the Abbey Craig that day. Moray also had another way of seeing this development. It was his instinct that these Scots nobles, and others like them, were even yet swithering as to which side to take when the talking stopped and swords were unsheathed. In the end a compromise was reached. Wallace would be present at the encounter, but the smooth talking would be left to Moray. In the event it had proved much as expected. The Steward and Lennox, accompanied by a mixture of English knights and Scots collaborators, had given voice to Warenne's "terms of surrender", the Steward being the actual spokesman. An immediate laying down of arms, handing themselves into captivity and unequivocally swearing future loyalty to Edward, would result in the lives of the Scots leaders being spared – there was no mention as to the fate of common soldiers.

Wallace had admired and respected the Steward, not only as his feudal superior, but as a man and a patriot. Now, however, as the nobleman eyed him almost beseechingly, his gaunt features somehow tragic, Will's blood boiled in his veins. He had agreed not to speak during this encounter, but words proved unnecessary. The sheer malevolence, the utter contempt which his features expressed, the murder in the giant's eyes, caused the Steward to visibly shrink before him. Lennox might as well have been some unnoticed insect. Moray also held his tongue eloquently. The envoys bowed their heads in a mixture of disappointment, shame and fear, and turning their horses around, galloped towards Stirling Bridge with undignified haste.

That starry night was a long one for the soldiers camped on the bank of the Forth and those under the trees of the Craig, endlessly watching, waiting and wondering.

The following dawn brought another deputation. When the failure of the first overture was reported, some of the shrewder brains among the English leadership belatedly realised that perhaps their choice of envoys had been tactless and least likely to elicit a positive response. So it came about that the central figures of the second group of diplomats were identified from afar by keen-eyed Scots as Dominican friars, by their black and white monkish garb. This time there was no discussion as to who would talk and who would remain silent. There would be straightforward and forceful plain-speaking. The message with which these churchmen had been sent differed substantially from

the first in that it was stated that if the Scots would surrender and
enter into "the King's peace", then they would receive pardon.

Having delivered this generous offer, the elderly friars awaited the
response with quiet dignity, while their escort of minor English
knights looked down long noses making no attempt to disguise
their feeling that these terms were too merciful by far. Out of
respect for the Church, Wallace had dismounted to meet the
friars. After a long and icy silence during which the other Scots
present – Moray included – naturally deferred to their leader, the
big man took long strides which brought him to but a yard from
the holy spokesman. Stooping so that his face almost touched that
of the alarmed cleric, he spoke quietly and with unexpected
restraint.

"Good brother, tell those who sent you that we, for our part, have
not come here to plead for our lives, but to fight to the death for
the freedom of our native land." He inclined his face even closer
and, almost at a whisper, added – "Tell them to come right ahead
and we will show them. Aye, into their very beards."

It was a curious thing, but those watching could have sworn that
the old Dominican's lips parted in a gentle smile of unspoken
approval.

The Scots party had scarcely returned to the summit of the Abbey
Craig when agitated lookouts clamoured to point out that the
English army appeared to be on the move. Sure enough, clearly
visible was the fact that a trickle of mounted knights and infantry
had actually crossed the narrow wooden structure and were
forming up on the Scots side of the river. That this was no mere
exploratory patrol was evidenced by the fact that it was led by a

royal standard bearer holding aloft the three golden lions of King Edward. Also visible were the banners of various English noble houses. Wallace and Moray could not believe their luck. Their eyes gleamed with exhilaration and anticipation. All around and behind them the assembled Scottish force became aware of this so long awaited development and realisation that action was imminent swept through the ranks.

"Fools… arrogant fools."
For all his relief and satisfaction, Wallace was furious. Indignant because the English were not treating him and his force with due respect.

Moray shook his head almost in disbelief.

"They are so assured of victory that they have cast common sense to the wind. Look at them. It is just as we said it would be. They manage but two abreast on yon bridge. Have they no notion of how they are cutting their own throats?"

The Scots commanders had feared that the English leadership, realising the danger of channelling their vast force over the Forth by that single narrow crossing, would have made provision to overcome this strategic weakness. They could, for example have built any number of makeshift bridges with timber abundantly available from the nearby Tor Wood. Or they could have taken the trouble to identify fording points. Either of these options would have enabled them to send men over in great bodies and retain the advantage of numerical superiority. Bizarrely, it had been the treasurer, Cressingham, who had prevailed upon the old soldier, Warenne, to order this rash advance over Stirling Bridge.

With an impatient army stirring restlessly behind them, this was the most trying moment for Wallace and Moray. They must calculate precisely how many of the enemy they should allow to cross the bridge before unleashing their own warriors. They waited… and waited. With every fibre of their being screaming to give the order for attack, yet they waited, thanking God for the strict discipline which held the Scots force at bay.

By noon fully one third of the English host had traversed Stirling Bridge and were fanning out on the marshland on the river's northern bank. At a certain moment, with an almost psychic mutual understanding, Wallace and Moray looked hard into each other's faces and nodded briefly and grimly. It was time.

A horn sounded. It was the signal for the Scots army, led by a large number of spearmen, to charge down the long slope of the Craig and into the unprepared English force, which was now effectively separated from the main body of Warenne's massive army. The English suffered from several fatal disadvantages. Firstly, the Scots had the element of surprise. Secondly, the English cavalry were hopelessly incapacitated in the boggy marshland. They were trapped within a tight loop of the winding River Forth, with the bridge far to narrow for them to make any effective retreat. Not least of the factors which counted against the ordinary English soldiers was the fact that their leaders were entirely at a loss, while the Scots fought with a focussed ferocity. The spearmen mercilessly fell upon the confused and panic-stricken chaos of English horsemen and infantry. A contingent of Scots pikemen, according to plan, closed off the north end of the bridge, causing fleeing English to take to the river where many of them, encumbered by heavy armour, drowned, and others were dispatched by well-aimed pike thrusts.

The Scots butchered these Englishmen, many of them attempting to offer up their arms in surrender, with the diabolical savagery of men at long last having a chance to settle the score with loathed oppressors. Many remembered Berwick. One of the English leaders slain was the detested Cressingham. To that man's credit, he had put his life where his mouth was and led the vanguard over the bridge. In the general carnage he was dragged from his mount and enthusiastically speared to death. His body was later to be skinned, with portions being retained as souvenirs by Scots dehumanised by the barbarity of warfare.

Warenne, seeing the slaughter of his men, appalled and hopelessly unable to bring the bulk of his force to bear, quite lost his head and fled the field followed by what remained of his defeated army. The Scots, using nearby fords, were able to pursue the fleeing English. Indeed, one party of the victorious force reached the length of Berwick and wrested the town from its demoralised English garrison. The Battle of Stirling Bridge had lasted but an hour, but the consequences of the rout were far-reaching indeed.

Neither Wallace nor Moray had been temperamentally capable of remaining aloof from the fray, as generals directing from afar. Rather they had both been very much in the thick of it all, roaring and hacking and slashing with the rest. One tragic result of this impetuousness was that young Moray sustained a wound from which he was shortly thereafter to die. It was to be a profound loss to Scotland and to Wallace.

A rather distasteful note was sounded by the Steward and Lennox. Seeing the way the wind blew, they turned their coats yet again, joining the Scots army in pursuit of the retreating English and ambushing their baggage-train.

By way of contrast, one English knight who came out of the conflict with a kind of distinction was Sir Marmaduke Tweng, a Yorkshireman. With remarkable gallantry, skill and determination, he led a party which successfully fought its way back over the bridge to the English side. While the rest of Warenne's survivors headed south, Tweng was instructed to take command of the garrison of Stirling Castle. Within days, however, the gallant knight found himself in chains in a cell on Dumbarton Rock – another fortress which the English had abandoned on receiving word of Stirling Bridge.

*   *   *

"Her cutty-sark, o' Paisley harn,
   That while a lassie she had worn,
   In longitude tho' sorely scanty,
   It was her best, and she was vauntie…"

He was a born thespian, and Gunner Irwin was making the most of this lively delivery, prancing around the little schoolroom, eyes flashing and arms waving. His dozen pupils were absolutely enthralled as their dominie gave his rendering of *Tam o' Shanter* by Robert Burns. It was a fitting way of rounding off what had been an extraordinary school-day.

"…Till first ae caper, syne anither,
   Tam dint his reason a' thegither,
   And roars out, 'Well done, Cutty-sark!'
   And in an instant all was dark…"

He was wringing every drop of drama out of the tale, with drunken Tam fleeing for dear life on horseback, while chased by a furious coven of witches, led by the fair young wench who was clad in but a short shirt which barely gave her decency – "Cutty Sark" being Scots for a scanty shirt.

Duncan Robertson was entirely familiar with this particular poem, his father being a devotee of the National Bard, and an enthusiastic member of the Dumbarton Burns Club, which had, as it happened, celebrated its tenth anniversary earlier that year.

Just an hour before, the children, with not a few of the townsfolk, had lined the chilly battlements of Dumbarton Rock to view the eventual launch of the great clipper. The ship had pulled through a tangle of financial, business and technical snares to finally and triumphantly slip into the waters of the River Leven on the afternoon of Monday the 22nd of November 1869. So large had the vessel been that a dredger had had to be hired from Glasgow to deepen the channel at the confluence of Leven and Clyde. The sleek craft, painted black with gold lines, had been launched by the captain's wife – Mrs Moodie. Named after the famous young witch from *Tam o' Shanter*, the ship had a figurehead which took the form of that wild maiden, hair flowing behind her and hand outstretched, as it were, in an attempt to catch Tam's steed by the tail. Thus Gunner Irwin's own spirited performance.

"…Whene'er to drink you are inclin'd.
  Or cutty-sarks run in your mind,
  Think! Ye may buy the joys o'er dear –
  Remember Tam o' Shanter's mare."

Most suitable, he reflected, that the work should end on a note of warning, to these young folk, of the evils of drink.

Clearly, from glowing eyes and broad smiles, it had gone down well – taking minds off the cold in a school-room warmed only by a single begrudged lump of coal – and in the Dumbarton of that time no translation of the broad Scots had been at all necessary. Now Gunner Irwin shared with many a teacher, before and since, a certain vanity – a weakness inasmuch as he loved to make known the extent of his knowledge. Especially so (to Duncan Robertson's increasing interest) in the field of history. So it was, on this occasion, that he permitted himself the surely forgivable liberty of wandering on to an only tangentially relevant line.

"Of course, boys and girls, Dumbarton has a long history of shipbuilding, going back some hundreds of years. Oh yes…"

Lips pursed, eyes lifted to some inner vision, coat tails theatrically tugged.

"Let us consider, by way of example, the reign of King James the Fourth. Scotland had, as you will remember, six kings called James…"

Few of the pupils, except Duncan Robertson, remembered anything of the sort, as the master well knew.

"…all of whom were interesting, but the fourth was a fascinating man and an extraordinary monarch. James reigned around the turn of the fifteenth and sixteenth centuries, which was a very significant time in the intellectual history of Europe. He became what is known as a "renaissance prince"…"

Dark eyebrows raised, he glanced enquiringly around the classroom, as though asking if anyone present was familiar with the term. The gesture was, of course, not only tacit but also rhetorical.

"Well, this meant that he was a widely educated man with a great range of interests. James spoke a number of languages, including our own native Gaelic. He was a patron of the arts – music, architecture, literature – for example, he introduced Scotland's first printing press. He had a keen interest in scientific enquiry and experimentation, for instance in medical matters."

The single lump of coal had quite entirely expired, and now, late in the afternoon, the room had become even colder, and the children, though well wrapped up in warm winter clothing, were becoming restive... except for the Robertson boy (sporting a brand new corduroy cap) who hung intently on Gunner Irwin's every word.

"But James was very much a man of action. He was athletic. He enjoyed tournaments. Indeed, he was a warrior king. Most importantly, though, for our purposes, King James the Fourth was very interested in ships. He was painfully aware of the need to protect his realm against an aggressive English fleet, so he was the monarch who built up a Scottish Royal Navy of some forty vessels."

Through the chimney, the whistle of a distant steam train could be faintly discerned by those who were not giving this lecture their undivided attention.

"Now, King James had other problems. This realm of Scotland was seldom entirely united. It is a sad fact that the Scots are a quarrelsome people, and these internal divisions were always exploited by the "Auld Enemy", which is to say – England. The clans of the Western Isles for centuries were unwilling to wholeheartedly recognise the authority of the King of Scots. Instead, they looked to the Lord of the Isles for leadership. The Lord of the Isles was the chief of the MacDonalds…"

With an indulgent twinkle in his eye, Irwin looked meaningfully at wee Alex MacDonald, a dark-haired lad with a squint, who coloured with embarrassment at being brought to attention in this way.

"…and they were proud men, jealous of their independence. John, the fourth Lord of the Isles, for example, became a vassal of Edward the Fourth of England, offering to fight for him, for the sake of a pension."

It occurred to the master that he might do well to get to the point.

"Anyway… the fact is that King James felt the need on several occasions to personally take his royal fleet into the Western Isles in shows of strength which eventually led to the submission of the rebellious chiefs. Now, at this time Dumbarton was one of the most important ports in the realm, and best placed as a base from which to launch these expeditions. It was a good place, also, at which to build ships, with its two rivers and a splendid supply of timber from the hills around Loch Lomond."

He glanced automatically through the small, north-facing window in the direction of the loch.

"During one particular winter – according to official records – the king's shipbuilders were working busily in Dumbarton at the repair of the great ship *Christopher*, and the construction of a grand royal barge. This was in preparation for one of the Western Isles expeditions. When such things were being done, the king spent considerable time lodging here in the castle. Of course, he visited the burgh… He was fond of the cards, you know, which he played in the town, but he was a religious man who gave generously to the Kirk here…"

He had wandered, he realised.

"Aye, well, there you are. Dumbarton has been a most important centre of shipbuilding for these hundreds of years."

Young Duncan locked away the details of this little talk in the growing brain that buzzed under the new corduroy cap.

*   *   *

From down in the Royal Burgh, the great black Rock could scarcely be discerned against the vast sky of winter, which was almost as dark. Accordingly the torches and lamps which shone high up in the castle had the appearance of fiery stars, enhancing the notion that the lofty ones who dwelt there lived in some exalted realm halfway between this world and heaven.

It was early December of the year 1505, and the king was in his castle.

With a sensible royal guard and a minimum of servants and courtiers, James had come to Dumbarton to kill two birds with one stone. Earlier that day he had heard Mass in the little Chapel of Saint Patrick. His company had later dined well from silver plate in the castle's Hall. As they drank goblets of white wine, they were entertained by the king's Italian minstrels. The king, himself, ate and drank sparingly – a habit which was remarked upon by Pedro De Ayala, the Spanish ambassador. Later, though, His Grace lost a large sum at the dice. The king's chamber was at the top of a four-storey building which was known as the Wallace Tower. It was to this room that he eventually retired with just two companions – the Keeper of the Castle, Sir John Stirling of Craigbernard, and John Smollett, a burgess of Dumbarton.

There had been, in the Spring of that year, yet another royal expedition to the Isles. It had proved reasonably successful, with the chiefs of Barra and Ulva entering into the king's peace. One man, however, Torquil Macleod, continued to be a thorn in James's side. It was the king's intention to have his Council summon Macleod to trial for treason, but in the meantime James had a secret, and related, mission which he wanted the man Smollett to undertake on his behalf in the Highlands. It did not suit the royal purpose that the Dumbarton burgess should appear at court. He wished their meeting to be as private as possible, and he needed little excuse to come himself to this western stronghold. The truth was that James was a restless man. He was given to bouts of melancholy, particularly in the dark winter months, and he kept his mind active with regular travel.

The three sat comfortably in the small but well-appointed chamber. A fire of pine logs blazed cheerfully. Beneath their feet there was a rich carpet. The thick stone walls were hung with beautiful tapestries. When the monarch had thus privily given the burgess his instructions, he spoke to the Keeper –

"Now, Johnny, let's be at yon ither wee matter."

The simple broad Scots was the natural mode of expression for this multilingual prince.

"As Your Grace pleases. Will I hae it broucht up, or would you raither see it doon by?"

Sir John was a darkly handsome man of middle years. Slim, smooth and with hooded eyes. A close and trusted friend of his king.

"Doon by, man… doon by. I hae the power o' my legs yet."

He spoke with an ironic laugh, this monarch now in his thirty-third year. He was a fine-looking man, with dark eyes, long aquiline nose, naturally-smiling mouth and a strong, pointed chin. Under a velvet cap he wore his thick, wavy, dark auburn hair to his broad and muscular shoulders. On this occasion he wore a rich crimson, fur-collared robe.

Smollett was politely but firmly dismissed with the king's good wishes, while king and keeper made their way down the winding stone stairway to the castle's armoury.

When they were alone, Sir John spoke.

"There yi are Your Grace. You'll see whit a meant…"

It was not the first time, by any means, that King James had looked upon the ancient sword of William Wallace. He had visited this royal castle on many an occasion and for a variety of reasons, and he had looked at this relic nearly as often. This year, as the king very well knew, was the two hundredth anniversary of the shameful and horrific execution of the national hero. As a devoutly religious man, James had a great belief in the power and the value of symbols. As he silently studied the long weapon before him, curiously, he found himself thinking, not of the great man who had wielded it, nor of the great cause in which it had been wielded, but rather he thought of endurance – the endurance of things, of ideas and of virtues. Here, indeed, was an object worthy of veneration.

Yet what he saw disturbed him a little. Here was neglect. Here was clear evidence that due and proper care had not been taken with a national treasure. He pursed his lips in an expression of distaste.

"Aye… aye, Johnny. This'll no' dae… no' dae at a'. Your predecessor has fair let us doon in this."

He rubbed the long chin gravely.

"I'll gie instruction tae Rab Selkirk… he's ma cutler, yi ken… in Edinburgh, tae hae this rectified. Aye, you hae done weel tae bring this tae my attention, Johnny."

With a final lingering look at the sword, the pair turned and silently left the armoury.

𝔓ower and tℏe 𝔚ritten 𝔚ord

"This was another supremely important radical departure, not only in Scottish history but conceivably also in European history... The Covenant was one of the great disjunctures in Scottish history. It marked, in a very real sense, the end of the medieval world."

(Ted Cowan: Professor of Scottish History and Literature.)

On the 15th of May 1975(I was twenty-two years old) my working life underwent significant change. I became an employee of the newly-created Strathclyde Regional Council, a massive chunk of the West of Scotland which was to become, in effect, a Labour Party petty kingdom. Arising from the Wheatley Report – a Royal Commission relating to reorganisation of local government in Scotland - the old counties and burghs were scrapped, being replaced by regions and districts. Accordingly, I no longer worked for Dunbartonshire County Council, but for the Dunbarton Sub-Region of Strathclyde Regional Council.

Initially I worked from the same desk in the same office, but some of the old faces were lost and some new ones gained. The rent collectors, of whom I have spoken, became members of staff with

Dumbarton District Council. Over a period of some five years, I had grown to like and to respect most of them. For by far the greater part, they had been warm and benevolent characters. They had given me much good advice which I had been unwilling or unable to accept and put into practice, but I did, nevertheless, appreciate their concern for me. I never came to share their political views. The generation gap remained real, but I eventually realised that these men and women had seen hard times but they had kind hearts. They were patient and understanding when I, in my youthful arrogance, made a fool of myself, as I did, more than once. I was sorry to see them go.

The new faces, as I remember, came mostly, but not exclusively, from Cumbernauld in the old East Dunbartonshire. As a result, then, of this upheaval, I became one of a circle of friends. Four men, one woman, all in our twenties... and every one a Scottish Nationalist. That it should work out this way was no fortunate fluke. The fact was that, at that time in the mid-Seventies, the SNP was the second strongest political force in Scotland, and almost half of young voters supported independence. The young woman, as it happened, was the one I'd known since our days in the same class in primary school. The one who'd expressed approval of my badge that night in the *Tudor Lounge*.

That old school – Main Street Primary – had been demolished around ten years earlier. On the site a new community leisure centre had been built. It was in a room in the centre that the monthly meetings of the Vale of Leven Branch of the SNP were held. I attended these religiously, but my main practical contribution remained leafleting, which I now undertook in a bigger and more systematic way. I became personally responsible for delivering all the party's leaflets in the area of the town known as Levenvale. This was an area of something just under half of a square mile of local authority housing, bounded by two main roads, a railway-line and a long street, with a western flank of semi-detached houses and sandstone villas. Approximately one thousand households. Over these five years, I became intimately acquainted with every letterbox, nameplate, garden gate and flight of stairs in the place.

Around the time of my change of employer, there was also a social change to my routine. On a particular summer's evening, after a long, hot day, I found myself in a cocktail bar in one of Balloch's hotels. I'd had a few lagers and I found myself standing at the bar with a man I'd thought of as a friend. He was a few years older than I was, a handsome ladies man with a reputation as a bar-room brawler. On this particular occasion both of us had had too much of the sun and too many pints – often a dangerous mixture. He made some sarcastic remark to me about the Scottish Nationalists. I do not remember how I replied, but my response was clearly ill-considered. He slapped my face, more insultingly than violently, but very publicly. With a rush of blood to the head, I punched him squarely on the jaw.

By this time I'd witnessed quite a few scraps in pubs and lounges, and it seemed to me that mostly there was an element of pretence about them. Two drunk men would flail their fists around, seldom making much contact, then they'd throw their arms around each other and stagger around the place upsetting tables and spilling drinks until they were (to their secret relief) hauled apart.

In the second or two during which my opponent recovered from my blow and took up a fighting stance, I made a conscious

decision that this display was going to look more convincing. I
made sure that several more punches landed on his face as we
horrified the genteel clientele with our barbaric interlude. Later I
was told that he hadn't landed a single clean blow on me. That
was just as well, because one punch would have been enough to
finish me off. I was not naturally a fighting man. I lacked the
hardness, nerve and aggression.

After what was probably only ten seconds or so of this fracas, I
was held from behind and unceremoniously thrown out into the
street. With a sleeve dangling loose from my torn shirt, I made my
way promptly homeward, before the police became involved. My
adversary had been an older and stronger man, experienced in
pugilism. I'd got the better of him in that brief tussle simply
because he'd been more drunk than I and because of the element
of surprise. It was the first and last occasion in my adult life that I
got involved in physical violence.

A few evenings later I was foolish enough to go back to the same
hotel. He got me in the gents toilet. Unfortunately we had the
place to ourselves. He grabbed me vigorously by the throat,
knocking my glasses from my face. I stood speechless and rigid as
he delivered an impassioned speech about my effrontery in
striking him on the previous occasion, while clearly working
himself up to set about me good and proper. To my inexpressible
relief another drinker eventually entered the toilet, which
intrusion blessedly brought about a cessation of these proceedings,
allowing me to slip away largely unscathed but utterly humiliated.

One positive outcome from these unpleasant encounters was that
I decided to avoid the pubs and lounges of Balloch for the
foreseeable future. Not an easy decision, for the various licensed

premises of the village had collectively been my evening "home" for several years. I recalled, however, an occasion from the time I'd briefly been a member of the Loch Lomond Rowing Club, when my crew had resorted, one evening, to a quiet wee public house in Alexandria. So it happened that one night I left the flat in Tullichewan and turned south instead of north and headed for the *Old Vale Bar*. My recollection of the place was that it was an old man's pub: a rather dull resort, but needs must when the devil rides, as they say.

It was situated on the old red sandstone edge of the town, at the corner of the Main Street and Albert Street. Walking into it was like stepping back in time. To my eye it had an Edwardian air. I was later to discover that it had originally been owned by a retired serviceman called Coates, who had served as a boy soldier in the Sudan. In my time it was owned and run by Lewis Montgomery, a droll, unhurried man in his fifties whom I came to regard with fondness and respect.

There was a wooden bar, the counter of which was worn to a shine by generations of elbows. Behind this was a large and impressive carved gantry which incorporated a clock with roman numerals. There was no carpet, but rubber matting on the floor. The chairs and tables harmonised with the rest of the place, in terms of date and condition. The ceiling was yellowed with decades of nicotine. There were large mirrors advertising ales which had long since passed out of production. The effect was completed by a tiny old gas fire which was fitted against the wall under a poster of the Scotland football team.

That evening the place was quiet. There were, I think, around half-a-dozen customers. By chance, as I ordered a pint of lager, I encountered at the bar an old school-friend. We exchanged ritual greetings and he left me and returned to the table in the south-west corner of the premises. Sitting there was a large, heavy man with thinning red hair. Apparently in his sixties, he had a round, florid and cheery face. Seeing me standing alone at the bar he gently berated my old acquaintance –

"Bring your friend over to join us, Jim."

Sheepishly I lifted my pint and went over... and that was the beginning of one of the least regretted chapters of my life – the half-dozen or so years during which I was a regular of Lewis' *Old Vale Bar*.

The big man turned out to be Jock Clark, a clerk at the local council's nearby Roads Depot. I was soon to make the acquaintance of a number of men whose company I would enjoy and value. Men from different backgrounds and age groups and with varying points of view. Interesting characters. It was very much a man's pub. Women very rarely entered these portals. Indeed, there were no facilities for them. It was nearly always around that table in the south-west corner that this company would congregate. The over-forties smartened themselves up for drinking sessions, perspiring uncomfortably in tight collars and ties, while we young fellows were as casual as possible. Out of all the precious memories I have of "sharing the social cup", one is particularly dear to me. Every time, to this day, that I hear the old tune *The Dark Island*, I recall with some emotion how, now and again, at a certain point in the evening, Iain Montgomery, brother of the owner, and I would whistle together that haunting air. I will be accused of the worst possible *Brigadoon* sentiment, but I swear that these shared moments spoke meaningfully to our common Highland ancestry. I recall one elderly gentleman referring to *Lewis's* as "the dream shop". How right he was – I dreamt many a great dream in those days, and have never felt more at home in any other public house.

Needless to say, politics was discussed regularly. As in my office, the older men tended to be ex-servicemen, but in the *Old Vale* there were more of that generation inclined toward independence. The younger men were also divided on the question and, with drink involved, debate was not always entirely dispassionate.

In quieter moments, when seated alone, perhaps before others had arrived, I could be seen poring over copies of the *Scots Independent*, particularly appreciating the contributions of my old favourites – Oliver Brown and Anthony J.C. Kerr. I have said that leafleting was my major political activity in those years, but it was at this time that I began to send letters to the local, and very occasionally, national press. The first political letter I remember having published in the *Lennox Herald* related to the referendum, introduced by Labour Prime Minister, Harold Wilson, on the United Kingdom's continuing membership of the Common Market (as the European Union was then known). In concurrence with the Nationalist party line, I argued that if government from distant London was bad enough, how much worse was interference from Brussels. I think the letter's publication caused my father a mixture of embarrassment and pride – perhaps, to be fair to him, more of the latter. Anyway, sixty-seven percent of the UK voters opted for continued membership.

Even more pretentiously, however, I began to contribute political poetry to the *Scots Independent*, constituency SNP literature, and our local papers. The first effort to go out in print, curiously, wasn't political at all. On the edge of my leafleting area, Levenvale, there was a small pedestrian bridge which crossed the railway-line. It was filthy (often bemired with dog's dirt), covered in graffiti, and seldom adequately lit. My verses on the subject graced the pages of the *Lennox Herald* in August of 1977. Very shortly after its appearance the council erected a new lamppost beside the bridge. I am under no illusion that my poetry had any literary merit. Such works as were published were used simply because of their political content.

In that latter half of the seventies, the main political issue was Devolution – the possible handing over of limited powers from Westminster to directly elected Scottish and Welsh "assemblies" (the Unionists of that time were careful not to call them parliaments, lest the Celts should get above themselves). For the Nationalists this was regarded as a stepping-stone to full independence, therefore we campaigned in favour. The Unionist parties were divided amongst themselves on the question. But those Unionists who did support devolution did so because they hoped that it would take the wind out of Nationalist sails.

1977 was the year in which Elvis Presley, Marc Bolan and Groucho Marx died. We listened to *Hotel California* by the Eagles, *How Deep is Your Love?* by the Bee Gees and *Dancing Queen* by Abba. Also Queen Elizabeth had her Silver Jubilee. Queen Elizabeth the *Second*. The second Elizabeth of England, admittedly, but of the United Kingdom assuredly, the *first*. But in spite of the logic, the historical reality, the English would have none of it, so when she'd been crowned in 1953, they'd ridden roughshod over Scottish sensitivities and named *their* queen Elizabeth the Second. Precisely the sort of arrogance which defined the relationship which was the Union.

In May of 1977, the strength and increased popularity of the SNP was given expression in the results of the Scottish local council elections. In my own constituency the Labour Party managed to return only two of its seven councillors. Old Labour stalwarts of many years standing were defeated by Margaret McGregor, a housewife, for Jamestown and Kilmaronock ward, Alistair Henderson, a retired headmaster, for Alexandria, Neil McEwan, a trade union official, for Tullichewan and Luss, and Ron Kirton, a school teacher, for Bonhill – all wards within the Vale of Leven. Particularly satisfying for me was the victory of Neil McEwan, because his ward included Levenvale, so I was able to tell myself that I had to a significant extent contributed to his triumph.

Such were the issues which determined the content of the many thousands of leaflets I delivered during these years. Night after night, I'd trail the streets of Levenvale, a black and white Adidas sports-bag slung over the shoulder of my cheap sky-blue cagoule. Every leaflet delivered, I told myself, largely in conscious self-mockery, was another thrust of the claymore. I did think of myself as being a twentieth century equivalent of one of the Jacobite clansmen at Culloden, or one of Wallace's people's army at Stirling Bridge, but I was mature enough to be hugely grateful that I might do my little bit without risk to life or limb.

The SNP had gone from being a party of amusing, harmless and indulged romantics to being a proven political threat which was now heartily despised by many of its Unionist opponents. One evening at this time, I was on may way to the *Old Vale Bar* with a drinking crony who was a reporter with one of the local papers. As we were passing the campaign headquarters of one of the Unionist parties (which I shall favour with anonymity) an official of that party recognised my friend and, knowing that he was a supporter of the SNP, asked him –

"Are you still working for the Nazis?"

Remarks of that nature were passed off as legitimate political rough and tumble by such people in those days.

*   *   *

The Hanseatic League was, in effect, a mercantile co-operative – a confederation of towns in northern Germany, banded together to further mutual trading interests. It was very successful, concerning itself with commerce with Scandinavia, the Baltic and Flanders. It took Moray a couple of months to die, but in those final weeks his wits were sharp and his commitment to Scotland's cause undiminished. In October, with Wallace, he wrote letters to the Hanseatic communities of Hamburg and Lubeck. In translation from the Latin, these read –

Andrew de Moray and William Wallace, Generals of the army of the realm of Scotland, and the community of that realm, to their worthy and well-beloved friends, the Mayors and common people of Lubeck and Hamburg, greetings.

We have been informed by trusted merchants of the realm of Scotland that you are giving aid and favour in all commerce concerning us and our merchants for which we thank you. We ask that it be made known among your merchants that they will now have safe access to all ports of the realm of Scotland with their merchandise, since the realm of Scotland, thanks be to God, has been rescued by force of arms from the power of the English.

Given at Haddington in Scotland, on the 11th day of October in the year of grace one thousand two hundred and ninety seven.

The amber seal bore the Lion Rampant because Moray and Wallace continued to act in the name of King John. On the reverse there was an image of Wallace's bow and arrow.

Lennox and the Steward were not the only members of the Scottish nobility to change sides again as a result of the Stirling Bridge victory. Others, such as Buchan, Strathearn and the Comyns also returned to the Scots army. At a council held in Perth, Wallace was knighted and elected "Guardian of the Kingdom of Scotland and Commander of its armies in the name of the famous prince Lord John, by God's Grace, illustrious King of Scotland, by consent of the Community of the realm."

It was one thing to drive the English out of Scotland, and to encourage a resumption of foreign trade, but years of occupation, warfare and rapine had left much of the southern part of the realm badly depleted of cattle and crops. Starvation faced many. For that reason, restitution, as it were, to ram home the new state of affairs, and out of a raw craving for revenge, it was decided to mount an extensive raid into England's northern counties. Mustering at Roslin Moor on Saint Luke's Day, the 18th of October, a properly assembled Scots force followed up on spontaneous raiding by driving deep into Northumberland and Cumbria. A terrified English populace, well-schooled with tales of the monster Wallace, fled southward as the Scots plundered cattle and grain, and indulged in an orgy of general looting and pillaging. An attempt to capture well-defended Carlisle was abandoned and the invaders reached as far south as Bassenthwaite

Lake before turning eastward in the direction of Durham. Severe winter weather brought blizzards to the Pennines, and in the face of these lethal conditions the Scots army was again diverted, this time back northwards eventually reaching Hexham Priory.

"Damn them!"

Wallace's face had turned crimson and his great fist hammered on the refectory table, causing silver plate to jump and goblets to spill.

"I'll have their heads for this. I swear it!"

All the monks but three canons had fled the Priory on receiving word of the approaching Scottish army. These three had been threatened with unspeakable torture unless they disclosed the whereabouts of the Priory's hidden treasures. With incredible courage they had refused to co-operate. Wallace had personally intervened, respecting their mettle and preventing atrocities being perpetrated against the churchmen. He'd then requested that they celebrate the Mass for himself and his soldiers. The Guardian had gone outside to remove his sword, in due deference to the sacrament. On returning, he was appalled to discover that in his absence some of his men – identity allegedly unknown – had actually made off with the chalice and other sacred items.

Seated around him were a number of the Scots nobility, his usual trusted lieutenants – Kerlie, Boyd, Gray – and Blair, his chaplain. His comrades of long-standing held their tongues and looked on tensely, but some of the lords looked cynical. It was one of the Comyns, an arrogant young man with golden hair and crimson velvet under his chainmail, who spoke out.

"My Lord Guardian, no one will betray these men. Who would see brothers-in-arms lose their heads over English priests? No common man in your army who suffered the humiliation of English clergy strutting in his own parish will care a fig for these holy ornaments, never mind see a fellow Scot hang for them. I strongly advise some other course, my Lord."

Kerlie jumped in quickly to head off an explosion of wrath from the Guardian.

"This is good advice, Will. There will be great resentment and ill-feeling among our men if any of their number are executed to humour these churchmen."

"In the name of God, Kerlie, this has to do with sacrilege... with discipline. I would not have King John's army seen as some heathen rabble lacking all respect for things sacred."

His listeners could hardly believe their ears, given the violent and mindless excesses of recent weeks, to say nothing of the countless English clergy who had been slain out of hand over the past year.

It was Blair, the chaplain, who ventured a suggestion.

"Some gesture, Will... A guarantee of future protection. On your word as Guardian. A charter, perhaps. Aye... that would impress these churchmen. A charter of protection and safe conduct."

And so, incredibly, after much patient and tactful persuasion, Wallace was prevailed upon to put his seal to a charter which guaranteed protection to the Priory and the Convent of Hexham, and curiously it did, indeed, impress the English clerics.

By Yuletide the sated marauders had trailed their weary and arduous way through snow-choked passes and over miles of frozen moors, back over the border and homeward with much-needed supplies of food, to say nothing of a fortune in loot.

*   *   *

"When James the Sixth, son of Mary Queen of Scots, eventually fulfilled his dearest ambition, and became king of the United Kingdom of England and Scotland, there were plenty who thought that it was a good thing, and of course in many ways it was. But, England being larger and richer, inevitably the king lost much of his interest in his native realm, wee, poor, distant Scotland. By the time his son, King Charles I, was crowned in Westminster Abbey, in 1626, that alienation from the smaller kingdom had increased. Charles, unlike his father before him, knew little of the Scots and their ways, and he cared less. So that when he became Head of the Church of England he entertained the notion that he should also be Head of the Church of Scotland. Well, you can imagine how the Scots and their Kirk felt about that."

Gunner Irwin was giving Duncan Robertson an account of the background events which had given rise to the Covenanters of the seventeenth century. The pair were in the Wallace Tower, where they had been trying, with some difficulty, to read an inscription cut into one of the stones surrounding a chimney piece. From the date "1694" and the words "persecuted for Christ", the school-master presumed that the writer had been a Covenanter prisoner who had been held in this part of the castle. At this mention of the Covenanters, Duncan had confessed that he had only a vague idea as to who and what they had been.

Over this past year, Irwin had begun to be increasingly impressed by this pupil's general intelligence and, in particular, his great interest in Scottish history. In fact, he'd begun to wonder if, indeed, young Robertson might have an academic future. The time was coming, however, and coming soon, when the boy would be expected to start working, perhaps as an apprentice to his father, or in one of the shipyards. But Irwin felt that such would be a great waste. This young fellow was university material. Perhaps he might have a tactful word with the father, James Robertson, the stonemason. Returning to the matter in hand, he continued –

"King Charles also intended to force the Scots into the same forms of worship as the English. As a start, he tried to impose *Laud's Liturgy* and then, effectively, the *English Book of Common Prayer* – on Scotland. This was what provoked the *National Covenant* of 1638."

It was a fresh Saturday afternoon, and the two of them stood alone on the battlement in front of the Wallace Tower, looking away beyond the Burgh, through the hills of the Vale of Leven, and towards the distant mountains and islands of Loch Lomond. As ever, the gulls swooped and cried, and an occasional spit of rain threatened to become a shower.

"Now this covenant was a very powerful document. The signing of it began in the kirkyard of Greyfriars Church in Edinburgh. Very soon copies of the Covenant were being signed by folk of all classes throughout the land. You know, it's said that some men actually signed in their own blood!"

Duncan twisted his lips doubtfully, unimpressed by this particularly macabre detail.

"The document insisted that those who put their names to it remained loyal to the king, but they were adamant that as Scots Presbyterians they would reject any return to Roman Catholic ideas and methods, and they were absolutely determined not to be swallowed up into the Church of England. Those who signed the Covenant lived and died to defend the independence of the Scots Kirk, and they became known as the *Covenanters*."

The school-master looked up as though suddenly something had occurred to him – something pleasing. His eyes lit up.

"Och yes. I must now tell you the story of Provost Sempill. Now there was a hero for you. D'you know, there might be no castle standing on this Rock today if it hadn't been for Provost John Sempill?"

Duncan looked suitably intrigued. The spitting rain was becoming heavier, but neither of them noticed the fact.

"Well, anyway – a kind of council was set up in opposition to King Charles's government in Scotland. This council was called *The Tables*, and your man – Sempill of Aikenbar and Stoneyflatt – as we should properly call him, was a member of it. He also attended the General Assembly of the Church of Scotland which sat in Glasgow Cathedral that year – the year the Covenant was signed."

Strictly speaking, Gunner Irwin was, at that precise moment, not on duty as the dominie, but as a soldier. He was in uniform, and unconsciously he replaced the tall, cockaded hat, which he had been holding under his arm, firmly back on his head.

"This Assembly audaciously deposed the bishops whom the king had set over the Kirk, and it did away with the new liturgy. Well, of course, the king could not stand for that and the stage was set for war."

Young Duncan, thoroughly absorbed, was scribbling furiously into a small notebook he carried on his person habitually.

"Charles got his generals together to plan an invasion of Scotland. An army of some twenty thousand English soldiers was to cross the border, and other sea-borne forces were to land at various places. The Earl of Strafford was expected to bring over an army of ten thousand from Ireland… to land at Dumbarton. The Scots, though, anticipated this, and they captured Edinburgh Castle, Stirling Castle, the Isle of Arran, and… Dumbarton Castle. So much for the Union of the Crowns ensuring peace."

On this point of high drama, that practised narrator decided that they'd be wiser to get out of what had become something of a downpour. Accordingly they retired hastily to the room in the Wallace Tower from which they had come.

"Now we come back to Provost Sempill."

They were, at that point, maddeningly interrupted by one of the guides conducting a couple of visitors – a rather genteel husband

and wife of middle years – on a tour of the castle. At length, having barely managed to keep civil expressions on their faces, they were left alone again and the Gunner continued.

"The King's Keeper of the Castle at that time was a certain Sir William Stewart. One Sunday in the month of March – this would have been the next year, after the Assembly – he attended the Parish Kirk, down by."

He nodded through the window, in the direction of the town's church, below in the High Street.

"At the end of the service, Sempill, with MacAulay o' Ardincaple and forty of the town's Covenanter militia, abducted the Keeper, his wife and one of his sons. They were all taken to Sempill's house where, under extreme duress, shall we say, the Keeper handed over the keys of the castle and disclosed the watchword."

The narrator, quite carried away with his own tale, smiled at some inner picture and continued.

"Sir William was made to strip out of his clothing, and one of the militia, a Covenanter of the same height and build as the Keeper, donned his garments. Then a body of men, with the disguised fellow posing as the Keeper, went to the gate of the castle, shouted the watchword to the sentries, and gained entry. Well, seizing the castle was really a simple matter, because it turned out that most of the garrison were either signed Covenanters themselves, or sympathisers."

Duncan smiled signalling his appreciation of the unfolding tale, but impatiently he asked –

"Aye, Sir… but what did you mean about there being no castle, but for this Provost man?"

*   *   *

John Sempill was short, overweight, and almost comically pompous. He was of late middle-years, round faced and with receding gingerish hair. Officious and conceited he might have been, but he was also courageous and an effective leader of men, as well as politically shrewd. His companion was William Crawfurd of Kilbirnie, a taller, younger and more handsome man. It had been the dark, hawk-featured Crawfurd who had raised the Covenanter militia in the County of Dumbarton. The pair stood in a small chamber of the Wallace Tower. It was May of the year 1644.

"Well, you can take it from me Crawfurd, I will do no such thing. Falling apart though this castle might be, it is sheerest madness to reduce a stronghold of such strategic value to rubble."

The fleshy jowls quivered with indignation. Crawfurd suppressed a smirk.

"Aye, John, but ye hae yir orders fae the Estates. Man, they're no' tae be ignored."

"There is not a man in this realm more loyal to the Covenant than I, Crawfurd, but I will not be remembered as the man who pulled down Dumbarton Castle."

After Provost Sempill had captured the Rock, in March of 1639, it had been held for but a matter of a few months for the

Covenanters. The attempt by King Charles to invade Scotland
had failed, principally because he had been faced by a strong and
determined Scots army at the border. In June of 1639 the king
signed the "Pacification of Berwick", a treaty which was short-
lived, but according to the terms of which Dumbarton Castle was
handed back to the Royalists. It was then garrisoned by English
soldiers, but in 1640 it had changed hands yet again when they
surrendered it to the Earl of Argyll, a general of the Covenanting
army.

Sadly, in a divided land, there were those on his own side who
mistrusted Argyll, and felt that he already held too much power
for one man. Control of Dumbarton Castle falling to Clan
Campbell was more than they were prepared to countenance.
Accordingly, by an act of the Scottish Estates, Sempill had been
instructed to remove the garrison, ammunition and cannon from
the fortress, and thereafter to demolish the castle's buildings and
walls. Provost John, however, was wise enough to know that earls
and acts came and went, but mighty rocks (and their strategic
importance) lasted forever.

A complex situation had become more complicated. In Scotland,
Roman Catholics, Presbyterians and Episcopalians were at each
others' throats. In England, the Civil War between Royalists and
Parliamentarians also had a religious dimension. There was a
certain amount of common purpose between the Scots
Covenanters and the English Parliamentarians, arising from
which, in September of 1643, the Scots had signed the *Solemn
League and Covenant*. This bond pledged the Scots to send
military aid to the English Parliamentarians in the hope (vain as it
was to turn out) that the Presbyterian form of worship would be
adopted by the English.

The first man to sign the original National Covenant, back in 1638, had been James Graham, Earl of Montrose. But Montrose, like many another, became hostile to his fellow earl, Argyll, and he changed sides. King Charles had made him a Marquis, appointed him Viceroy of Scotland and sent him northward to raise an army against the Covenanters. Such was the situation that May morning, when Provost Sempill and Crawfurd of Kilbirnie were having their private conversation in the chamber fast within the Wallace Tower of Dumbarton Castle.

"Madness, it would be sheerest madness, I tell you, to abandon such a position of strength here, dominating the Firth of Clyde and holding the key to the West."

The portly warrior glared at his listener as though defying him to contradict. Kilbirnie was disinclined to say so aloud, but in truth he tended to share Sempill's view.

"With Montrose scouring the North and the Isles for Highland men and Irish to pit against the Godly army of Christ's True Kirk, there has never been a more dire need to hold this landing place against the war-galleys of the MacDonalds and their like. Mark my words, Kilbirnie, these rag-tags are motivated neither by religion nor by any other principle, but by desire for plunder and sheer hatred of Argyll's Clan Campbell – as is Montrose, himself. Well, let me assure you…"

He snapped chubby fingers in a gesture of dismissal.

"…I give *that* for the Estates and their instructions. By the time Montrose gets this length with his Highland Host, I will have this fortress mightily strong against him, even if I have to pay for every block of stone and plank of timber out of my own purse."

Sempill had become quite puce through his emotional outburst. He paused to draw breath and settle himself, so Kilbirnie took the opportunity to change the subject.

"The inventory, John? D'ye mind that?"

Sempill ignored the possibility of sarcasm in that question.

They had, in the company of three of the garrison's officers, been touring the fortress, building by building, making an account of their various contents. They had meticulously examined the Hall, the Pantry, the Brew-house, the Armoury... and now they were alone (the officers having been dismissed in order that these two might talk privately) in this room high in the Wallace Tower. The dusty chamber showed all the signs of neglect and decay which were evidenced throughout the castle, and from somewhere there lingered a distasteful odour of sour milk.

Sempill unlocked the long chest which lay on the stone floor and they looked down on the ancient sword within it.

"A wee touch o' rust there, John. It's just as well some o' the previous occupiers had nae knowledge o' whit this kist held."

"Just as well, indeed, my old and trusted friend."

"Are yi goin' tae pit this oan yir list, then?"

Sempill's piggy eyes devoured the large, two-handed sword.

"It is here, so it must go into the inventory. I'll have no inaccuracy."

"And d'ye think that's wise, then?

"Well…"

Kilbirnie interrupted the Provost.

"Ah mean, can yi imagine whit Montrose wid dae wae this, if he wis ever tae get his haunds oan it? He'd mak a richt symbol o' it for his Royalist heathens tae rally aroon – the sword o' William Wallace."

Sempill frowned, deep in thought.

"Right, we'll simply list it as a rusty old double-handed sword. That's what it is, after all. It's a perfectly truthful description, without betraying its … greater significance, so that it doesn't get into the wrong hands."

Kilbirnie looked doubtful.

"Should we no' pit it in wae a' thae ither swords in the Armoury?"

"No, no, man. If certain powers get their way, every weapon in there will be flung in the river. I'll lock it up and you can help me put it back in its place here."

So saying, Provost John Sempill picked up quill and parchment and began to write slowly and with care –

"Ane auld twa-handed sword without a scabbard."

Betrayal and Defeat

"…never two nations, that had so much affinity in circumstances, have had such inveteracy and aversion to one another in their blood."

(Daniel Defoe: 1709)

It's a Saturday evening. I've just watched *All Creatures Great and Small* on the television and now I'm getting ready to catch the bus for Dumbarton. On with the dark blue pinstripe suit with flared trousers and wide lapels, a carefully chosen tie, gold-plated digital watch, and a splash of *Blue Stratos*. As I leave the flat and walk carefully on snow-covered pavements a song called *Sweet Talkin' Woman* by the Electric Light Orchestra plays in my head. Now I'm standing under streetlights in the High Street, looking up at a tearoom window and waiting for a girl – a dark-eyed, raven-haired beauty – and I'm thinking – "I'll remember this moment when I'm an old man." The winter of 1978-1979 is one which I do remember fondly.

Around this time my writing pretensions were notably rewarded when a couple of big name Scottish folk groups set some of my lyrics to music and then recorded them. These were not political works, but historical ballads. Especially thrilling for me was when one of the songs was sung on television and another was reported by a friend as having been heard on the radio. Although I received complimentary albums, I recall going into Woolworth's to buy a copy of one of them. Playing over the sound system, as I proudly made my purchase, was the Abba song, *Super Trouper*. Curiously, this reminds me of an almost bizarre example of the way in which a sense of low self-esteem seems to permeate the Scottish collective psyche. On a number of occasions I heard people arguing, quite indignantly, that the song did not contain the word "Glasgow". The line of reasoning being, apparently, that a supergroup with the international standing of Abba were hardly likely to mention the likes of *Glasgow* in a song. I was twenty-five years old, and my swagger was a cover for the profound self-doubt I shared with my nation.

Politically it was an interesting but rather strange time. It was the run-up to the referendum on whether there should be a Scottish "Assembly" – a directly elected body with certain powers devolved from Westminster. Parties were split on the issue, and so, to an extent, was I.

It seemed to me that only one party actually believed in the thing for its own sake – the Liberals. Unionists who supported it tended to do so reluctantly, fervently hoping it would put a stop to any desire for outright independence. It was, in fact, a cynical device. The Nationalists who supported it (and there were some who didn't) hoped, with equal fervour, that it would be a step on the way to absolute sovereignty. I swung round to the latter point of view, but with reservations.

The background to all of this was the "Winter of Discontent". A Labour government, under Prime Minister James Callaghan, had run the United Kingdom so ineptly that British society was in a shambles. There had been high inflation, with the pound losing value so dramatically that in September of 1976 Britain had humiliatingly been forced to apply to the International Monetary Fund for an unprecedented loan of some 3.9 billion dollars. The IMF had made the bail-out conditional on the UK government applying drastic cuts in its public spending. These claw-backs had affected economic and social policies profoundly. The relationship between the Labour government and the trades unions deteriorated dramatically and during this 1978-1979 winter a series of bitter strikes broke out, badly affecting public morale and any residual confidence in Labour's ability to govern. Devolution was, at least in part, a bribe to the SNP to help keep Labour in power.

Devolution as an idea had an interesting pedigree. Historically Scottish socialists had supported "Home Rule". In 1919 parliamentary reports suggested a devolved assembly for Scotland with tax raising powers. Nothing was done about this, of course.

In the 1930s the Labour Party was divided on the question. There was a split, with the Independent Labour Party in favour. In 1932 *the Scottish Daily Express* held an opinion poll in which 113,000 participants voted for Home Rule, and just 5,000 voted against. The Scottish National Party, it will be remembered, was established in 1934.

Again, it might be recollected, the Scottish Covenant, asking for Home Rule, was signed in 1947 by some 2,000,000 persons... but totally ignored.

The emergence of the SNP in the 1960s forced Unionist British parties to reconsider devolution, so that, at the Conservative Conference of 1968, Edward Heath uttered a pledge to establish a Scottish Assembly. More pressure from the Nationalists throughout the 1970s resulted in a measure of commitment from Labour Prime Minister, Harold Wilson, but his party was still divided and unenthusiastic. James Callaghan succeeded Wilson as Premier, but the first Devolution Bill he introduced failed, having been defeated by Tory and Labour MPs alike… Then there was the second Bill.

George Cunningham, Labour MP for Islington South and Finsbury, was a Scot. You can always depend on one. It was he who introduced the "Forty Per cent Amendment". In effect, this device meant that in order for the Scottish Assembly to become a reality, it would have to be voted for by no less than forty per cent of all persons entitled to vote in the referendum. This, at first glance, may sound not unreasonable, but to put it into perspective it should be noted that most United Kingdom governments had been voted into power by less than forty per cent of the electorate. The figure had been chosen deliberately to kill off devolution. Indeed, there were Labour MPs who were prepared to see their own government pulled down, rather than support a measure of home rule for Scotland. One anti-assembly diehard Scottish Labour MP was reported as having hilariously said that "under an assembly the real problems of Scotland – poor housing, unemployment, deprivation – would be no less grim than at present." Presumably his detestation of devolution made him blind to the way in which these words reflected on his own government's record.

The Forty Per cent Amendment was described at that time by Alex Salmond as – "the most disgraceful distortion of democracy in Britain since the rich were able to vote twice." He added that "everybody who doesn't vote be they dead, on holiday, or at home in the bath, is counted as being against Devolution."

Anyway, all of this meant more meetings and more leaflets. There were the SNP's own leaflets and those of the all-party "Yes For Scotland" campaign. This time the nights were dark and cold… and the opinion polls were not kind to the Nationalists. I recall attending one party meeting in our wee room in the leisure centre, and being so disheartened by the deviousness of our opponents and the apparent lack of enthusiasm among the Scottish public that I voiced the opinion that we would never see any Scottish Assembly. The silence which followed wasn't shocked, it was just disappointed. One councillor looked me in the eye and asked –

"So Jimmy has fought all his life for nothing then?"

Jimmy Muir must have been in his eighties. A Nationalist since the days of the "Red Clydesiders". He looked at me sadly but without reproach. I could have bitten my tongue off.

On the 1st of March 1979, 1.23 million Scots voted for the Assembly. 1.15 million voted against. A perfectly clear majority in favour of Scottish Home Rule, but under the Westminster terms of the Forty Per cent rule, YES meant NO. As dirty a swindle as ever stained the history of the Union of the Parliaments.

*   *   *

"He is returned from Flanders. That servant of the devil set foot back in England on the fourteenth day of this month and he has moved his court to York. You know what that means."

The speaker was a dark, heavy man of early middle years. Beaky and rough of complexion, but with brown eyes which shone with compassion and sincerity, William Lamberton, Bishop of St. Andrews, wore the full vestments of his office as he sat opposite the man who had appointed him. It had been one of Wallace's first duties as Guardian to select a replacement for William Fraser, who had died the year before. Lamberton, then Chancellor of Glasgow, was a patriot in the mould of Wishart himself. Indeed, the Church in Scotland remained the strongest supporter of independence... apart from the common people themselves. Churchmen were also the swiftest and most sure sources of information.

"He made peace, of a sort, I understand, with Philip of France, and he may now turn his full attention to Scotland, which means, my Lord Bishop, that our sorry realm needs the prayers of her Church as she has never needed them before, for Edward has turned quite mad, I fear, and should he prevail with his multitudes then our fair land will be turned into one vast Berwick, with indiscriminate carnage on a scale hitherto unseen. His vengeance will be terrible to behold."

"Sir William... Lord Guardian, every priest, monk and nun in the realm will be hoarse with praying, you may be assured, but... but how stands the army of King John?"

By this, of course, he meant the people's army led by the Guardian in the name of King John Balliol, who was at that time a prisoner in Edward's Tower of London.

A new Wallace was emerging. The previous cold, heartless, indeed murderous, agent of revenge, was giving way to a more sensitive personality, perhaps with unexpected skills in diplomacy and administration. The sensitivity had always been there, showing itself occasionally and in unexpected ways, and the iron fist would always be ready to strike, velvet glove or none, but the balance had subtly altered. Time would tell, but William Wallace might turn out to have the qualities of a statesman.

The two men were seated in a chapel in the Abbey of Cambuskenneth – the Abbey of St. Mary of Stirling, in which town Wallace had established his government. The peace, quiet and relative solitude of these ecclesiastic surroundings were appropriate to the delicacy of their discussion. Essentially, Edward Plantagenet was about to visit his terrible wrath on the Scots with a major invasion, and until the Guardian had prepared his forces, organisationally and psychologically, the fewer people who knew the extent and immediacy of the danger, the better. A particular and enduring problem for Wallace, and therefore for Scotland, was the nature of his relationship with the realm's nobility. He frankly held most of them in contempt, and they, for the greater part, bitterly resented him as a social inferior who had been unnaturally raised above them in the leadership of the nation. It was true that the great majority of those nobles who mattered had, since the Battle of Stirling Bridge, realigned themselves with the cause of independence, but Wallace knew that the slightest reversal in the fortunes of that cause would have them scurrying back with their tails between their legs craving Edward's pardon and renewed favour. To make matters worse, from the point of view of the aristocracy, was the fact that Wallace had been actively working to undermine the very feudal system which supported them and all their privileges. To their credit, however, and almost unbelievably, when Edward summoned them to a council in York, not one had attended. The Plantagenet promptly forfeited their lands out of spite.

"What of Edward's strength, his numbers?" Wallace enquired.

"My information is that he has assembled some eighty thousand infantry and three thousand armed horse. There are reports, though, of over ten thousand Welsh archers – these using the new longbow…"

"Aye, mercenaries!"

The giant snorted his disgust, eyes staring distantly southward through the tiny chapel window. These figures were obviously exaggerated.

"But there is more than that, Lord Guardian. It is said that Sir Aymer de Vallance and Sir John Siward will shortly sail from France with another force which is to land in Fife…"

Wallace's great auburn head spun round, eyebrows raised.

"You say so? Then we must make ready for them."

When the time came the Scots army was, indeed, ready. On June the twelfth they vanquished the English force of Aymer de Vallence, Earl of Pembroke, in a battle which took place at Black

Earnside near the Abbey of Lindores on the bank of the River Tay. It was a bitterly fought engagement and the Scots lost many men. At one point the Guardian was to be seen scooping water from a burn into his helmet to slake the thirst of some of his wounded. Sir John Graham was one of the injured, and for a while Wallace feared that he might lose another of his dearest friends and most staunch lieutenants.

In the following month Edward crossed the Tweed at the head of a formidable English force (though by no means of the numbers suggested by the Bishop of St. Andrews) which was determined to punish Wallace and his Scots for Stirling Bridge. The populace fled before them as the English mercilessly laid waste to the land between the border and the Firth of Forth. There was scarcely a handful of grain, a sheep or a cow left to feed a hungry army. Wisely, Wallace, expecting his foes to starve, had pulled his own force back and back, drawing the English onward over the desolate and barren land. Camped just a short distance west of Edinburgh, Edward, however, had made wise provision – or he thought he had – but the ships which should have contained food, for some reason arrived instead with holds filled with casks of wine. The inevitable drunkenness among the soldiery led on to vicious fighting between English and Welsh. At this point things looked desperate for Edward's campaign, and abandonment and retreat were the realistic options. Then he got the break it seems the English could always depend upon.

Two Scottish earls – Angus and Dunbar – galloped into Edward's camp with the information that the Scots army was deployed in the forest outside Falkirk – not twenty miles away.

Edward of England was much given to very public displays of piety. On receiving this incredible piece of luck, he is reported to have said –

"May God be praised, for He has solved all of my problems."

Curious talk from a man who had just burned down the abbeys of Kelso, Dryburgh and Melrose.

It had been Wallace's intention to carry out a surprise attack on a weakened, demoralised and divided English force, but the two informers had put paid to that.

As it happened, however, the Scots were in a reasonably well defended position. They were deployed on the side of a hill, with a densely wooded area to their rear. Between them and the approaching English army there was a burn and a small loch.

It was dawn on the Feast of St. Mary Magdalene: the 22nd of July. Will heard what he took to be an unseasonable rumble of distant thunder. He was reminded, sweetly yet heartbreakingly, of that first time he and Mirren had made love on the hillside outside Lanark. He shook the memory out of mind and was turning in the saddle to address the Earl of Lennox – now back with the Scots army – when a couple of scouts came galloping out of the woods and uphill towards the Guardian and the group of knights who surrounded him. The first scout to reach the party threw himself off his horse and nearly fell in his haste to report to Wallace.

"My Lord Guardian, the English are near upon us…"

"Curse them! How many? Foot? Horse? Speak, man!"

"Both, my Lord. Many hundreds… thousands – the English host."

"Where are they? How far?"

"About a mile yonder, Lord…" the scout gesticulated towards the direction from which he and the others had ridden.

"A *mile*! Mercy of Christ!"

He glared around at the earls of Lennox, Menteith and Buchan. Without a further word he wheeled his horse around savagely and rode at a gallop towards the bulk of his army, the others not far behind him.

In the night, as the monarch slept on the ground, Edward's horse had astonishingly and inexplicably trampled over his recumbent form. The king had been badly (and noisily) injured, sustaining two broken ribs. The word had passed swiftly through the English camp, the story becoming exaggerated as it spread. Many came to believe that Edward had been killed and something close to panic had swept through the army. A number of units prepared to flee. Edward, brought urgent word of this, courageously had himself strapped up, mounted, and made himself highly visible riding among the ranks – in silent agony. He was no longer a young man, and this was a supreme effort of courage, will… and sheer obsessive hatred. Now the dawn had come, and the time for action.

Squinting his eyes and peering toward the hillside the Plantagenet perceived the Scots deployment. There were four schiltrons spaced out with bodies of archers between them. The schiltrons were densely-packed formations of infantry armed with long, metal-tipped spears, formed up in such a manner as to appear like vast hedgehogs, bristling with lethal sharpened steel. Behind these, between schiltrons and the woodland, was a body of lightly armed cavalry. Directly in front of the spearmen Wallace had ordered sharpened stakes to be placed, with ropes between them, as a defensive palisade. Between these and Edward's host a wide burn ran through sodden marshland. Although the English outnumbered the Scots by at least two to one, the strength of the latter's position gave Edward pause for thought.

As the sun climbed into the sky, with tension mounting as the two armies eyed each other, English leaders grew impatient with their king, and starving English soldiers fretted to be let loose on the enemy. But Edward remained undecided. He didn't like the look of these schiltrons. Nor was he happy about the marshland.

His own force consisted of some fifteen thousand foot, which were divided into four brigades, two thousand armed horse, and around a thousand Welsh archers (the loyalty of whom was now highly suspect). There was also a body of mercenaries from Genoa. These were armed with the crossbow – a weapon deemed so heinous that it had been outlawed by the Second Lateran Council of Churches.

Between the palisade and the schiltrons, Wallace rode out in front of his men. Noon was fast approaching. The day grew hot. Men sweated in the sun… and with fear. The Guardian removed his helmet, took a long look at the English army across the marsh, and rubbed his beard with the back of a gauntleted hand. Turning his horse around to face his Scots, he drew his great sword from over his shoulder, raised it high and roared in a voice that the furthest off man could hear.

"I have brought you to the ring... Let them see how you can dance."

He laughed, then slowly, hesitantly at first, a ripple of response turned to a roar as his people's army voiced its answer to their leader's joke.

Hearing this, the Earl of Surrey, Warenne, snapped and led his contingent of armed horse in a charge towards the Scots line, as a furious Edward looked on. The first of the heavily armoured mounts to reach the marshland began, inevitably, to sink and flounder in the bog. Seeing this, those behind wheeled around, avoiding the hazard, and skirted the waterlogged field in order to attack the Scots army in the flank.

The other wing of Edward's heavy horse was commanded by Antony Bek, Bishop of Durham. Taking note of these developments, he now led his force in a charge which avoided the marshland and clashed with the Scots' other flank.

The well-drilled and determined schiltrons stood their ground magnificently, inflicting dreadful casualties on English knights and horses alike with the razor-sharp heads of their long and skilfully-wielded spears. Frustrated by the sight of this, Edward gave the order for the Welsh archers to let loose a rain of arrows from their longbows. To his fury, the order was totally disregarded.

At this point, with the conflict seemingly going well for the Scots, an inexplicable and calamitous development took place. The Scots cavalry, to the rear of the schiltrons, commanded by no lesser a figure than John Comyn, the Red, of Badenoch, suddenly wheeled around and left the field of battle.

Wallace, with other key leadership figures, was situated with the royal standard at the rear of the schiltrons and to the fore of where the cavalry had been. In becoming aware of this apparent desertion he was almost convulsed with rage and disbelief. He cast around looking for some suitable messenger. Discerning one of the sons of MacDuff of Fife, the Guardian barked –

"You... young MacDuff. To me, man!"

When the mounted youth reached him through the mass of milling figures, Wallace, pointing towards the retreating horsemen, ordered him –

"Get you after these. Speak with Comyn. Order him in the name of the Guardian to bring the cavalry back this instant, or by God I'll have all of their heads for treason. Off with you, man. Swiftly!"

No sooner had he uttered the words than the English knights, observing the changed circumstances, turned their futile attention away from the schiltrons and began to systematically annihilate the archers who were on foot in the spaces between the great hedgehogs of deadly spears. The Scots bowmen, led by Sir John Stewart, brother of the Steward, consisted predominantly of contingents from the Forest of Selkirk and the Isle of Bute. From horseback, with sword, battleaxe and mace, Edward's knights set about butchering these archers who should have been protected by Comyn's cavalry. At last, the Plantagenet smiled.

In defiance of their orders, and in spite of Wallace's hard training, the schiltrons began to break so that the spearmen would be free to assist the archers. They were too late. Almost all of the men from Selkirk and Bute lay horribly slaughtered – including their commander, Sir John Stewart of Jedburgh. Seeing this, Edward at once gave the command for his cavalry to withdraw. When this had been accomplished, he then instructed his own English bowmen to turn their fire on the men of the schiltrons. The result was diabolical. The iron-tipped arrows, falling from a great height, cut through leather, chain-mail, breast-plates and helmets. An English chronicler was later to write that "bodies covered the ground as thickly as snow in winter". Seeing the turn of events, the Welsh turned their bows on those Scots who still stood. There were the dead, and there were those who would pray for death.

Wallace, with Sir John Graham on one side and Sir Robert Boyd on the other, sat astride his horse with tears of impotent rage running down his cheeks and into his beard. He heard a man who had been blinded howling for his mother. He saw another screaming man trying to pull an arrow from his ruined genitals. Behind him, in spite of the clamour of battle, he clearly heard one of his own knights vomiting. He turned to see his friend and brother-in-arms, Sir John Graham, dying horribly with a crossbow bolt in his throat.

"For Christ's sake Will, you have to get out of this. You are the Guardian. They must not get the Guardian."

It was Kerlie – Kerlie who had never been far from his shoulder. Before Wallace could give him an answer they saw wave upon wave of English foot advancing toward the remnants of the schiltrons. Such Scots as were still able began to flee and Edward gave the order for his cavalry to pursue them.

Before it was too late, the Guardian of the realm, with a small band of loyal supporters, turned and galloped into the woodland, Lion Rampant trailing behind them. It was true. Even with his mind distorted with grief and fury. He could see it. As long as Wallace lived, Scotland had hope.

*   *   *

It hadn't been so much of an entrance examination as an unofficial way of demonstrating his precocious ability. Of course, it had been Gunner Irwin who'd set it all up. It had really begun one day on the Rock, when Duncan and the school-master had been talking about the big Union Flag which flew above the castle. The old soldier had a curious tale to tell. The design of the flag had been devised, he'd said, not long after the Union of the Crowns, when James the Sixth of Scots had become James the First of the United Kingdom, in 1603. Apparently Scots had been offended that the red cross of St. George, representing England, had been boldly featured on top of the white saltire of St. Andrew, which, of course, represented Scotland. A request had been sent to London asking for permission to superimpose the saltire on top of the cross of St. George when the flag was used in Scotland. Apparently such usage had been tolerated until the time of the Union of the Parliaments, in 1707. At that time, while the Treaty of Union was being debated, the Scots Privy Council had sent a request to the government of Queen Anne asking that the Scots version of the Union Flag be made official, for use in Scotland, under the terms of the treaty. This had been refused and from that time onward only the English version had been permitted. The cross of St. Patrick had not been added until 1801.

Duncan had found this both fascinating and a little offensive. A distinct blow to Scottish national pride. This had been Gunner Irwin's cue to bring up the whole subject of the history of the Treaty of the Union. Just as he'd been about to launch off on what seemed to be a personal hobby horse, a certain notion had occurred to the dominie.

Some weeks earlier, Irwin had approached Duncan's father with the suggestion that, given proper encouragement and support, the boy might, in due course, win a place in the University of Glasgow. James Robertson had been dumbfounded. He, himself, had been born in a small croft and brought up in virtual poverty. He had been extremely fortunate in gaining an apprenticeship in his craft, and even more so in being eventually able – mostly with the financial backing of his wife's family – to establish himself in a modest business. The thought that a son of his might become a man of letters and thus climb several rings on the social ladder thrilled him in a manner befitting a man who now belonged to the Victorian lower middle-class. Irwin had pointed out that although Duncan clearly possessed the required intelligence and scholarly virtues, he would be much better placed for university if he were enrolled in the Dumbarton Academy.

Later – after Gunner Irwin had had his bright idea – father and tutor paid a respectful visit to that venerable seat of learning, and spoke persuasively to Rector Hugh Dickie. The long and the short of it was that Dickie listened sympathetically and then the master of the castle's school played his trump card. He presented the rector with a lengthy essay, which, he assured Dickie, Duncan Robertson had, at fifteen years of age, personally researched and written. The subject – the history of the Treaty of the Union: 1707.

When King James the Sixth left Edinburgh for London, in 1603, he initiated a process of neglect and decline in his northern kingdom. In effect, Scotland was from that time governed by the English ministers of King James and of subsequent London-based monarchs – either by these or by Scots appointees dependent on their patronage. Scotland's natural leaders flocked to the seat of power – London – where they competed for office, titles and honours, and the remuneration which went with them. Policy in matters such as foreign affairs and trade were, of course, decided on the basis of the English interest, often to Scotland's detriment. Scotland was habitually required to contribute men and money for English wars which were declared without reference to Scotland and sometimes contrary to Scottish policy. The English parliament was, in fact, actively hostile towards Scottish trade, regarding it as inconvenient competition. In 1660 and 1663 it introduced, for example, the "Navigation Acts", the purpose of which was to exclude Scots from trade with the plantations.

Scotland became steadily poorer until William Paterson, the Scot who effectively founded the Bank of England, came up with the idea of setting up a trading colony in the isthmus of Panama in Central America. The idea was that such a venture would be able to trade in goods from both the Pacific and the Atlantic, selling, as it were, commodities from the one sphere to the other, and saving merchant ships the time, expense and danger of sailing thousands of miles around Cape Horn. The idea was put to the Minister of

Scotland, Lord Tweeddale, and on the 26th of May 1695 the Scots Parliament passed an Act for a company trading to Africa and the Indies. The colony was to be established on two conditions – that it was with the consent of the native inhabitants, and that the territory was not already claimed by any other European power. Fifty per cent of the shares went to Scots, with the remaining fifty per cent going to English investors. Known as the Darien Scheme, it was seen by the English as a threat to their East India Company. Accordingly, the English Parliament instructed English investors to withdraw their money from the scheme. They wrote to the governors of the plantations ordering them not to give any kind of assistance to the Scots in their endeavour. Further, they encouraged Spanish hostility to the venture.

The response to this, from all classes of the people of Scotland, was to raise some £400,000 – fully a half of the money in the nation's economy at the time.

The ships set sail for Darien on the 17th of July 1698. The colony was abandoned on the 30th of March 1700.

Incompetence, disease, Spanish military action, and not least – the malevolence of Scotland's English partners in the Union of the Crowns – killed off the nation's attempt to reverse the process of its impoverishment. The result was national ruin. Many were left literally penniless. Scotland's virtually bankrupt ruling class was now more vulnerable than ever before to bribery and corruption.

Queen Anne had no surviving children, and the question of who would succeed her as monarch of the United Kingdom was complex and difficult, with no obvious leading contender. The English Parliament, however, without any consultation whatsoever with the Scots, decided in 1701, through its "Act of Settlement", that the thrones of England and Ireland would, pass to Sophia, Electress of Hanover. The English took it for granted, in the manner so natural to them, that the Scots would meekly accept their decision and share their choice. Whatever the attitude of the nation's supine aristocracy, the Scots as a people had other ideas.

When they realised that the Scots were going to be tiresome over this matter, the English decided that enough was enough. Their answer was to gain once and for all complete control over Scotland by means of an "incorporating" Union of the Parliaments. It was a scheme which William had sought and which Anne now favoured. Negotiations commenced in November of 1702. In the following year the Scots Parliament passed an "Act of Security", by which it asserted that the Scots Parliament would nominate its own successor to Queen Anne for the Scottish Crown. It further insisted that the Scots would not share a monarch with the English unless they were granted equal trading rights and real power was returned to the Scottish Parliament. This latter was considered necessary because since 1603 acts passed by the Scottish Parliament had required royal approval from London, and that had largely depended on whether or not it suited English interests.

The English responded with an "Alien Act" which stipulated that unless the Scots had accepted the English decision on the succession by the 25th of December 1705, then from that date all Scots in England would be treated as aliens and would be unable to inherit property. From that same date the English would cease to import cattle, sheep, linen and coal from Scotland. The inheritance element was particularly aimed at the Scottish aristocracy who in many cases owned estates in England. In the same year twenty-four English warships were deployed to prevent Scottish trade with France.

Commissioners participating in the treaty negotiations, from both English and Scottish Parliaments, were hand picked by Queen Anne's ministers, with only those Scots being selected who could be relied upon to act in the English interest. In the treaty as it was proposed, in another clear expression of the English mentality, the new and united parliament would consist of the English parliament just as it stood (with all its existing members), but with some forty-five (out of the existing 147) Scottish members added to it. This was approximately the same representation as Cornwall.

The people of Scotland were massively and fervently opposed to the Union. Hundreds of addresses expressing this opposition were sent from every corner and every class of the realm. Counties, burghs and parishes, craft guilds... There was a single exception – the Burgh of Ayr, which was not so much in favour as equivocal. By way of an example, the following address was sent from the community of Dumbarton to their member of the Scots Parliament and Commissioner in the negotiations –

The council having considered the proposal for union of the kingdoms, to be discussed at an ensuing convention in Edinburgh, resolve that the same is a matter of the greatest weight and moment, and, in their judgment, of the most dangerous consequence to all the interests civil and sacred of the nation, and in appointing Sir James Smollett to be their commissioner, instruct him to declare their dislike of and dissent from the said union, as in their judgment inconsistent with, and subversive of, the fundamental laws and liberties of their nation, and plainly evacuating all the publick oaths this nation lyes under; and, further, they expect and desire of their commissioner to have due regaird to the judgment of his constituents, the laws and liberties of the nation and the established government of the church.

Sir James Smollett of Stainflett and Bonhill, however, went right ahead and voted for the Union. He was rewarded by being made one of the forty-five Scottish members of the new united London Parliament.

Roman Catholics opposed the Union because they feared the House of Hanover. Episcopalians rejected it for the same reason. But the most powerful and most authoritative voice against it came from the Kirk. Sir John Clerk of Penicuik wrote at the time – *In a corner of the street you may see a Presbyterian minister, a Popish priest, and an Episcopal prelate, all agreeing in their discourse against the Union...* The General Assembly of the Church of Scotland was much closer to being a democratic national forum than the compromised Scots Parliament, which represented only the aristocracy, the lairds and the merchant class. Daniel Defoe, the English spy in Scotland, at the time wrote – *The most dangerous rock of difference on which the Union could split, and which could now render it ineffectual, was that of religion... Rigid and refractory clergy who are the worst enemies of the Union.* The Earl of Mar commented – *One thing I must say for the Kirk, that if the Union fail it is owing to them.*

Another interesting feature was the English "Sacramental Test". In effect this meant that, should the Union come about, any Scot in England could neither hold office, nor enter a university, unless he first took an oath of allegiance to the Church of England.

But in the end the views of the many were utterly disregarded and the matter was settled by the bribery and intimidation of a corrupt few. Regarding the bribes, Sir Walter Scott put it very well –

It may be doubted whether the descendants of the noble lords and honourable gentlemen who accepted this gratification would be more shocked at the general fact of their ancestors being corrupted, or scandalised at the paltry amount of the bribe.

And regarding the threats, Godolphin, the English Lord Treasurer, in a letter dated 17th July 1703, made it very clear that the alternative to Union was war, and that the Scots would certainly lose. In 1706, while the treaty was being "negotiated", it was reported that three regiments of English foot had been stationed on the border, and, in the North of Ireland, one more regiment of foot, three of horse and one of dragoons were awaiting orders to sail for Scotland. These preparations were no doubt explained away as necessary precautions to "restore order" in the event of a popular uprising resulting from the signing of the treaty.

The Act of Union was finally passed on the 16th of January 1707. There had been anti-union rioting and violence in Edinburgh, Glasgow and throughout the country during the period of the negotiation. After signing the treaty, the men who had sold their nation's independence dared not show their faces in the streets.

Robert Burns, writing over eighty years later, by which time the much promised "benefits of Union" should have been abundantly evident, said

– Alas have I often said to myself, what are all the boasted advantages which any country reaps from a certain Union, that can counterbalance the annihilation of her independence, and even her very name.

The particular individual who must be regarded as the champion of the fight against the Union was Andrew Fletcher of Saltoun. He was a small laird of Haddington in East Lothian, and a member of the Scots Parliament. His democratic instincts led him to oppose the despotism of Charles II. Fletcher fled into exile, but was sentenced to death in his absence for the part he played in the Monmouth rising. When King William took the throne, however, Fletcher was, in a manner of speaking, off the hook. He also supported the Darien Scheme, but is best remembered for his determined, courageous and eloquent opposition to the incorporating Union. In March of 1708 a French fleet attempted to land in Scotland in the hope of restoring a Stuart to the throne. The exercise (the first of several) was aborted, but the now-British government made a number of arrests. Although innocent of involvement, Andrew Fletcher was, because of his anti-Union record, incarcerated in Stirling Castle. Fortunately he was treated well and released after a relatively short time.

In the years after the enactment of the Union, to the humiliation of the Scots, its articles were broken routinely and repeatedly, as and when it suited the English. So bitter and widespread was the disillusionment of the Scots representatives that in 1713 a motion to have the Union dissolved was put before the House of Lords… and defeated by just four votes.

This was the story written by Duncan Robertson in the essay which was presented to Rector Dickie. It was perhaps not so detailed nor so long-winded, but substantially and eloquently it set out the important facts. Gunner Irwin had taken the lad into the well-stocked library of Dumbarton's Mechanics' Institute and shown him the ropes of research. Duncan had found, in the various works of history available there, all the information necessary for a project which at once fascinated him and left him indignant.

It had, frankly, been an odd choice of subject, on Irwin's part, with which to impress a pillar of the burgh's community who presumably shared the general belief that the Union with England had led to prosperity and progress, Scotland having previously been a poor and backward country which was now fortunate in being allowed to be a junior partner in the biggest empire in human history. But Gunner Irwin knew his man. Hugh Dickie had a sense of history and he had no illusions about the true nature of the present relationship between the junior and senior partners. He knew the score and was prepared, in discreet conversation with selected listeners, to voice certain sentiments which in the not too distant future would gather support and take on a political expression in the call for "Home Rule". When the rector read Duncan's essay he was impressed, not simply with the research, intelligence and skill behind it, but also by its patriotic tone. He instantly warmed to the boy. Before that month was out Duncan Robertson was enrolled in Dumbarton Academy.

The school was housed in the impressive neo-mediaeval Burgh Hall which was situated just yards from the Robertson home, at the top of Church Street. This was, indeed, a huge step on his way to a place at Glasgow University, but something even more wonderful had happened to Duncan – he had met Hannah Paton.

Despair and Hope

The right of self-determination is enshrined in the United Nations Charter. If that right is weakened, small countries the world over would be at risk. (Margaret Thatcher)

The failure of the Labour government to deliver a Scottish Assembly led to a vote of no confidence which brought the Callaghan administration down. In effect, it was those Labour MPs who had voted for the treacherous Forty Per cent Rule who brought about the General Election of May 1979 – and the reign of Margaret Thatcher. It is seldom pointed out that if the Forty Per cent Rule had applied to Thatcher's Conservative Party she would not have won that election. Although the Tories won 53% of the United Kingdom's seats, they did so with the votes of a mere 30% of the total electorate, and I remember having a rather unpleasant exchange with a policeman acquaintance who simply refused to believe that this was the case.

No United Kingdom General Election could ever be regarded as a referendum on Scottish independence. For one thing, Unionists would be the first to claim that a vote for the SNP was not necessarily a vote for independence. Equally, however, a vote for a Unionist party did not necessarily indicate a rejection of independence. Never was this more clear than in 1979 when Scots voters, faced with the immediate threat of a Conservative government led by Thatcher, flocked back to Labour in the vain hope that the party would save them.

Just a matter of weeks after Thatcher took office – piously quoting a prayer of St Francis of Assisi – there was a big change in my personal circumstances. At the age of 26 I was still living with my parents. None of the few young women I'd had relationships with had put up with me for any length of time, and I had no particular wish to live alone. No doubt this situation gave rise to speculation and rumour, but that's how things were. My mother was an assistant at that time in a shop in Balloch. This involved a long walk to and from her place of work twice a day and she wasn't getting any younger. My father, having been made redundant when the Royal Naval Torpedo Factory had closed almost a decade earlier, was effectively retired. They were looking for a shift to another council house, but in Balloch. So it came about that in the summer of '79 the three of us moved into an end-terrace house in Beaton Road, Dalvait.

I realised then that my parents were actually getting elderly, and this was a depressing thought. I came, however, to love this new home. On the edge of the village, we were placed conveniently for shops, post office, railway station and buses. When I looked out of the window of my upstairs room there, about thirty yards away, beyond a magnificent oak tree, was the A811 road to Stirling. On the other side of this there stretched a huge golden field, all the way to the Main Street of the village and the gates of Balloch Park. Forming the horizon was the gentle curve of *Ledrishmore*,

the hill which always made me think of Robert Burns. 1979 was
also, as it happened, the year when I finally read Robert Louis
Stevenson's *Kidnapped*, which became one of my favourite books,
and which to my mind somehow expresses so much of the
Scottish soul.

The move also brought about a change in the public houses I
frequented. Now I began to do the rounds of the *Doghouse Bar*,
the *Glenroy Hotel*, the *Balloch Hotel* and, in Jamestown, the
Locheil. I enjoyed socialising in these places after a day in the
Finance Department, but the truth is that habitual drinking was
good for neither my body, mind nor soul. I had embarked on a
long and sterile chapter of lonely bachelorhood.

I was, naturally, profoundly disappointed with the failure of the
Labour government to deliver a Scottish Assembly, and I was
bitter about the manner in which Scotland had been cheated. Also
at the '79 election, the SNP had lost nine of its eleven MPs. In my
early twenties, I had come around to a decidedly Socialist political
position. I became convinced, as I remain to this day, that
Capitalism is an economic system based on greed and
exploitation. During the course of the 'seventies the Scottish
National Party adopted a left of centre stance which reflected an
understanding that Scotland, especially the nation's working class,
inclined instinctively toward a collective attitude. Historically, or
so it was perceived, the Scots had always been community-
minded, emphasising the need for the individual to contribute to
and work toward the common good. The Scots believed in
society, where Margaret Thatcher infamously did not. The
Conservative regime, which all parts of the United Kingdom now
lived under, was one which exalted the individual to the point of
making a virtue out of selfishness. Thatcher was seen as the enemy

of the Welfare State, she was a ruthless destroyer of trades unions, favoured private enterprise over public-owned services and industries. Very much a centralist, she was an opponent of devolution and, of course, she zealously set about the job of destroying any vestige of Socialism left in British society. She made much of patronisingly praising traditional Scottish qualities of thrift, industry and inventiveness, but in truth she despised what was referred to as the Scottish "culture of dependence". Surprisingly contradictory in one so utterly opposed to Scottish *independence*.

In January of 1980 the government introduced the "Right to Buy" legislation. This meant that tenants of council houses could purchase the homes they had been renting at a discount. The purpose of this measure, from a Tory point of view was probably two-fold. Firstly, it significantly depleted the stock of public sector housing, and this led to the power of local councils – mostly Labour-controlled in Central Scotland – being diminished. Secondly, there was a psychological factor. People who became house owners were likely to entertain the notion that they had stepped up a rung on the social ladder, and just might be that bit more likely to vote Conservative in the future. I used to be vastly entertained when, having bought their council house, most folk seemed to immediately buy a fancy new front door, as though to tell the world that they were no longer council tenants. It was a very tempting offer, and very many were tempted. My parents and I were against the idea in principle. I don't recall how long we held out, but a rumour was circulated that local authority houses were going to be handed over to private landlords, and the thought of finding ourselves at the mercy of some Rachman caused us to reluctantly cave in. Shortly after we'd made the purchase my mother insisted that we buy a fancy new front door.

I recall coming home from my work one evening in April of '82 and catching an item on the television news. Some Argentinian soldiers had overpowered a small company of Royal Marines in a remote and unheard of island called South Georgia. Apparently the Argentine forces had been preceded by a bunch of scrap merchants who'd raised the Argentine flag on this British "dependency". I actually laughed. At the time it sounded to me like the plot of some old British comedy from the 'fifties. Of course, I didn't know then that it was the start of the Falklands Conflict. The dispute was over the "sovereignty" of these far-flung and hitherto obscure islands in the South Atlantic. Both Britain and Argentina claimed a historical right of possession. Undoubtedly, the overwhelming majority of the Falklands' 1,800 inhabitants wanted to remain British, and Thatcher's government, amid an orgy of Rule Britannia "jingoism", sent a massive military taskforce to retake the islands. The ensuing conflict, which did recover the islands for the UK, cost the lives of 655 Argentinians, 255 Britons and 3 civilian islanders.

At the time I was horrified: totally against the military response, thinking, perhaps naively, that a diplomatic solution was possible, disgusted by the "send a gunboat" mentality which was hyped up by an almost hysterical media and embraced by the great majority of the population, and, if I am absolutely honest, I was frightened in case I'd be conscripted if a wider conflict resulted. I knew very few people, in my circle of friends and acquaintances, in my workplace or in the pubs, who did not approve of the military action. I had presumed that the Scots would not support this post-imperial madness, but I was mistaken. There was a particular occasion, one evening in *Smith's Lounge* in Jamestown, when it was all under discussion and an old school-friend made some remark along the lines of not being able to look at himself in the mirror if we'd let the Argentinian "dictator" away with this. I don't remember my exact words, but I responded with disgusted sarcasm. We did not speak to each other for several years after that. Oddly enough, however, not many years passed before a lot of those who had enthusiastically supported the task force began to speak as though they had been very much against the military response at the time. Curiously, in 2007 I read a book called *Vulcan 607*, by author Rowland White, which caused me to reconsider my opinion and be a little more sympathetic to Thatcher's position. I still believe a diplomatic solution should have been sought more determinedly, and I cannot think that the loss of life and the terrible injuries with which people have had to live since were a fair price to pay to show the world that Britain was still a force to be reckoned with.

There was one utterance made by Thatcher at the time which I consider to be, in the light of her attitude to Scottish independence, a classic expression of hypocrisy –

The right of self-determination is enshrined in the United Nations Charter. If that right is weakened, small countries the world over would be at risk.

*   *   *

Whatever the rights and wrongs of it, the Falklands War undoubtedly kept Margaret Thatcher in power. The Conservatives won the General Election of June 1983 with a majority of 144. In Scotland they held on to their 21 seats, with the SNP doing no better than retaining their own 2 seats.

I had continued to attend SNP branch meetings at the community centre, but my days of leafleting were finished and sometime in the early 'eighties I allowed my membership to lapse. My contribution was then limited to writing occasional poetry and short stories for a political magazine called *Radical Scotland*. This was a left-wing, pro-independence, bi-monthly publication. From the few copies I still have in my possession, I see that I contributed poems which were written in opposition to the Trident nuclear weapons system, commenting on Thatcher's presentation of the Scottish Cup at the final of '88 (when the fans sang – "Denis Thatcher's wife's a whore" – or something which sounded very like it), and a short story which spoke against anti-English racism.

In the 'eighties I was (as I remain) a firm believer in trades unions, convinced of the need for workers to be organised and united in defence of their common interests in the face of attacks from employers, either in the private or the public sector. Accordingly I served for a number of years as a shop steward with my own clerical union, the National Association of Local Government Officers – NALGO.

In March of 1984, Ian MacGregor, the Scots-born hatchet man who had "rationalised" the British steel industry, was appointed by Thatcher as head of the National Coal Board. He promptly announced that twenty pits and some 20,000 jobs were to be axed. This provoked a national strike which involved around 93,000 coal workers. It became a bitter dispute which descended into violent clashes between police and strikers. The majority of Scotland's 14,000 miners from pits in Fife, Stirlingshire and Lanarkshire, stuck with the strike for its entire year-long duration. There was hatred and brutality on both sides, but the miners were fighting for their livelihoods and their communities, whereas Thatcher was motivated by a loathing of trade unionism and everything it stood for. She deliberately provoked what became a class war, misusing the police force, the security services and the law. Even though Thatcher was cheered on by a gloating and biased media which resorted to demonising NUM leader Arthur Scargill, there was enormous public support for the miners. I remember on a number of occasions seeing people on the streets of my own community filling collection tins in support of the NUM. Thatcher divided British society and destroyed the lives of countless individuals and communities, in the light of which her sanctimonious recitation of the Prayer of St Francis became a hypocritical blasphemy.

But she won… and sadly the British people let her win. The Labour Party, which had been founded by the trades unions to protect the working class, was from start to finish, under the weak leadership of Neil Kinnock, more of a help than a hindrance to Thatcher in her fanatical persecution of working people.

A week after being literally shown the red card by thousands of Scottish football supporters at Hampden in May of '88, the "Iron Lady" insisted on addressing the General Assembly of the Church of Scotland. There she treated her listeners to a personal interpretation of Christianity which supposedly justified the Capitalist priority of the accumulation of wealth. This condescension became notorious as the "Sermon on the Mound".

A wonderfully exhilarating ray of political hope shone through the dark winter clouds of that November. Jim Sillars had been a Labour Member of Parliament. After his party's failure to deliver a Scottish Assembly, he left Labour to take a leading role in the newly-formed *Scottish* Labour Party. Then, in 1980, Sillars embraced independence and joined the SNP. A charismatic personality, shrewd politician and inspiring orator, Sillars stood for the Nationalists when the resignation of Bruce Millan created a by-election in Glasgow's Govan constituency, right in the Labour heartland. In the event Sillars won the seat, achieving a 33% swing from Labour to the SNP. I recall coming home from the pub and sitting alone until the early hours watching the count on television. My tipple of the time was, I think, *Alloa Ale*, and I was carrying my usual cargo, which was generally enough to see me off to sleep, but that night I was so elated by the result that I barely got a wink. I suppose I had managed to suppress the extent to which the hope of independence sustained me, until this apparent breakthrough brought it back to the surface. For a number of years I believed that one day Sillars would become the first Prime Minister of an independent Scotland.

The Community Charge, or as it was unpopularly known, the "Poll Tax", was introduced in Scotland on the 1st of April 1989. Previously local authority services had been funded by domestic and non-domestic rates. These had been property based and calculated on the basis of the notional value of the property. There was a myth, much entertained by mortgage payers, that the tenants of council houses paid no rates and therefore made no contribution to the services from which they benefited. In fact this was untrue. Local authority tenants paid rates along with their rents, and a rebate scheme operated for those (both tenants and owners) who were deemed unable to pay the full rate. This form of local taxation was unpopular with those in the Tories' natural constituency, and the Community Charge – a tax which applied to individuals rather than properties – was regarded by the Conservatives as fairer. A revaluation of the Scottish rates in 1985 had caused such a howl of rage from the nation's propertied class that the Poll Tax was brought to bear in Scotland one year earlier than in England. It is now said that the Tories did not inflict this tax on the Scots in order to test its effectiveness or popularity, but Conservative politicians at the time spoke of Scotland being a "guinea pig". The tax was resented bitterly by so many that even prior to its introduction there was organised resistance and mass refusal to pay. Widely perceived as robbing the poor to benefit the rich, it was seen as yet another Thatcherite attack on the working class and Scottish local authorities had a difficult job in collecting it. It placed Labour-controlled councils in an especially embarrassing position – did they collect it, or did they show solidarity with the class they were supposed to defend and refuse to implement it? Of course, they collected it.

Which brings me to my own role in this. I was one of those who did the collecting. I remember it as though it was a lot less distant than a quarter of a century ago. I sat at a desk in a long room known as the "Collection Hall". On my left, running the length of the room, was the counter at which members of the public paid their Poll Tax and other debts. There were three of us. The boss – an attractive and able young woman in her mid-twenties – her assistant, myself, then in my late thirties, and Brigid, an intelligent and dignified Irish lady close to retirement. I recall the light grey walls, the pale lime doors, the metal filing cabinets which partitioned our little section from the rest of the office, the yellow, blue and white Strathclyde Regional Council calendars hanging on the walls, and the shiny black surface of the public counter. It was all cash and cheques in those days – plastic rarely used. Was it hypocritical of me to collect a tax of which I disapproved in principle? I suspect I was on a similar moral level to the many folk who worked at the Naval Base at Faslane while personally being opposed to nuclear weapons. Most of my friends on the left knew what I did for a living, but I don't remember receiving criticism from them. On the other hand, members of the public occasionally approached me about it outside working hours. I'd be standing at a bus-halt, or sitting at a table in the pub, and some stranger (whose Poll Tax I'd presumably collected) would come up and starting asking me to explain this or that aspect of how the Poll Tax operated. It got to the stage that when somebody found out that I worked for the Council I'd tell them I was with the Sewerage Department.

The detestation of the Poll Tax brought together some unlikely bedfellows, and the ravages of Thatcherism undoubtedly created a much keener demand for "Home Rule" than had hitherto existed, but I found this point of view morally deficient. These people, mostly Labour politicians and supporters, entertained the notion that a Scottish "assembly" would protect them from all the nasty elements of the Union with England while they'd be able to cling on to the alleged benefits. An attitude which seemed to me to be devoid of principle.

To my mind, Margaret Thatcher, with her nauseating aura of arrogant superiority, was the utter personification of all that was worst about the English middle class. It may be, as Unionist politicians are now anxious to point out, that she did not single out Scotland for especially harsh treatment, but the point is this: England elected Thatcher, re-elected her and elected her yet again. The Scots consistently rejected her, but Thatcherism was the price Scotland paid to stay in the Union with England.

One unexpected feature of the 'eighties for me was my infatuation with Dundee United Football Club. It began in a strange and perhaps silly way. At the time in question Aberdeen FC and Dundee United FC began to be referred to in the sporting media as the "New Firm". This was because these two teams were then seriously challenging the previous dominance of Glasgow's "Old Firm" – Rangers and Celtic. In spite of having many friends who were Celtic supporters, and a few who followed the Rangers, I personally had never been in the least attracted to either of these clubs. I detested the sectarian element of their support, and I considered the emergence of the "New Firm" as healthy and very welcome. One evening, as I stood in the public bar of the *Locheil*, my eye was drawn to the television screen on which a football match was being shown. It was the team's bright tangerine strips which attracted me – that and this "New Firm" thing. From that moment onward I was an "armchair supporter" of Dundee United. I even went so far as to become an agent for the cub's "Taypools", collecting money from around thirty of my friends and colleagues in the Finance Department. My most glorious football memory (apart from Dave Narey's goal for Scotland against Brazil in the World Cup Finals of 1982) was United's second-leg game against Barcelona in the Nou Camp stadium in 1987. The Scots reached the semi-finals of the UEFA Cup by beating Barcelona 3-1 on aggregate. When the final whistle blew that evening the Spanish fans were howling derision at their club's English manager – Terry Venables. I was walking on air when I entered the *Doghouse* that night.

My fascination with United lasted through the 'eighties until the Scottish Cup Final of 1991. My team were up against Motherwell, and I watched the match on television in my grandmother's house. Dundee United lost, and as I was walking homeward past the Haldane School, I realised that there were tears running down my cheek. Enough was enough. This was just foolishness. At that moment I made a conscious decision – no more football. It is only from this distance in time that I can see that the whole Dundee United supporter thing was really a subconscious substitute for political fulfilment. But I will always retain a soft spot for Paul Sturrock, Dave Narey, Hamish McAlpine, Paul Hegarty, Davie Dodds etc... and of course manager Jim McLean.

As previously suggested, the 'eighties were something of a personal wilderness. Even in small things there was dissatisfaction. The fashion of that decade seemed dull and unimaginative to me after the colour and flamboyance of the 'seventies. I was unmoved by the music, at the time. Curiously, though, it was when I listened to the brilliant television series, *Ashes to Ashes*, all these years later, that I belatedly realised how good some of that music, and how expressive some of these clothes, had really been. It had clearly been down to my own very negative frame of mind.

My grandmother died in 1982, aged 91. Throughout my teenage years and up until not long before her death, every so often she would ask me if I ever thought of going back to the Church. I used to get uncomfortable and try to shrug the question off. I do not doubt now that in all of those years she must have prayed regularly that I would return to the faith of my upbringing. But in 1982 it would still be a good few years before those prayers would be answered in any obvious way.

At some time when I was living in Beaton Road, a supermarket was built on the big field which had been the central feature of the view from my room. I considered this to be a kind of desecration. I wrote a poem about it then. Reading over some of the lines now,

I can see that essential vestiges of spirituality remained within me,
and that an element of hope endured.

Then
the field was broad
and long enough
for the unfenced range
of a child's mind.
Among golden,
breeze-blown grasses,
ran secret,
often-changing paths,
through different moods
and seasons,
through many worlds.

Beyond,
against a sky
which still had room
for Heaven,
rising as a grand cathedral,
stood trees,
whose venerable presence
preached
by their height, the authority,
and in their depth, the mystery,
of all religion.

The profound ritual
of death and resurrection
was worked through every blade of grass,

each leaf and fruit,
while the feeling,
knowing mind
grew slowly
out of the rich, protected promise
of infancy
into the scorchings,
the freezings,
and the drenchings
of maturity.

Now,
through a small window,
a man stares
with spent purpose
and only dregs of hope.
Heavy clouds
suffocate the old horizons,
a threatening growl
of earth-devouring steel
takes the place of thunder
as giant, nerveless claws
tear and bury
every blade of grass,
each leaf and fruit.

Cruel, twisted metal thorns
of barbed-wire
ensnare, wounding,
while, behind the glass,
caught in a tightening vicious circle
of self-defeat,

the man bleeds
from the shame of wasted years
and the weight of disappointments.
He sees
the hard lines
of rigid girders,
a reality
casting shadows over ruined faith.

Yet
he has learned,
of life and hope,
that from a single, trampled seed,
or dream,
there comes deliverance.
When walls have crumbled
and the powdered rust of iron and steel
surrenders to the soil,
in due season
every blade of grass, each leaf and fruit,
will triumph
in a field, broad and long enough...

*   *   *

As it turned out, although the English army had won the Battle of
Falkirk, they suffered such casualties and had been in such a
weakened state prior to the conflict, that Edward was quite unable
to consolidate his victory. His army occupied an inhospitable
Stirling for a couple of hungry weeks, then ravaged Fife, but
exhausted, starved and utterly demoralised, the summer months
saw them back over the border. Christmas found them still at

Carlisle. In reality there were few parts of Scotland actually under Edward's control, and none of these were north of Clyde and Forth. His appetite for conquest was, of course, undiminished, but his nobles were now refusing to raise men for further invasions.

Wallace's opinion of the Scots nobility having reached even greater depths, after their various displays of calculating self-interest and treachery at Falkirk, he decided that he could no longer co-operate with such people. Accordingly, he resigned the Guardianship and returned with the hardcore of his support to their familiar lairs deep in the Forest of Selkirk. One chapter of resistance had closed and another was soon to open.

Meanwhile, in August of 1298, with the ruling class – or elements of it – now apparently leading the fight against Edward, new Guardians were chosen: the unlikely and volatile partnership of Robert Bruce and John Comyn. Young Bruce had changed sides, and would continue to do so, backwards and forwards, in and out of Edward's rule and, indeed, his friendship, so often as to make the Carrick man's role of Guardian almost farcical. His priority had always been his family's pursuit of the Scots crown, his grandfather having been one of the "Competitors". In this regard he was a sworn enemy of the Comyns, who were supporters of King John Balliol. Equally bizarre was the choice of the Red Comyn, the man who had led the Scots cavalry off the field at Falkirk and handed victory to Edward on a plate. These two, paired as leaders of the realm and community of Scotland – it was madness... but it happened.

Of course it didn't last. After actual personal violence between the pair, William Lamberton, Bishop of St Andrews, and Sir Ingram de Umfraville, were made Guardians, until finally, in May of 1301, Sir John de Soules, son-in-law of the Steward, was appointed sole Guardian. It was a sound choice. De Soules was a dependable and proven patriot, steady and uncontroversial.

Lamberton was consecrated in Rome in June of 1298. His diplomatic endeavours to secure papal support for Scotland against Edward's aggression sowed seeds which were later to bear fruit. One year after the bishop's consecration, Pope Boniface VIII issued a Bull which declared Scotland a fief of Rome. Apparently, because the realm had been Christianised by the relics of St Andrew, Scotland was under the Pope's protection. Edward alleged that he did not receive word of this pronouncement until a year later, from the Archbishop of Canterbury, while the king was campaigning in Galloway. In response to the Papal Bull, legal "experts" from the universities of Oxford and Cambridge, unsurprisingly, assured the Plantagenet that he had absolute right in law to the possession of the realm of Scotland. So much for the Pope.

William Wallace gloried in the scene which spread out before him. The sky was a gentle, cool blue, enhanced rather than spoiled by the feathery layer of benevolent cloud, silver, pink, with an underside of light grey, which sailed over the distant coastline to the north. The sea itself was a deeper azure, ruffled but little by the warm breeze of the season. The salt tang of that brine wafted up from the sand and seaweed far below. The sound of the waves and cry of the gulls, combined with sights and smells, satisfied the man's senses and in some impossible to define, almost mystical, way, spoke to him of his love of, his identification with, his native land. There was a purity, a cleanness, about this natural world which existed aloof from and untouched by the squabbles and petty ambitions of men.

He sat in an upper chamber of the Bishop's Castle of St Andrews. The Church Fathers maintained that St. Andrew had preached the Gospel in Asia Minor, Scythia, the Black Sea, Greece, Hungary and Russia. It was in Patras in Greece that he was martyred by being crucified on a diagonal cross. An ancient tradition held that a Greek monk called St. Regulus (also known as St. Rule) had been the custodian of St. Andrew's bones in Patras. Through a vision he was inspired, it was said, to hide some of the relics just before the Emperor Constantine moved the remainder to Constantinople. An angel then appeared to Regulus, instructing him to take the bones and sail westward. Wherever his ship ran aground, Regulus was to establish a church. It had come to pass that the monk's boat was driven by a storm into the little port of Kilrymont in Fife. There he had founded a religious community and the town had become known as St. Andrews.

A monastery was established by King Oengus of the Picts in the middle of the eighth century, and the Culdees of the old Celtic Church had a church near the site. The Culdees were succeeded by Augustinian monks early in the twelfth century, and Bishop Robert of St Andrews added the beginnings of the reliquary church at that time. In the great tower here fragments of the bones of the apostle were believed to be kept in a special casket called the *Morbrac*. Because of the relics, St. Andrews, ecclesiastical capital of Scotland, became a major European centre of pilgrimage, second only to Compostella. Many thousands of pilgrims, from all over the British Isles and the Continent, flocked to the town seeking absolution of crimes and miraculous cures.

Wallace turned away from the great stone archway from which he had been drinking in the magnificent view. Facing him were five churchmen – his old mentor, Robert Wishart, Bishop of Glasgow, his appointee, William Lamberton, Bishop of St Andrews, and three others who were vaguely familiar to him. It was Wishart who spoke first.

"Will… we want you to leave Scotland."

Wallace's features seemed to turn to stone. The old bishop smiled crookedly and held forward the open palm of his hand in an arresting gesture.

"There is a great service you must do for the realm and for King John, Will. Not this time with your sword, or your bow. Not with an army, but with words, Will. Well-chosen, effectively-delivered words."

Wallace stared around the various churchmen, mystified. Lamberton took over from Wishart.

"Sir William… the papal protection of our ancient realm, the Bull of His Holiness, has, we are reliably informed, been challenged, contradicted, by Edward of England. He is sending a delegation to Rome to put his case before a Papal Court."

Wallace shook his head in frustration.

"The man is a pariah. He is unhinged, demon-possessed. Why should the Pope listen to him or his lackeys?"

Wishart looked pained, glanced around at the others.

"It is not straightforward, Will. It is complicated. There is much politics involved…"

In exasperation Wallace interrupted him.

"Be that as it may, what has this to do with me? Why must I leave Scotland? What is meant by this?"

"Do you not see, Will? You must go also to Rome, to state… to *restate* Scotland's right to independence. You must counter Edward's deceptions with truth."

Wallace stood aghast. Silent. Wordless.

"What does it benefit Scotland to have you hidden away in Selkirk Forest when the nation's fate is decided in the courts of distant lands?"

Incredulous, the giant found words.

"I am no talker, no lawyer or clerk. Nor am I a courtier. Why do you not send one of Scotland's great ones – the Steward, or one of these new Guardians?"

Wishart's features softened.
"Will, to some of us, to the common folk and the Church, you will always be Scotland's Guardian."

Much moved by these words and by the manner in which they had been spoken, Wallace remained silent again. Lamberton spoke into that silence.

"Sir William, you will not go alone. These…"

Wallace glared at him and interrupted again.

"But why send *me* at all?"

"Because, since you force me to speak bluntly, Sir William, these nobles to whom you refer, they cannot be trusted to put the interests of King John and Scotland before their own ambitions. Some of these seek the crown for themselves, they fear Edward and play a double game. You, on the other hand, have never sought anything for yourself. You might have *seized* the crown – many would gladly see you wear it – but ever you have been loyal to John Balliol and acted in his name. All men, at least all true Scots, know that Wallace can be trusted."

"I have been loyal, and remain loyal, yes, to the rightful King of Scots. All I have done, I have done to put him on his throne again, in a free Scotland."

Old Wishart broke in.

"Aye, Will. You hit the nail on the head. Edward, under pressure from the Pope, released King John from English captivity, and since July he has been under the supervision of Philip in France. You must persuade His Holiness to instruct Philip to return our king to his own realm, and you must counter any more English talk of 'overlordship'. You can accomplish more at this Papal Court than ever you could on a field of battle."

Forgetting himself somewhat, Wallace snarled his response.

"Are you deaf, man? I say I am no lawyer. No purveyor of words. I am a man of action, of deeds!"

"You are an educated man, Will. You have Latin. You were destined for the Church. You have presence, and you have inspired men with your words more than any other in the land. Who could more eloquently speak from the heart of Scotland's right to be an independent realm? As for law…"

He gestured to those other churchmen present whom Wallace had been unable to place.

"…Master Baldred Bisset, Master William Frere, Archdeacon of Lothian, and William of Eaglesham."

The giant nodded at each stiffly as they were introduced. Wishart continued.

"These will go with you. They have the law, Civil Law and Church Law, at their fingertips. They will be at your shoulder to advise. But you… Rome will listen to William Wallace."

Lamberton fluttered a hand.

"Go first, Sir William, to Philip of France. As you know, I spent some time at his court on my way back to Scotland from Rome. Philip will give you a letter of introduction to His Holiness. Such would not be needful, of course, but it should help."

Wallace compressed his lips and turned his back on the company, staring unseeing at the distant Firth of Tay. It was in his mind to refuse, but before that summer had turned to autumn he was aboard a ship for France.

*   *   *

A rather curious incident occurred at the end of October in the year 1872. The Keeper of Dumbarton Castle received a letter from the War Office. From the Surveyor General's Department of the War Office, to be precise. As it was signed by a certain *E. Reilly, Colonel Royal Artillery, Assistant Director of Artillery*, the Keeper at first assumed that it would relate to the garrison's ordnance, but no, it concerned the Sword of William Wallace. It read (in part) –

"I am directed by Mr Secretary Cardwell to remind you that this sword was sent to the Tower of London in the year 1825 for repair…"

(This had been almost half-a-century earlier.)

"…and to be fitted with a new hilt, and was, by direction of the late Duke of Wellington, Master General of the Ordnance, submitted for the opinion of Dr Meyrick. That gentleman was of the opinion that the sword never could have belonged to Sir William Wallace… This opinion having been concurred with by the Tower Authorities, Mr Cardwell therefore desires me to state that there appears to be no truth in the belief that has been entertained by many persons that this sword was that of Sir William Wallace. Accordingly he would be obliged to you if you would ensure that directions be sent to Dumbarton Castle to refrain from exhibiting it as such in future."

This letter and its content became known to Duncan Robertson through Gunner Irwin, but thoughts of such matters were not, at that time, his immediate priority.

Hannah Paton had thick, curling red hair which tumbled onto her shoulders. She had the bluest eyes Duncan had ever seen. Her complexion was creamy-white and lightly freckled. Her chin was delicately pointed. Her mouth... Duncan spent a lot of time thinking about Hannah Paton's mouth. Although, at sixteen, she was a year older than Duncan, Hannah was in his class at the Academy. She was the eldest daughter of the Provost's gardener. Duncan found that he could not take his mind off her for any great length of time. The way she was formed. The curves of her body. The graceful manner of her movements. That certain mystery of budding womanhood. Her facial expressions and the music of her voice. He found that he wanted to be in her company as much as possible, and he was forever thinking of ways to bring himself to her attention. Even when she was bossy or stand-offish with him, which she generally was, he found that, curiously, it made her all the more desirable. Of course, he was acutely jealous of any attention she gave to other boys in the class. Indeed, there was one boy in particular, Peter Connell, in whom she seemed to have far too much interest... Duncan had noticed that, for some odd reason, girls seemed to make more of a fuss over tall boys, and Duncan himself was barely of average height. No, he'd have to find some area of common interest between himself and Hannah Paton. Some activity or place where he could get her away from the likes of Connell. But what activity? Which place?

At fifteen, Duncan, apart from his fascination with Scottish history and his ambition to get to Glasgow University, had only one other notable interest. He loved watching Dumbarton's football team. The club had been formed that very year and to date Duncan hadn't missed a single home fixture. Oddly enough, he had seen the Paton family – father, mother and Hannah, attending one or two of the games. Dressed to the nines, they seemed to have a special interest in one of the players. Not one of Hannah's brothers, some other relative or neighbour perhaps. But it was not beyond the bounds of possibility that somehow Duncan might at least initiate some kind of casual encounter at the football…

Priority or not, the subject of the Wallace Sword came up for discussion, nevertheless, in the Robertson household, however indirectly, at the turn of the year. It all had to do with the Dumbarton Burns Club. The club's gatherings and organisation had been allowed to become rather informal, not to say casual, so a special meeting was to be held on Friday the 24th of January in the town's *Elephant Hotel*. New officer bearers were to be appointed, and proper minutes taken and so forth. Duncan's father, being one of the club's leading lights, was wondering if he'd be proposed for some position. Around a couple of dozen members could be expected to attend and it was the usual requirement for each to contribute some sort of "turn", be it a recitation, a song or perhaps a brief talk on some aspect of the Bard's life and work. James Robertson intended to say a few words about the Burns song, *Robert Bruce's March to Bannockburn.*

SCOTS, wha hae wi' WALLACE bled,
Scots, wham BRUCE has aften led,
Welcome to your gory bed,
Or to victorie!

James' *basso profundo* rang around the small kitchen as the family sat at the supper table, but he was interrupted by a curious Duncan.

"So, did Robert Burns know about the sword… Wallace's sword, being here at the castle?"

James raised a bushy and quizzical eyebrow.

"Whit makes yi ask that, Lad?"

"Well, I never heard of him visiting it when he was here yon time, Father."

James smiled a wry smile.

"Ah… there's a bit o' a story there, young Duncan. Aye, there is that."

Mrs Robertson sniffed disapprovingly and bustled about her domestic business. She had little regard for Robert Burns or any of his doings. A rascal if ever there was one. Ignoring this frostiness, the stonemason pushed his papers aside and settled comfortably into the tale.

"As you know, the Bard received his Burgess Ticket here in the toun on the 29ᵗʰ o' June in the year 1787."

Duncan nodded sagely, and all around the table the younger siblings knew to hold their tongues while Father spoke.

"Burns was daen' a bit tour o' the Western Highlands. Noo, the morn afore he cam tae Dumbarton he was up in Arrochar. He cam through by Tarbet and doon the lochside tae Archibald MacLachlan's hoose at Bannachra. Noo, as yi also mind, Bannachra is jist doon fae the mooth o' the glen – Glen Finlas, where I was broucht up, so the story passed doon the family."

A light of ancestral pride shone in Robertson's eye.

"Noo, the terrible sad truth is that in thae days gentlemen wir richt terrible heavy on the bottle – the demon drink – yi tak my meaning. They drank, some o' them, mornin', noon and nicht. Well, nae mistake aboot it, young Rab wisnae slow in learnin' fae them."

He paused and gave young Duncan a stern look, full of tacit warning.

"Anyway, the Bard's visit wis a rare feather in the cap o' MacLachlan, and he made guid an' certain that the hospitality under his roof wisnae skimped. We hae it fae Rab's ain pen – by way o' private letters, yi follow – that the company danced and drank till three in the morning."

Another pause to allow the full measure of this debauchery to sink in.

"No' content wi' this, they were back at it first thing wi' the sunrise. Oh aye, they wir doon at the watter-side, actin' the goat and scoopin' up mair drink!"

A sorry shake of the head.

"Well, you may imagine the state oor National Bard was in when he mounted his horse yon morn. Himsel' and twa ither young braves – fu' as monkeys, yi may be sure – cam doon the loch-side fae Bannachra, jist by Arden, headin' tae mooth o' the Leven. Well, a certain heilantman came gallopin' past them on his bit garron, an' Burns an' his cronies wir fair affrontit. So aff thae chased, roarin' drunk that thae wir, and before ower lang it wis jist between the Bard an' the heilantman."

A quick look around his listeners to make sure that the drama of his rendering held their undivided attention. He was not disappointed.

"By the Bard's way o' it, the heilantman went tae pu' oot in front o' his horse – *Jenny Geddes*, he ca'd her – an there wis an almichty stramash. The heilantman cam aff his garron an' flew ower a hedge. But Burns fell in atween the twa brutes an' got fair trampled."

At this James Robertson pursed his lips judiciously and gave Duncan a look that said – so there's your answer. The expression on his son's face, however, did not suggest enlightenment, so his father spelled it out.

"The day Robert Burns got his Burgess Ticket in Dumbarton, Duncan, he was in such a state wae the effects o' the drink wearin' aff him, and the bruisin' an' batterin' he took fae yon twa horses, he was in nae fit state tae walk the length o' the High Street, ne'er mind climb the steps o' Dumbarton Rock. Mind you, I'd wager he'd have been fair disappointed no' tae have seen Wallace's Sword."

"Do you think so, Father?"

"Indeed, I do, Lad. Jist you haud oan here the noo."

And with that James rose from the table and disappeared briefly into the tiny room he dignified with the name of his 'study'. When he returned he was leafing keenly through the pages of a book.

"Oh aye. The Bard was fair inspired by William Wallace… fair inspired."

He trailed off, distractedly looking through the pages. The strong workman's fingers seeking the relevant lines.

"Aye. He tells us that the first twa books he ever read wir *Hannibal* an' Blind Harry's *History o' William Wallace*. Noo listen tae this –

At WALLACE' name, what Scottish blood
But boils up in a spring-tide flood!
Oft have our fearless fathers strode
By Wallace side
Still pressing onward, red-wat-shod,
Or glorious dy'd.

"Indeed, he speaks o' Wallace in *The Cottar's Saturday Night*, in his *Vision*… Och, Burns wrote monie a line aboot the Guardian o' Scotland. In his *Parcel of Rogues in a Nation*, yon poem he wrote against the Union, he gies us –

Oh would, ere I had seen the day
That treason thus could sell us,
My auld grey heid had lain in clay
Wi' Bruce and loyal Wallace!

"Sure, he e'en mentions him in his *Ode for General Washington's Birthday*."

To his father's satisfaction, Duncan gave every indication of being suitably impressed. Closing the book, James Robertson concluded profoundly –

"Robert Burns must have been richt pit oot aboot no' seein' Wallace's Sword. Aye... but such are the evils o'drink!"

Cause and Conversion

We have come to the inescapable conclusion that Scotland's destiny lies as an independent nation within the European Community.

(The Sun)

1990: It was the year in which Alex Salmond was elected leader of the Scottish National Party and Margaret Thatcher resigned as leader of the Conservative Party.

Elected Member of Parliament for Banff and Buchan in 1987, Salmond won a leadership contest against Margaret Ewing by 486 votes to 146.

On the 31st of March 1990 (the year in which Glasgow was the European Capital of Culture) over 200,000 anti-poll tax protestors attended a rally in Trafalgar Square. It deteriorated into a bloody riot arising from which there were some 339 arrests. The English expressed their opinion rather more forcibly than the Scots, and the English, of course, were heeded. Thatcher's personal popularity in the opinion polls plummeted and the

Tories began to regard her as a liability. After a leadership contest
in which she was effectively rejected by her party, Thatcher
resigned, shedding bitter tears as she left Number 10 Downing
Street.

Three years later I became forty, which depressed me a little. At
that time I began to question my priorities in life. Was I using my
time, talents and energy wisely and well? Up till this year I had
entertained quite serious notions of making my mark in the world
as either a painter or a writer.

The Tony Hancock film – *The Rebel* – was about a young man
who had a deadly boring job with a firm of accountants. In his
own time he pursued the life of the amateur artist – as painter and
sculptor. Utterly devoid of authentic talent he packs in his job and
heads for Paris to live a bohemian life in Montparnasse (where he
is farcically "discovered"). I first saw this film with my father
when I was around eight years old. There is a scene in which
Hancock enters a studio which he is to share with an artist friend.
Something of the atmosphere of that room, with its canvases,
easels, brushes and tubes of paint, its disorder, its space and its
vast window looking out over the chimneys of Paris at night,
spoke to my young soul. Its romance fascinated and thrilled me. It
seduced me. From that moment I longed to be a painter and
believed that such was my destiny.

Two books later inspired me enormously. The first was called
Colossus. It was a novelised biography of Goya. At the time of
reading I hadn't painted anything since I left school, having lost
all my confidence when I failed to get into Art School, but after
devouring that book I went out and bought a half-dozen brushes
and got to work on a watercolour, applying the paint thickly and

vividly like oils. The subject was Robert the Bruce sitting on his war-horse at the Battle of Bannockburn (I was in my early twenties at the time of that first painting). Some workmates in the office praised it, so I started on a second then a third... Now, every time I pass the door of the shop in which I bought those paintbrushes so many years ago, I look into the distance, up to the hill on the eastern side of the Vale of Leven. On the horizon I see a certain line of trees. The sight of them invariably makes me think of Goya, sitting at a campfire with a company of Spanish soldiers, as he is inspired to paint his *Colossus* during the Napoleonic invasion of his native land. These trees are my symbol for that kind of life.

The other book was entitled *The Master Painter* and was about El Greco. Mr Fraser, my old Vale of Leven Academy art teacher, recommended that one. I was impressed by the way El Greco received commissions from the Church of his day and I became curiously and rather quixotically motivated by a desire to work for the Church.

By 1993, however, I'd painted no more than a dozen watercolours and drawn a few charcoal sketches. I'd sold just one painting – an image of the three Bonhill Bridges – to my employer, the local council. So, by any realistic assessment, I'd failed to become a noted painter.

As regards the writing: I'd had the very minor publications of poetry and short stories previously alluded to, but to this day I possess a shirt box filled to overflowing with rejection slips and letters from literary magazines and publishing companies. Most painful, however, was the experience I had with a novella which was initially accepted for publication by a small publisher. The sense of affirmation and achievement this brought me was intoxicating. Particularly, I looked forward to making my parents proud in this way. Month upon month went by, though, with excuse after excuse as the actual date of publication was pushed further and further into a never to be reached future. Eventually, and foolishly, I had thrown the rattle out of the pram and withdrawn from the non-contracted "agreement".

This was the frame of mind, then, that I was in as I reached forty. It seemed clear that I could carry on, year upon year for the rest of my life, seeking artistic recognition which would never come my way, or I could do something more realistic and worthwhile. I was looking for a cause. Around this point I chanced to see an advert, in (I believe) the *Observer* newspaper, for the work of Amnesty International. As I read I became interested then impressed. Amnesty members campaigned to abolish the death penalty, to put an end to torture, and to gain freedom for "prisoners of conscience". The thought came to me then that a time might come some day when I'd change my mind about socialism. One day I could come to think that energy spent in pursuit of Scottish independence might be wasted, but I could not imagine that I would ever believe that any effort to prevent someone from being tortured would be mistaken. I decided to join Amnesty International and become an activist.

I recall that I wore a brown leather jacket and a scarf of the *Culloden* tartan as I stood on the platform of Alexandria railway station waiting for the old lady. The train drew in, and although I'd never seen her I recognised her at once. Elizabeth Burnett was tiny, in her eighties and wearing a big red velvet hat. I remember thinking that she was a Scottish version of Margaret Rutherford. In fact, she was a founder member of the Dumbarton group of

Amnesty, and she had agreed to meet me to explain how the organisation worked and how I might contribute to that work. We had lunch in the nearby *Station Bar*, which was fortunately quiet on the occasion. I must have known that this was going to be a significant moment in my life, because I actually kept the wee bill which I have before me as I write – *2xFish £7.70*. Elizabeth – or Bea, as her friends called her – was an incredible person whom I came to like and respect enormously. The outcome of our meeting was that I joined the "Urgent Action" scheme. This involved committing to receiving regular Urgent Actions (in my own case about two per week), which were in those days delivered by Royal Mail. These were A4 yellow pages which contained case notes relating to what would become known as "Individuals At Risk". These were human rights victims of various kinds - typically it would be a non-violent political activist who had been jailed by an oppressive regime, possibly tortured, sometimes sentenced to death.

Those of us in the Urgent Action scheme would write letters and send them to officials of the offending authority basically asking them to release the prisoner, or to stop torturing him or her, and so on... Surprisingly, in many cases the cumulative effect of hundreds of people from all over the world sending messages to Heads of State, Government Ministers, Governors of Prisons etc., did at least improve conditions for the victim. Many were actually released. This activity became my substitute for political and artistic activity, and I continue to participate in the Urgent Action scheme these twenty years on.

That year of my fortieth birthday was also when the Council Tax replaced the Poll Tax. So, I was now helping to collect a new form of property-based local revenue which, though not of course popular, was less detested than its forerunner. That year my trade union, NALGO, combined with NUPE and COHSE to become *Unison*. A change of office, a change of union, working with different colleagues, but no more job satisfaction. I was still going to the pub every evening – the *Balloch Hotel* now being my resort of choice –   but in my free time, during weekends and public holidays, I did a lot of walking out in the countryside. There was a particular estate – forestry and farmland – which stretched along the south-eastern shore of Loch Lomond, that was my favourite stalking ground. *Boturich* was owned by a Mr Robert Findlay whose ancestors had been successful East India merchants. The Findlays had generously made available a considerable part of *Boturich* estate to the Scout movement when the *Rob Roy* campsite was opened in 1960. Thereafter several generations, countless thousands of boys from all over the world, had had their lives enriched by times spent in those fields and woodlands on the shores of Loch Lomond. This, indeed, had been how I came to know and love the place as a boy.

Politics, of course, was still happening. I was still aware of it and interested in it. For example, it was in 1993 that Ravenscraig, the last of Scotland's steelworks, was closed. I talked about politics to workmates, to fellow-drinkers, but for a number of years there was a Sunday afternoon arrangement by which I met a group of friends, half-a-dozen middle-aged men, all left-wingers, with whom I did most of my political talking. We would meet in Balloch, usually at the bottom of Mollanbowie Road, and then head uphill, past the North Lodge of Balloch Park, by *Over Balloch* farm – with my beloved *Ledrishmore* rising to the right – and down through the old green gates into the estate itself. There was a point, at the top of one of the braes, from which one could look northward and, over green fields and through the trees, the great tower of Boturich Castle could be seen. Beyond that, on the western side of the loch, the magnificent contours of Glen Finlas formed the horizon. Further on, past *Meikle Boturich* farm, a vista opened out – Loch Lomond, her islands and the soaring mountains which surrounded her – a panorama which I continue to think of as surely one of the finest views in Europe.

As we pounded this beat, week after week, year after year, we spoke of little but politics. Two unemployed Clyde shipyard workers, a retired plumber, a storeman with the MOD at the Faslane Naval Base, a bus driver… and a tax collector. *The Last of the Summer Wine*, we called it. One summer we decided to have a change of scenery, and the Sunday walk was rerouted from Kilmaronock parish to Jamestown parish. We'd rendezvous in Jamestown and head out on the Auchincarroch Road, through more farmland, for five miles or so. On one occasion, as we reached the farm of *Mid Auchincarroch*, I interrupted a discussion about the Labour Party's "Clause Four". Pointing to the farm buildings, I said –

"It was in there they found Robert Nairn's secret room."

"How d'you mean, Willie? Robert Nairn's secret room?" This was from Campbell, one of the redundant shipyard welders: quiet, unassuming, reasonable and principled, one of the most gentle men I ever knew.

"Well, Robert Nairn was one of the Bonhill Covenanters during the 'Killing Times'."

"The *Killing Times*? Sounds like something out of a John Wayne movie." Added his fellow welder with a cynical laugh.

"The Killing Times were in the 1670s and 80s, when the king in London was imposing bishops on the Scots Presbyterians. It was illegal not to attend the church services which had been officially sanctioned by the government, but the Covenanters took to the fields and worshipped at open air 'conventicles'. To preach at a conventicle, and then even to attend one, was punishable by death."

Big George, a craggy-featured, remarkably well-read man and profound thinker, chipped in.

"Aye, c'mon, fellas. Robert Nairn was a Covenanter. He's buried in Bonhill Churchyard."

"That's right. Nairn was a local shoemaker who lived at Napierston in Bonhill. For not attending the services of the Episcopalian minister who had been foisted on the Bonhill congregation, Nairn was hunted onto these hills."

I gestured to the moorland which stretched above us.

"He was even shot at by dragoons on patrol from Dumbarton Castle. For a while he was sheltered by friends and neighbours – which was pretty courageous on their part – but eventually, after a cruel winter in the woods, Nairn died of starvation and exposure."

George, frowning thoughtfully, took up the tale.

"It didn't end there, though. The minister of Bonhill Church was loyal to the king, so he wouldn't allow Nairn even to be buried in the churchyard, but the locals took matters into their own hands and made sure that their Covenanter got a final resting place beside the Kirk after all."

"Aye, but what's this about a secret room?"

"Oh, well, the MacAllisters of *Auchincarroch* here, they were one of the families that gave food and shelter to Robert Nairn from time to time. Well, sometime early in the nineteenth century, a barn was demolished in there, and a false wall was pulled down and they discovered this wee secret room… and they actually found some of Nairn's cobbler's tools. Some story, eh?"

They all looked suitably impressed. Much gratified I carried on, pointing uphill a little.

"D'you see the wee quarry up there, behind the farm?"

All eyes turned in the required direction.

"Well, the red sandstone of Jamestown Parish Church…"

I turned and pointed back westward the couple of miles to the clearly visible steeple.

"…was dug out of that hillside – the hillside on which Robert Nairn was hounded and where he died for his faith."

I just couldn't explain exactly why, but I felt there was something very wonderful about that.

Returning to the politics of the 1990s: There were the complex moral questions arising from British participation in wars in the Gulf and Bosnia.

In 1989 the Scottish Constitutional Convention had been set up to continue the campaign for a devolved Scottish Assembly. Its first meeting was held in the Church of Scotland's Assembly Hall in Edinburgh, with political parties, local government bodies, trades unions, business organisations and churches, all represented. The Conservatives were opposed from the outset. The Scottish National Party were at first interested, but withdrew when the Convention rejected independence as an option. Under the chairmanship of Canon Kenyon Wright, of the Episcopalian Church, the Convention eventually published, on St Andrew's Day 1995, its proposals in *Scotland's Parliament: Scotland's Right.*

The SNP, (which enjoyed around 30% support in opinion polls) was, in 1990, to some extent divided between "fundamentalists", who argued straightforwardly for independence as soon as possible, and "gradualists", who were prepared to play a longer game using, perhaps, the stepping-stone, of a devolved parliament. Leader, Alex Salmond, was a gradualist. Meanwhile support for outright independence had been growing, and in some unlikely places. In January of 1992, the *Sun* newspaper declared –

We have come to the inescapable conclusion that Scotland's destiny lies as an independent nation within the European Community.

One opinion poll went so far as to rate support for independence at 50%.

At the General Election of April 1992, however, the Nationalists were disappointed to hold only three seats, with Jim Sillars losing Glasgow Govan. It was a fourth consecutive victory for the Conservatives, and the fourth consecutive time the Scots had rejected them. Shortly after this election Neil Kinnock resigned as Labour leader. Kinnock was, to my mind, a vain man and a weak leader who, in his eagerness to be politically "respectable", gave Thatcher an easy time, refusing to give unambivalent support to the miners during their strike, and making himself a more passionate opponent of "the far left" than of Thatcherism.

In May of 1994 the Channel Tunnel was opened. John Smith, the new Labour leader, from whom great things were expected, died of a heart attack and was replaced by Tony Blair, a man whose style and appearance made me think of an English public school sneak. In fact he was born in Edinburgh and went to Fettes College, distinctions which were wasted on me. The following year Roseanna Cunningham of the SNP won the Perth seat at a by-election.

The first half of the '90s featured a lengthy period of tension between the SNPs fundamentalists (independence, nothing less) and Alex Salmond's gradualists (who saw a devolved parliament as a second best which would hopefully lead on to full independence). Personally, I was inclined to the fundamentalist position, harbouring serious doubts about devolution and the motives of the Unionists who offered it.

In April of '96 I found myself with yet another employer. The Tories had got around to carrying out another major local government reorganisation by which they had been able to abolish the massive Strathclyde Regional Council – which they regarded, not without good reason – as a Labour Party petty kingdom. I now worked for West Dunbartonshire Council, which was rather more like the old Dunbartonshire County Council to which I had been recruited all these years before, in 1970. As someone who was historically minded, I was conscious of an element of consistency in the heraldic device which decorated the wall of the Council Chamber in our Garshake Offices. It was the red saltire on white, with the four red roses of the ancient earldom of Lennox, an area which roughly corresponded with Dunbartonshire. When I had commenced my working life a flag bearing that powerful symbol had flown in the grounds of Garshake. Now, a quarter of a century later, a similar flag, based on that Lennox heraldry, was flying once more.

Later in that year an unexpected gesture was made by the Conservative government. As a symbolic recognition of Scottish national (not to say *nationalist*) sensitivities, the Stone of Destiny, which had been appropriated by Edward I seven hundred years earlier, was returned with much ceremony to Scotland. On St Andrew's Day, 30th of November, the Stone was placed with the *Honours of Scotland* in Edinburgh Castle. Representing the Queen on the occasion was Prince Andrew. A condition of this loan was that the Stone would be returned to Westminster, as and when required for future coronations.

*   *   *

It had all been in vain. A complete and utter waste of time and effort. All those endless miles by sea and by land. All the frustrating months spent waiting in courts and palaces. All the smooth talking, the smiles that never reached the eyes. The luxury. The sophistication. The enforced idleness. The vast grandeur of Paris and Rome. Princes, cardinals and the Pope himself. The pirates and brigands they had encountered on the way had been paragons of virtue compared with the fork-tongued serpents of church and state. Words, words, words... all empty words.

In July of 1302 Philip's French army had been defeated by the Flemings in the Battle of Courtrai... and Scotland was the loser. It was no longer in the French interest to side with the Scots against the English. The Pope, who was now in dispute with Philip, but warming towards Edward, had sent brittle instruction to Scotland's churchmen – they were to live at peace with Edward of England – and there was only one way the Plantagenet would ever interpret peace – submission on his terms.

The following summer the French king signed a treaty with Edward. Scotland was now on its own. The ink had not dried on the document before the English king had commenced yet another invasion of the northern realm. Shrewdly bypassing Stirling, his army forged onward through Perth, Brechin, Aberdeen, Banff and Elgin, eventually drawing to a triumphant halt at Kinloss Abbey in Moray. At this time the Guardian, Sir John de Soulis, was on the Continent, seeking to recover support by continuing diplomacy, and Red Comyn was acting Guardian in his absence.

Edward spent the winter months in Dunfermline. When he left the town in March, he made a point of burning its Abbey, burial place of Scotland's kings and queens – including that of his own sister. This act of desecration was perpetrated in spite of the fact that, in the previous month, the Red Comyn, in his capacity as Guardian, had, on behalf of the community and realm of

Scotland, surrendered to Edward. The terms of the capitulation were such, however, that the great majority of the Scottish nobles were allowed to hang onto their lands and their positions.

Edward promptly held a parliament at St Andrews. He appointed his nephew, the Earl of Richmond, Viceroy of Scotland. Wallace was (yet again) outlawed, being exempted from the general amnesty, and the Planagenet ordered the Scots to "exert themselves until twenty days after Christmas to capture Sir William Wallace and hand him over to the king..." A price of one hundred pounds was put on his head.

Word of the burning of Dunfermline Abbey reached Wallace in the hills of Menteith. He and a small band of his closest and most loyal veterans were concealed in the deep, wooded gully which ran between Ben Dearg and Ben Gullipen. There was no outburst of rage on receipt of the news, just a weary sadness. The man who had been Guardian was yet brooding darkly about this latest surrender to the English. He knew that however the realm's nobility might stoop and crawl to Edward, he, Wallace, and these men around him now, would fight the oppressors to their last breath. Comyn, Lennox, the Steward and all their kind, they did not speak for the common folk of this land, and Wallace had had enough of words. It was back to deeds.

He looked at the company around him – that mere dozen of cold and hungry men. His cousin, Adam Wallace. Thomas Gray, the Liberton priest. Steven MacGregor of Strathcashell on Loch Lomondside. John Blair, their Benedictine chaplain... and Kerlie, now with scarce a tooth in his head, God bless him... and the others. He had trusted these men with his life a hundred times

over, and he feared he would surely lead them to their deaths...
sooner rather than later.

"Dumbarton... We'll strike Menteith at Dumbarton. We have no
chance of taking the castle, but we'll singe his beard in the burgh.
Damned if we don't."

Sir John Menteith had been singled out by Edward, after the
surrender, being conspicuously favoured with the sheriffdom of
Dumbarton and the keepership of its castle.

As they descended cautiously and silently down the burnside, the
vast lowland plain opened out before them, in bleak, grey, late-
winter tones. These Menteith Hills formed a part of the Highland
Line, and immediately below them, stretching around and beyond
the little Loch Menteith, was the great sweep of Flanders Moss, a
huge marshland through which the River Forth meandered.

The Benedictine spoke –

"D'you think they'll watch the Fords of Frew?"

They had been reliably informed that Edward had ordered Sir
Alexander de Abernethy to take a force of men and patrol the
course of the river in case Wallace and his band might be captured
attempting to cross it.

"Aye. It's a possibility. We would, in their shoes. But maybe
Abernethy will just go through the motions with horsemen, from
Stirling eastward."

Kerlie, recovering quickly from a stumble on an icy boulder, steadied himself with a hand on Blair's shoulder and added breathlessly –

"We'll be heading the other way, anyhow, so it doesn't signify."

Climbing now in a south-westward direction, out of the gully, the company carried on through a long and shallow valley, which ran along the top of the ridge. Eventually they followed the course of another little burn steeply downhill by *Nether Glenny* and onto the edge of the Moss, just west of Menteith Loch. Darkness was falling and the night grew colder. Wallace walked in a moody silence. He knew the Moss reasonably well, but for the company to win through it without so much as moonlight to illuminate their path required the intimate knowledge which few but a member of Clan Gregor possessed. They were lucky, then, to have Steven MacGregor among them. For several hours they progressed but slowly, taking pains to avoid, where possible, habitation. Keeping to a general south-westerly direction and entering into the Earldom of Lennox, they crossed the Kelty Water, winning out of the Moss and covering the miles through the parishes of Drymen, Kilmaronock and Bonhill, to the south of Loch Lomond. These men were well used to hardship: to walking in all weathers on empty stomachs, often to find themselves in combat at the end of it.

Dawnlight was teasing the horizon of the Kilpatrick Hills when the weary company came softly like shadows upon the farmhouse of *Aikinbar*, on the outskirts of Dumbarton. The burgh was by no means unknown to Wallace. It was, after all, an important port, none so far from his home town. Many a time, in his earlier years, he had come over the Clyde with his father to purchase imported luxuries. This *Aikinbar* was home to a certain widow who had no fewer than nine sons, two of whom had fought at Falkirk. These folk were friends.

Making a great fuss of their arrival, the mother posted a couple of sons on lookout duty while she went about the urgent business of feeding her ravenous visitors. Before long they were greedily devouring chunks of bread, hard-boiled eggs and salted fish, washed down with large quantities of small beer and small cups of whisky. The effects of this latter, on filled stomachs and exhausted limbs, would have rendered the grateful recipients sound asleep where they sat, had not their hostess fretfully steered them into a large barn where they might slumber to their hearts content concealed by stacked piles of winter fodder.

They slept until mid-afternoon and spent the few remaining daylight hours keeping out of sight and making plans. The widow and her sons assured them that the burgh was crawling with English soldiery; not only was the castle well garrisoned, but many of the town's houses had had the occupiers billeted on them. Apparently families of any means had been forced to pay tribute to the sheriff, and this, on top of other routine indignities, had made the soldiers who enforced this taxation particularly detested. Wallace was struck by how dramatically the widow had aged since he had last seen her.

Aikinbar lay little more than a mile from the town cross, and the great Rock was clearly visible to them looming over the Clyde shore. Not till near midnight did the company split up into groups of two and three, these making their way separately at intervals to the burgh, with an agreed time and place of rendezvous. Some of the widow's sons were keen to accompany them, but Wallace forcefully ruled this out. He wanted no reprisals coming the way of these loyal folk.

In the darkness of that March night the townsfolk seemed to have settled into their beds, apart from the light and sounds which came from two inns, one at either end of the High Street. The various groups had met up as planned just to the north of the ferry which crossed the River Leven. Even from the distance of some couple of hundred yards, they could discern strident English accents cutting through the stillness of the night. With practised stealth they fanned out and moved in to surround the inn. It was a long, two-storied building with a thickly thatched roof. Wallace and his men had no way of knowing exactly how many English soldiers were occupying this inn, but irrespective of the strength of the enemy – which was unlikely to be more than a couple of dozen – the plan of action would have been almost monotonously inevitable, except for one almost absurd factor.

Since gorging himself on a large quantity of the salted fish that morning, Wallace had been experiencing a quite insatiable thirst. The very thought of slaking this with a tankard of ale quite overcame all common sense imperatives of self-preservation. To the surprise, not to say alarm, of his company, the tall warrior strode through the open door of the building and into the light and warmth of the inn.

Present were a darkly-bearded English captain, nine soldiers sprawled around a long trestle-table, and a harassed-looking inn-keeper. Curiously, there were no women in evidence. Naturally conversation ceased abruptly and the seated men stared with astonishment at the giant in their midst. Wallace spoke resoundingly into the tense silence in what he hoped would be taken for an Irish accent.

"God bless all of you. I take it you are English soldiers? Aye. I have sailed over the sea from my native Tirconnel, just for the honour of serving King Edward. I pledge my sword in his service."

With which, in a swift and fluid motion, he drew his great blade from over his shoulder, causing some of the English to involuntarily draw back. The captain, after a long and penetrating inspection of the speaker, found his voice, however dry his mouth.

"Don't take me for a fool, Scotchman…" as he spoke he made a slight lifting gesture with both hands spread out at his sides. Interpreting him, his men began to rise slowly, reaching for their weapons.

The captain never finished his sentence. There was an incredibly swift blur of swinging steel, then the bearded head rolled over the straw-covered floor and bounced into the flickering log fire. The decapitated body remained grotesquely seated. Only one of the soldiers kept his nerve, raising a crossbow and taking aim at Wallace's chest as the inn-keeper retched noisily. An arrow from MacGregor's bow sped through the open door and cut through the soldier's leather jerkin, killing him instantly.

In the ensuing melee, Wallace's company, having the advantage of surprise, got the better of the remaining English, their bodies being dragged the few yards to the riverside – sufficiently downstream from the numerous tied-up sailing craft – and slipped without ceremony into the swiftly-flowing Leven, the captain's macabre head bobbing along in their wake.

Returning to the inn, Wallace remembered his thirst. The ashen-faced innkeeper, a bald Highlander of middle years, wearing a soiled plaid of some drab green tartan, had swept the straw from the floor and was now sloshing it with buckets of water to remove the considerable amount of shed blood. Blair had been left behind to keep an eye on him, and a third figure had appeared: a tall, dark, rather hard-looking young man who turned out to be the innkeeper's son. They were all duly provided with ale and bread. While they ate and drank, Wallace questioned the pair as to the dispositions of the other English military in the burgh. It transpired that there were over two hundred of them in the town. They had been imposed on a number of households, but there was one large property, which belonged to a particularly prosperous shipbuilder, in which were lodged around three dozen of them.

The son, whose sweetheart had been abused by soldiers, was avid to assist Wallace and company in any way that would hurt the English. Accordingly he eagerly volunteered to guide them to the house in question. In the manner of experienced campaigners who knew not to stand when they could sit, and not to sit when they could lie, they all – with the exception of two men who stood guard outside – sprawled on new, fresh, dry straw, and made careful plans.

The shipbuilder's house was situated well back from the river, to the east of the High Street. Rather than draw attention to themselves by carrying flaming torches through the streets, they took with them flint and tinder. At a discreet distance from the property, they soundlessly encircled it, then at a prearranged signal began to rain flaming arrows on the huge thatched roof from all sides. It did not take long before the night sky was lit up by a good-going blaze. Timing was now of the utmost importance. It was essential that they deal with the occupants before the fire was spotted, either by sentries on the Rock, or by other English in the town itself. Before many minutes passed, however, howls of alarm could be heard above the crackling of wood and thatch.

It was the usual, cynical and merciless procedure. Panic-stricken, semi-clad men, some of them little more than boys, were cold-bloodedly butchered as they attempted to flee the burning building. It was all over in less than ten minutes. Some thirty men were killed – some perished horribly in the inferno, others died by sword, dagger or arrow at the hands of the Scots.

"Edward won't be so impressed with the stewardship of his new Sheriff of Dumbarton, now, I'm thinking."

Wallace observed with satisfaction. Kerlie and the MacGregor snorted in unison.

"Sir John Stewart of Menteith will have a bit of explaining to do to his royal master, right enough."

They had appropriated three small boats in which they'd crossed the Leven, and the company, having suffered not so much as a scratch among them, were now drawing their collective breath, as it were, in a small cave on the shore of the Clyde, a couple of miles to the west of the confluence of the two rivers.

Will smelled the water, and looking out over the mile or so of the Firth in the direction of his native Renfrewshire, invisible in the darkness, he began to recall episodes from his childhood. He fell to thinking of his father... again.

Blair the Benedictine remained silent. He could not stop thinking about how young some of the English boys had been.

*   *   *

Dumbarton's ageless Rock glowered behind the carefully arranged group of characters which represented local wealth and power in the year 1847. Smolletts of Bonhill. Ewings of Strathleven. Campbells of Tullichewan and Colgrain (in Highland regimentals). The pair stared intently at the large group portrait. Duncan could appreciate the skill which had captured such detail as the collar and cuffs on the red tunic of James Colquhoun of Luss. Hannah admired the fine lace which covered Victoria's bright tartan scarf.

"The Landing of Queen Victoria at Dumbarton", painted by a certain Hope James Stewart – of whom neither had ever heard – to commemorate the visit by Victoria and Albert to the Royal Burgh, some twenty-seven years earlier. Ten feet by eight, in oils. The painting hung in the hall of the County Building. They were looking for a ghost...

"Of course, I don't actually believe in ghosts." said Hannah – in a manner which very self-consciously spoke of mature dignity.

"Don't you? I'm not so sure. My father has told me some stories..." He let that trail away. This was perhaps not the time to develop such a theme. They were not, after all, alone. Mrs Paton stood rather uncomfortably just a few yards behind them.

Duncan's notions of encountering Hannah with her parents at a football match had been misplaced. There were very clear rules about courtship in Victorian society. A young man and a young woman did not meet socially (even if they had been in the same class in Dumbarton Academy) until they had been formally introduced. Generally such introduction would be made by their parents at a ball or some similar social occasion, and this would happen only if both sets of parents approved of the match. The boy's parents would be looking for a girl from a family of some means, for if it reached the stage of marriage – as would most certainly be expected – then such inheritance as came to the wife would, in law, be the property of the husband, for him to invest or squander as he willed. For their part, the parents of the girl would be looking for a boy of sound reputation and good prospects, who would give wife and children comfort and security.

In the case of Hannah and Duncan, the Patons were reasonably satisfied to anticipate the marriage of their daughter to the son of a well-to-do local craftsman. The Robertsons, on the other hand, only grudgingly accepted the idea of their son marrying the offspring of a local gardener. To be fair to James Paton, he was not only gardener to the Provost, but also to various other of the town's leading families, so it might be considered that he was in the way of small business himself.

It had happened then, that when Duncan's parents learned of his interest in Hannah – through the mischievous loose talk of one of his sisters – they stage-managed, after appropriate discussion with the Patons, the required formal introduction at a Christmas Ball in the Burgh Hall. What were Hannah's feelings in all of this? It must not be thought that the expected marriage was "arranged", in the sense of the bride-to-be having no say in the matter. Hannah had, to her excruciating embarrassment, been questioned as to her feelings regarding a match with Duncan Robertson, and she had been secretly thrilled – after all, he was a fine-looking boy, with obvious intelligence, but mostly he could make her laugh and he had that certain indefinable something which stirred her heart. So she had quietly and with great dignity assented. Duncan and Hannah were now seventeen and eighteen respectively. Duncan's father had shrewdly decided that it would be a good thing if the lad had a trade to fall back on just in case the academic life fell through. Accordingly Duncan was learning his father's skills of stonemasonry while waiting to be informed if he'd been accepted by Glasgow University. Hannah was in domestic service with the family of one of the burgh's glass manufacturers.

A young woman could not "keep company" with a young man unless she was strictly chaperoned, usually by her mother. Hence the presence of Mrs Paton on the occasion in question. Or rather, Mrs Paton, had had reason to visit the County Building and it suited her to allow the couple to accompany her.

Duncan had seen this painting before and he was familiar with a rather curious feature of it. An intriguing detail. The "ghost". He pointed to a space just to the left of the little empress, and to the right of Miss Cecilia Smollett. There, just barely visible, was a face. A young lady whom the artist had decided to over-paint had refused to be lost and she haunted the scene for evermore.

"There… Do you see her?" His eye twinkled roguishly.

Hannah bent forward to peer closely at the indicated figure. On perceiving it she jumped back with mock indignation.

"You clown. That's not a ghost... But it is strange, isn't it?"

She was rigged out stunningly in an emerald, fur-trimmed coat, which set off her fiery red hair quite gloriously, purple and gold paisley pattern scarf and black knitted woollen stockings. Duncan could barely stand the frustration of being so close to her without being able to throw his arms around her and cover that milky complexion with passionate kisses – though one would never have known this from his composure.

Returning to the painting, Duncan's attention was drawn to the gun salute which was depicted blasting against the sky, high above the roof of his old schoolhouse on the Rock. This brought to his mind Gunner Irwin and the numerous conversations the pair of them had had over the years on the subject of the Wallace Sword. Ever since that moment when Duncan, at the age of four years, had seen the sword raised aloft at the laying of the foundation stone of the Wallace Monument, it had taken a powerful hold over his imagination. It was a fascinating story, but one which had a frustrating element of mystery, causing his thoughts to return to it again and again. Looking at this impressive image of the visit of Queen Victoria to the Rock set him thinking afresh. There was something he'd very much like to check out... if he could.

But this was a distraction to be dealt with some other time. For the moment he returned to the infinitely more potent spell of Hannah Paton.

At first he'd assumed he'd have to make the train journey to Glasgow, but in the event – and it should not by now have surprised him – he'd found what he was looking for (more, indeed) in the library of the burgh's Mechanics' Institute. Firstly he discovered that three great literary figures: William Wordsworth, Dorothy Wordsworth and Samuel Taylor Coleridge, had visited the castle in August of 1803 and been shown the Wallace Sword. In her recollections Dorothy described the sword as a large, rusty weapon. William Wordsworth must have had a keen interest in the relic, having but a few years earlier written –

How Wallace fought for Scotland; left the name
Of Wallace to be found, like a wild flower,
All over his dear Country; left the deeds
Of Wallace, like a family of Ghosts,
To people the steep rocks and river banks,
Her natural sanctuaries, with a local soul,
Of independence and stern liberty.

Then, as Gunner Irwin had told Duncan, in 1825 the sword had been sent to the Tower of London where it had been examined by the man Meyrick, who had declared it bogus. It had, at that time, been cleaned and repaired, with a 15th century handle being added to it.

Further, Duncan had discovered a publication dated 1840: *Strath-Clutha: or the Beauties of the Clyde*, by John M. Leighton. In this work the author spoke of his visit to Dumbarton Castle in the course of which he had been shown an ancient relic: a large, two-handed sword which was regarded as that of William Wallace.

The writer added that there was nothing improbable about the weapon being genuine.

But then came the more weighty piece of evidence which came from the pages of a carefully preserved copy of the *Glasgow Herald*, dated 20th August 1847. During the visit that year of Queen Victoria and Prince Albert to Dumbarton Castle, the royal couple *had* been shown "Wallace's sword". Victoria and her Consort inspected and actually handled the weapon, marvelling at the strength Wallace must have possessed to wield such a large and heavy sword. The writer of the piece emphasised the identity of the relic by repeating in a subsequent paragraph that the queen had marvelled and examined "his well-kept sword".

It would have taken, Duncan considered, a brave official to consciously deceive no lesser a personage than Queen Victoria in such a matter... if, indeed, Meyrick's verdict of 1825 had been taken at all seriously. This evidence would suggest it had not. Why, then, after a lapse of almost half a century, did the War Office forbid the showing of the sword as that of William Wallace?

End and Beginning

There was a "Great Comet" in the sky at the time of the 1997 New Year. By coincidence it heralded a time of profoundly positive change in my life. For several years, in the winter months, I had been experiencing periods of painful swelling and inflammation in one of my big toes. This usually lasted for just a week or two, so I never sought medical advice. At the beginning of 1997, however, a particularly severe bout coincided with my going out with a nurse. The combination of the pain, the inconvenience and the silly notion that the nurse would be impressed, caused me on impulse to drop in on a doctor one miserable January morning. He examined the foot, asked me several questions, told me that it was most likely gout, and took a blood test to be certain.

When I returned to the surgery, several days later, he confirmed that it was, indeed, gout, and he asked me more questions about my lifestyle. In particular my drinking habits. It turned out he'd run a liver function test, and I remember the phrases he used to this day –

"It's up the Swanee." "We're getting flashing lights."

I'd been drinking too much for many years. This was no surprise. The doctor instructed me to drink no alcohol at all for a month, and then cut down to half of the level I'd been used to. I got such a fright I didn't touch a drop for three months, and when I resumed drinking I stuck to the reduced levels, and have done so religiously ever since. In fact, the older I get, I find the less I drink.

Since my late twenties I'd been aware of a certain spiritual hunger. I studied Buddhism and, to a lesser extent, Hinduism, becoming fascinated and impressed by both. At length, however, I accepted that I could never fully embrace any faith other than the Christianity in which I'd been brought up. In my early forties, therefore, under various good influences, not least the writings of a Stirling-born Victorian evangelist called Henry Drummond, and those of Professor William Barclay, I began to have a fresh look at the Bible. I was surprised to learn how generally reliable the Gospels and other New Testament books were as accounts of the life and teaching of Jesus and the early Church. I was, I think, surprised to find myself persuaded of the historical truth of the Resurrection. This is not to say that I didn't have problems with orthodox Christianity. I had, and continue to have, for example, a complete aversion to the doctrine of "eternal punishment".

Perhaps the warning I'd been given about my unhealthy lifestyle had concentrated my mind wonderfully, because one day, as I read Mark chapter 9, verse 24 – *"...Lord, I believe; help thou mine unbelief."* I realised that I could, in all conscience, join the Church.

It would have been natural for me to go back to Jamestown Parish Church. It had been the church of my family and of my childhood. Not only that, but the minister of Jamestown had been hugely supportive and instrumental in my spiritual homecoming. I had read, however, a book entitled *By the Rivers of Water*, by Iain Galbraith, which was a wonderful history of Bonhill Church and Parish. I was so affected by this work that I decided Bonhill would be the church for me. So it happened that on Maundy Thursday, 27th of March, 1997, I joined Bonhill Church, and in this way – I suspect – my grandmother's prayers were finally answered.

The United Kingdom General Election of May that year produced a Labour landslide. No Conservative MPs were elected in Scotland, but the SNP, with a disappointing 22% of the Scottish vote, sent only six MPs to Westminster.

The Labour Party of Tony Blair was very different from the Labour Party my parents and grandparents had voted for. I believe that by this time certain politicians had reached the conclusion that getting elected was not about persuading voters that your policies were right, but rather it was a case of gaining the approval of capitalist newspaper proprietors. Many Unionist Labour politicians who supported the setting up of a Scottish parliament had come round to that position because of the long years during which they'd been impotent against Thatcher rule. These people seemed to think that a Scottish parliament, albeit with carefully limited powers, would be some kind of defence against this situation arising in the future. I found this attitude rather dishonourable. They seemed to want all of the alleged "benefits" of the Union, but with an opt out clause when the English vote went against them. Either you were in a Union and accepted the first past the post on a UK basis, or you weren't and didn't.

I recall a particular occasion. It was a Sunday afternoon. The "Last of the Summer Wine" company had completed its patrol of the *Boturich* estate and we were about to part and go our separate ways. I remember we were standing just beside the tiny bridge where Dalvait Road crosses the Inler Burn, and I remarked that it was no longer a question of *if* we were going to get a Scottish parliament, but *when* we were going to get it. One of the others answered that, yes, we'd get it, but it wouldn't be worth having. There were those in the new Labour government, however, some of them Scots, who were bitterly opposed to the establishment of a Scottish Parliament at all. Even so, motivated by principle or otherwise, Labour had committed to setting up a Scottish parliament if the party was elected. Indeed, previous leader John Smith had famously described this as "the settled will of the Scottish people". In 1996, however, this was modified: they would hold another referendum. Scots had voted for an assembly in 1979. They were to be asked to vote for a parliament in 1997. Not only this – there would be two questions: Did they want the parliament? Did they want it to have tax varying powers?

It was not difficult to reach the conclusion that the second question had been devised to make the proposed parliament appear considerably less attractive. Any mention of taxation is unlikely to be regarded as encouragement. The "Forty Per cent Rule" was far from forgotten.

Alex Salmond persuaded the SNP to campaign with Labour and the Liberal Democrats for a "Yes-Yes" vote. That much beloved of Scotsmen, Sean Connery, took part in the campaign, most effectively quoting passages from the *Declaration of Arbroath*. The poll was held on the 11th of September. As it happened, this was 700 years, to the very day, after William Wallace won the Battle of Stirling Bridge. 74% voted Yes for the Scottish Parliament. 63.5% voted Yes for the tax varying powers. Donald Dewar, Secretary of State for Scotland, was at least one Labour politician who seemed genuinely delighted with this outcome.

Any sense of triumph or fulfilment which I personally might have experienced was absent. After a long illness, my father, aged seventy-nine, died six days after the referendum.

*   *   *

Far from remaining in the shadow of Edward's displeasure, following Wallace's relatively minor incursion into the Burgh of Dumbarton, Sir John Menteith quickly earned the English king's gratitude and favour. Like most of the Scottish nobility, Menteith had been inconsistent in his loyalty. He had fought on the Scots side at the Battle of Dunbar, being taken prisoner. He was released to fight for the English in France, after which he'd come back over to the Scots. In February of 1304, however, he joined in the general submission to Edward and, as has been noted, was rewarded with the Sheriffdom of Dumbarton.

Menteith had a nephew, a small man called James Stewart, who had been, unlike his uncle, a loyal follower of William Wallace for several years. Throughout the realm men of all stations and in all walks of life were having to come to terms with the new reality of what appeared to be a final English victory. Scotland, it now seemed, was firmly held in Edward's cruel grasp. It was no great difficulty for the chameleon-like nobles, such as Menteith, to adjust and prosper in the adjusting, but for lesser folk choices were not always so easily made. In the end, though, and under cruel pressure, James Stewart, commonly known as "Jack Short", had agreed to betray William Wallace to the Sheriff of Dumbarton. And so it had happened, at Robroyston on the Glasgow Muir.

In order to minimize the danger of attempted rescues, Menteith arranged for the prisoner, as a matter of urgency, to be taken by sea from Dumbarton Castle, down the Firth of Clyde and up into the Solway Firth. At Bowness-on-Solway Wallace was handed over into the custody of Sir John de Segrave who was Edward's Warden of Scotland south of the Forth. On the seventeen-day journey from Carlisle to London, Wallace was kept tightly bound, and of course well-guarded, on horseback. As he was led through the northern counties of England he was, quite naturally, a figure of loathing and detestation. The further south they travelled, passion gave way by degrees to curiosity. However, in London the crowds which gathered in vast numbers reviled and abused the Scots captive.

On the 23rd of August in the year 1305 Wallace was taken to a crowded Westminster Hall for what was to pass as a trial. When he was taken before the Court of King's Bench he was mockingly made to wear a crown of laurel leaves. The sacrilegious parallel with Christ's Crown of Thorns would not have been lost on the prisoner. He remained silent, as to all intents and purposes he had since the day of his betrayal. Those officiating included Sir John de Segrave, Sir Peter Mallory, Justiciar of England, Ralph de Sandwych, Constable of the Tower of London, John de Bacwell, a judge, and Sir John le Blunt, Lord Mayor of London.

A list of charges were read out. These included all manner of criminality, from the mundane to the barbaric, most of which Edward himself was equally guilty, and which could justly have been placed under the general heading of mediaeval warfare. Only one of the charges caused Wallace to break his silence – the charge of treason. He scathingly pointed out with impregnable logic that since he had never sworn allegiance to Edward, and that since Edward had never been and never would be rightful King of Scots, there could have been no treason.

This was, of course, utterly disregarded.

Sentence was pronounced –

That the said William, for the manifest sedition that he practised against the Lord King himself, by feloniously contriving and acting with a view to his death and to the abasement and submission of his crown and royal dignity, by bearing a hostile banner against his liege lord in war to the death, shall be drawn from the Palace of Westminster to the Tower of London, and from the Tower to Aldgate, and so through the midst of the City, to the Elms..."

The "Elms" was Smithfield. Wallace was tied, completely naked and face-upward, to a hurdle which was fastened at the tails of two horses. Following a deliberately circuitous route, to expose him to the maximum number of citizenry, he was dragged four miles through the streets of London, being fouled by the beasts and unspeakably tormented by the mob which was glorying in this opportunity to mock and defile the hated Scot. Arriving at Smithfield, Wallace was placed before the gallows. In meticulous observance of the sentence he was first hanged by the neck until he lost consciousness. He was then revived. His genitals were cut off – at which point it is to be hoped and presumed that he mercifully lost consciousness again – his intestines, lungs, liver and heart were drawn out of his body and ritually burned. Finally what was left of the man was decapitated.

His corpse was, on Edward's express command, quartered, which is to say, the arms and legs were hacked off.

The head of William Wallace was placed on a pole which was raised above London Bridge. His limbs were transported to and publicly displayed, one each, in Newcastle, Berwick, Stirling and Perth.

It is said that on the point of execution Wallace asked to be shown a Bible. Edward, we are told, had forbidden the English clergy to minister to the condemned man. Present, was Sir Robert Clifford. The English knight was an old adversary of Wallace, with no reason whatever to love the defiant Scot, or to risk the displeasure of the Plantagenet. Yet Clifford turned to a nearby priest and took from him a Bible, which he held open for the bound Wallace to read during his last lucid moments. If true, and one likes to think that it is, this is a shining example of human decency in an episode otherwise utterly diabolical.

Edward, surely quite insane, had intended to mete out to Wallace the most humiliating, debasing and inhuman extinction. Little did he know that in making his arch-enemy a martyr who would be loved and revered by Scots, and indeed by countless others, for centuries to come, he was bestowing immortality on him.

*   *   *

At first it had been closely guarded, for it was fully realised that his supporters – and that meant almost the entire community – would seek to recover it and reverence it with a Christian burial. And that was quite entirely contrary to the will of the King of England. Time passed, however, the flesh decomposed and fell away, priorities changed and the guards grew lax in their duty. Taking advantage, therefore, of a particularly wild and stormy night, a group of six Augustinian brothers from the Abbey of St Mary the Virgin, at Cambuskenneth, cut down the arm, hand and finger bones, which had been chained on a gibbet above Stirling Bridge.

Returning to the Abbey, the monks, in due course, interred these remains with the appropriate Christian rites. The arm and hand of William Wallace was buried in such a way as to point in the direction of the nearby Abbey Craig, from which height the great man had directed his people's army's greatest victory.

*   *   *

The Reverend Doctor Charles Rogers was a complex man. Erudite, passionate, patriotic and prolific. Clergyman, author and antiquary. His portrait in sepia tones depicts a heavily bearded Victorian gentleman. A force to be reckoned with, but with something of petulance in the purse of the lips.

He was born in 1825 in Dunino, Fife, the son of a minister. He went to St Andrews University becoming a minister himself in 1846. He assisted in various parishes before founding a preaching station at Bridge of Allan, in the shadow of the Abbey Craig. From 1855 till 1863 he was chaplain to the garrison at Stirling castle. He initiated a number of literary and religious institutes and publications. As has been noted, Rev Rogers was a prime mover in the project to build a National Wallace Monument. The committee which steered this endeavour was, throughout its lengthy deliberations, torn between two opposing camps. There were the straightforward Nationalists, those who were dissatisfied with Scotland's treatment within the Union, and there were those who might be termed the patriotic Unionists. The former group stood for the historical Wallace who lived and died in order to liberate Scotland from the English. The latter group invented, in tune with the mood of their age and for their political convenience, a fantasy Wallace who had bizarrely given his all for a vision of the future Union and Empire. Not surprisingly, as these two forces struggled to determine the character of the monument and its message to the world, there was emotional and acrimonious conflict between them.

The Unionist establishment was generally suspicious of the project, suspecting that it was essentially a device of Nationalist malcontents, such as the National Association for the Vindication of Scottish Rights. The endeavour was described as anti-English, and the sneering comments in a *Times* editorial have been cited earlier. Ascendancy would appear to swing from the Nationalists to the Unionists and back again, with one obviously crucial area of dispute being the actual architecture of the monument. The Nationalists favoured what was known as the "Lion and Typhon" design, which featured a lion breaking its chains and fighting off a crowned typhon. This was clearly expressive of the enslaved Lion of Scotland resisting the domination of Edward Plantagenet. As such it was far too near the bone for the Unionists. They, naturally having more clout given the predominant attitudes of their day, won the struggle, giving us the monument which stands today with its "imperial" crown.

The foremost personality among the Nationalists was William Burns, a Glasgow lawyer and historian. The Reverend Rogers sided with the Unionist camp. He was the secretary and chief fundraiser for the project, and, after the foundation stone had been laid, funds were slow to come in. This led to serious criticism of the minister which in turn led to his departure from both these offices and from Scotland. He settled thereafter in London, devoting himself to journalism, literature and founding yet more literary, religious and historical societies. He seems, in his lengthy career, to have drawn considerable negative comment, and he has been described as having a persecution mania. His dedication to Scottish history, however, is irrefutable, and he continued to make an active contribution to the National Wallace Monument project.

Specifically, after the eventually completed tower was officially opened in 1869, the Revered Doctor began to campaign for the transfer of the Wallace Sword from Dumbarton Castle to the monument at Stirling. At this time the Dumbarton fortress came under the jurisdiction of the War Office, and it was to this authority that the Reverend made his appeal in the year 1872.

Whether it was for political reasons – the entire Wallace project being regarded with suspicion and disfavour in certain corridors of power – or not, we will probably never know, but Rogers received a negative reply which repeated the opinion given by Sir Samuel Meyrick forty-seven years earlier: that the sword in question was not old enough to have been wielded by William Wallace.

It was that very month – October 1872 – that an almost identically worded letter was sent to the Keeper of Dumbarton

Castle, with instruction from the War Office, this time, that the weapon was no longer to be referred to as the Wallace Sword.

Mystery solved… at least in part.

But Duncan Robertson did not yet know of the Reverend Doctor's involvement. He had, however, heard an interesting if distasteful tale relating to the history of the relic. This was related to him, not by Gunner Irwin, his usual informant, but by Master Gunner Wiggins, whom he'd encountered at a Dumbarton versus Queen's Park football match. Apparently, not long after the royal visit of Victoria and Albert to the Rock, one of the "visitors", a particularly large and forceful Cockney, had insisted on removing the Wallace Sword from its place in the Armoury and, foolishly gripping the weapon by its point, attempted to swing it around in a supposed demonstration that his own strength was the equal of any "Scotch" hero. The result had been that the sword's handle had clattered off the wall and the blade broke at a weak point. Fortunately the sword had been mended by Robert Reid, one of the burgh blacksmiths.

When Duncan mentioned this story in the passing to Hannah, she at first chided him for his obsession with the sword and then expressed concern that it was not better looked after. Duncan hotly denied that he was obsessed and quickly changed the subject.

It was a crisply pleasant morning in late October. A fresh breeze stirred golden leaves against a clear blue sky. The couple were walking in the countryside just a mile to the east of the burgh. They made their way in a leisurely manner uphill on Garshake Brae, surrounded by hedgerows, majestic trees and golden fields.

Hannah wore a gorgeous outfit of some subtle green and purple tartan (she knew how to make the most of her fiery red-gold hair). The cut accentuated her bosom, was tight around her narrow waist and shapely buttocks, then flowed billowingly to the ground. Duncan was resplendent in a black frockcoat, golden waistcoat, dove-grey trousers and black top hat. According to the rules which governed Victorian courtship, they should not, of course, have been in each other's company unaccompanied. But in matters of the heart rules were, Duncan felt, made to be broken. A matter of the heart, that is, for him. He had no doubt whatever that he had fallen in love with Hannah Paton. She, on the other hand, knew that she had grown fond of Duncan, found him attractive and enjoyed his company. She respected him and looked forward to marriage in the hope that perhaps true love was something which would develop within matrimony. Their times alone together had been recent and few, and they had been gained at the cost of so-called "white lies". Hannah had been unhappy about deceiving her parents, but Duncan had been persuasive, insistent. It was true, though, that in these few hours they had achieved a degree of intimacy – not physical, of course – which had a certain sweetness, like some precious secret.

There was one unspoken bone of contention between them. Duncan, now twenty years old, had fulfilled not so much his own ambition, but that of his father and Gunner Irwin, of getting to Glasgow University. He was not entirely comfortable in an exclusively academic environment, missing to some extent the feel of the tools of the stonemason's trade, but he was well on his way to gaining degrees in English Literature and History. The tension arose because women were not expected to receive any education beyond the basics. Their lives were required to be spent in the domestic sphere, bearing children and running a home. Hannah, who was at least as intelligent as Duncan, if not more, indeed, resented bitterly, if secretly, the fact that Duncan, as a male, was allowed, no, encouraged, to spread his intellectual wings and soar to the heights of academic achievement and recognition, where she, as a mere woman, would be caged in a kind of oversized doll's house in Dumbarton.

They had turned and were heading back towards the town by Round Riding Road. Hannah hoped they would not be recognised and their liaison spoken of, but only one carriage passed them, and pedestrians were few, far between and strangers. Duncan had been importantly telling her of some new business venture which was, he assured her, the talk of the burgh. Some of the big shipbuilders and engineers, people like the Dennys, Inglis and Brock, had been in league with some Dutchman and they'd bought a rope works from a man called Hamilton. It was deadly dull to Hannah and her mind addressed a more pertinent matter. What the Robertson and Paton families had, with regard to Duncan and Hannah, at this point was an understanding. There had still been no formal engagement. No actual proposal. She wondered when he'd get around to it. Duncan, a much less confident young man than he appeared, wondered too.

Fulfilment and Frustration

The sky was stark white and snow lay thick on the ground when I arrived outside the semi-detached house in a quiet, tree-lined crescent in Clydebank. This was Sunday the 1st of March 1998. This was the first time I'd been here, and as I rang the doorbell I was startled by the overhead roar of a low-flying jet which was coming in to land at Glasgow Airport.

Mary opened the door and was, to say the least, surprised to see me standing there, my face glowing with embarrassment. She asked me to come inside. No, I said. I had to rush away because someone was waiting for me, and with this I pressed a small, soft parcel into her hand. "This is just a wee something for you." I blustered and quickly retraced my steps along the path to the front gate.

Mary and I had worked in the same department for a number of years. Latterly we'd spent many lunchtimes sitting together in the office canteen. Mary's mother and father were from Donegal. When she opened that parcel she discovered a brushed wool scarf in the "St Patrick" tartan. This was my first clumsy step in our courtship.

Browsing through old diaries I can see that during the years 1997 to 1999 I had somewhat broadened the range and intensified the extent of my work for Amnesty International. As well as carrying out my Urgent Action Scheme duties I was playing a part in specific campaigns for the release of certain prisoners of conscience. On the last day of 1997 I met the Reverend Ian Miller of my own Bonhill Parish Church, and the Reverend Ken Russell, of Jamestown Kirk, in Balloch's *Princess Rose* Chinese restaurant to sound them out about the potential for setting up Amnesty support teams within the two congregations. The outcome of the meeting was the establishment of a group of half-a-dozen elders at Bonhill who worked on various Amnesty campaigns over a number of years. Also, a standing arrangement was entered into whereby I'd address the Jamestown Congregation each year around Christmas and dozens of greetings cards with messages of encouragement would be sent from them to various human rights violation victims. I continue to do this on an annual basis.

As well as this sort of thing, I was addressing different interest groups from time to time trying to drum up support and recruitment.

After the YES-YES vote in the Scottish Parliament referendum, the Nationalists enjoyed high levels of support, with opinion polls indicating that over 50% of the voters favoured independence. This was not to last, of course. When Alex Salmond courageously voiced strong criticism of British participation in the NATO bombing of Serbia, Unionist politicians and media made the most of it. The campaign for the first election to the new Scottish Parliament was largely a battle between Salmond for the SNP and Donald Dewar, Secretary of State for Scotland, for Labour. By April of 1999 Labour had a clear lead. The Nationalists went into the contest with a promise that, if they were given control of the Parliament, they would call for a referendum on Scottish Independence.

The election took place on May 6th 1999. Labour won 56 seats, SNP 53, and the Liberal Democrats 17. A coalition of Labour and the Lib-Dems took control of the parliament, and Donald Dewar became Scotland's first "First Minister". The new Scottish Parliament sat in the General Assembly Hall of the Church of Scotland, in Edinburgh. It was officially opened by the Queen on the 1st of July. Her Majesty wore tartan.

I took the day off work so I could watch the opening on television. The Queen presented the Parliament with a new, specially designed mace, as the symbol of its authority. This was placed alongside the *Honours of Scotland.* These are the Scottish Crown Jewels, which are, in fact, older than the English Crown Jewels, although one would not think it, given the manner in which the latter are referred to routinely as *the* Crown Jewels, as though they were the regalia of the United Kingdom as a whole.

The proceedings were generally in good taste. First Minister Dewar, in his speech said – "This is about who we are, how we carry ourselves, and in quiet moments of today, we might hear echoes of the past."

Alex Salmond asserted that the Scottish National Party's primary loyalty was to the Scottish constitutional tradition that sovereignty belonged to the people.

Two particular aspects of the occasion impressed themselves on me very profoundly. The Queen sat listening with great dignity as Sheena Wellington sang "A Man's a Man For a' That" by Robert Burns –

Ye see yon birkie ca'd a lord,
Wha struts, an' stares, an' a' that,
Tho' hundreds worship at his word,
He's but a coof for a' that.
For a' that, an' a' that,
His ribband, star, an' a'that,
The man o' independent mind,
He looks an' laughs at a' that...

I suspect it could only have happened in Scotland.

The other thing was much more meaningful and emotional. All the Members of the Scottish Parliament sang the 100th Psalm –

All people that on earth do dwell,
Sing to the Lord with cheerful voice...

Even at that time the United Kingdom was showing signs of corporately distancing itself from Christianity. Political Correctness was flexing its muscles. We were reminded that ours was a multi-cultural, multi-faith society. I do not know what the official intention was, but it seemed to me that here was little

Scotland, at a very vulnerable yet powerful moment, having the unexpected courage to, boldly and with quiet dignity, tell the world that we were still a Christian land – that from our earliest beginnings we had been built on Christian foundations and Christianity was of our essence.

Soon after that great day – a day which I wished many had lived to see – Mary and I went on a car run to Aberfoyle. The *clachan of Aberfoyle* in Rob Roy's country of the Trossachs. On a long, downhill stretch of road which swept over the western edge of Flanders Moss, I put on a carefully selected piece of music. It was from an old Jimmy Shand album and came under the heading of "strathspey and reel". It was an exhilarating tune which I could never listen to without visualising a young Jacobite clansman galloping on horseback, plaid flying, through a beautiful green glen on a fresh spring morning. It was just so in keeping with time, place and mood. Earlier I had presented Mary with a single white rose – the little white rose of Scotland, as so profoundly written of by the poet MacDiarmid.

*   *   *

Robert the Bruce belonged very much to that class of the Scottish nobility which William Wallace held in contempt. The family had originated in Brix, Normandy, but King David I granted lands in Annandale to Robert Bruce in 1124. Several generations later, a subsequent Robert Bruce married into the Scottish royal line. The sixth Robert Bruce, grandfather of he who was to become Scotland's "Hero King", was one of the "competitors" for the throne when Edward of England nominated John Balliol. Accordingly, where Wallace had fought out of patriotism and loyalty to King John, Robert the Bruce was motivated by the desire to win the crown of Scotland for himself. Bruce had been born in Scotland, as had been his father and his father before him. His mother was a Celtic countess.

In fact, however, the Bruce's father, the Earl of Carrick, had at one time been Chief Justice of England, and Bruce himself was for a time something of a favourite of Edward. The Comyns were kin to King John Balliol and hugely powerful in Scotland. As such they stood between Bruce and the throne, hence the antagonism between these two great houses. Robert the Bruce changed sides several times, now fighting on the side of resistance, now loyal to the Plantagenet, as policy and ambition dictated. The execution of Wallace, however, galvanised the Bruce into decisive action.

In February of 1306, Robert the Bruce met John Comyn in the Greyfriars Church in Dumfries. A deal had been made between these two bitter rivals. Bruce was to have the crown, but Comyn would take ownership of all the royal lands. Bruce had reason to believe that Comyn had betrayed him to Edward. A furious row broke out between the pair and, there, in front of the altar, Bruce stabbed the Comyn fatally.

Knowing that he would almost certainly be excommunicated for such an act of sacrilege, and that an excommunicate could not be made king, Bruce moved swiftly. Just as it had supported Wallace, the Scottish Church, perceiving Bruce to have committed himself finally and irreversibly to the Scottish cause, gave him its backing. He was absolved by the Bishop of Glasgow before excommunication could be pronounced, and on the 27th of March he had himself crowned at Scone. According to tradition the actual crowning should have been performed by the MacDuff Earl of Fife, but the present earl was with Edward of England.

The earl's aunt, however, Isabella of Fife, courageously took on the role. As punishment, when she was later captured by the English, she was imprisoned in a cage which was suspended from the walls of Berwick Castle for four years.

Officiating at the coronation of Robert the Bruce were the Abbot of Scone and the Bishops of St Andrews, Glasgow and Moray. Wearing a crown, however, was not the same as possessing a kingdom. Bruce was up against the might of Edward, the power of the House of Comyn and all their various allies.

The excommunication of Scotland's new king was pronounced by the Archbishop of Canterbury on the 5th of June.

The first real trial of strength was the Battle of Methven. Preparing to challenge a joint English and Comyn force led by the Earl of Pembroke, outside Perth, Bruce's force was taken by surprise and routed, though the king managed to avoid capture and went to ground in Atholl, being given sanctuary in the Priory of St Fillan.

The MacDougalls of Argyll were kin to the murdered Red Comyn, and in the Pass of Brander by Loch Awe, they ambushed Bruce and his small company. Yet again, the king was lucky to escape with his life, and this time he was forced to take up the life of a fugitive.

In the meantime, several members of Bruce's family had been captured by the English. His wife, Elizabeth de Burgh, Edward's god-daughter, was simply imprisoned. His daughter, Marjory, and his sister Christian, were put into nunneries. Another sister, Mary, was given similar treatment to Isabella of Fife – for four years she hung in a cage from the walls of Roxburgh Castle. The king's brother, Nigel Bruce, was hung, drawn and quartered at Berwick.

Scotland's new king was, however, a courageous and determined fighter. In 1307 he returned with a vengeance. Over the next seven testing years he proved to be an inspiring leader and a highly skilled guerrilla warrior. Men rallied to him and there were Scottish victories at Glen Trool and then Loudon Hill in Ayrshire.

When Edward had heard of the murder of John Comyn he was beside himself with fury. At once he began to prepare yet another invasion of Scotland. By this time the Plantagenet was aged, in poor health, and in no fit state for military campaigning. But, realising that his life's work of crushing the Scots was yet in vain, he was a man obsessed. In July of 1307, at the head of his army, he died at Burgh-on-Sands. An indication of his state of mind on the point of death is that he instructed his son to have the flesh boiled from his body, so that his bones could be carried at the head of the English army which would march into Scotland.

It had been hoped, even believed, that with the death of the despotic "Hammer of the Scots" the English might leave Scotland in peace and return to minding their own business. But, of course, it hadn't just been Edward. His son, a much less aggressive individual, lacking his father's hunger for constant conquest, was managed by nobles who felt entitled to possess Scotland.

Even so, Bruce defeated garrison after garrison, captured castle after castle, and recovered town after town. His army grew in

strength and effectiveness until, by 1313, only one important
Scottish stronghold remained in English hands – Stirling Castle.

A Scottish force led by the king's brother, Edward Bruce, laid
siege to that ancient fortress rock which was generally regarded as
being to all intents and purposes impregnable. This left, as the
only realistic option, the long haul of trying to starve out the
occupying English garrison. After six long and frustrating months
there was still no sign of capitulation, and Edward Bruce, a rash
and impatient young man, did a foolish thing. He entered into a
pact with Sir Philip Mowbray, Edward II's Constable of Stirling
Castle, under the terms of which if an English army had not
arrived to relieve their besieged compatriots by Midsummer's Day
– the 24th of June – then the English garrison would surrender.

On hearing this news both kings were furious. Robert the Bruce
had made great military advances by scrupulously avoiding a set-
piece pitched battle with any large English force. Now his
impetuous brother had placed him in such a position that he had
little choice but to prepare to meet a mighty English army.
Edward II, equally, had no desire to lead any major force onto the
field of battle, but under irresistible pressure from his warlike
nobles, he was now forced to act.

He instructed his earls and barons to muster all the men they
could raise and bring them to Wark, near Berwick. An English
army around twenty thousand strong crossed the border on the
17th of June. Accompanied by some two hundred wagons, they
marched northwards, reaching Edinburgh by the 19th. Four days
later found them making their way through the Torwood, a forest
which stretched over the land between Falkirk and Stirling.

A Scottish army of little more than five thousand men was waiting for them by the Bannockburn, to the south of Stirling. Their position had been cleverly prepared with a defensive line of pits and traps designed to foul the English cavalry. Bruce's lieutenants were his nephew, Thomas Randolph, Earl of Moray, Edward Bruce and James Douglas. The Scottish cavalry was commanded by Sir Robert Keith. Also present was the Abbot of Arbroath, bearing the ancient reliquary which contained the bones of St Columba. As with Wallace's people's army, the main tactical weapon of the Scots was the schiltron – the densely-packed hedgehog of men wielding long spears.

Late in the afternoon of Sunday the 23rd, an English vanguard led by the Earls of Gloucester and Hereford sallied out from the Torwood. They immediately charged across the Bannockburn, heading towards the Scots army. Robert the Bruce was riding a small pony a short distance in front of one of the schiltrons. Sir Henry de Bohun, a nephew of the Earl of Hereford, identified Bruce at a distance by the gold circlet he was wearing. On impulse the English knight raised the tip of his lance and charged.

It was one of those heart-stopping moments when the course of history hangs by a thread.

Just an instant before Bohun's lance made deadly contact, the Bruce made an agile and perfectly-timed side-stepping evasive movement with his pony, simultaneously bringing his battleaxe downward from the shoulder, slicing through the metal of Bohun's helmet and shattering his skull.

An exultant roar came from the throats of the Scots and the schiltrons surged forward unbidden to bear punishingly on the

English horsemen. Meanwhile another company of some five hundred English cavalry, led by Sir Robert Clifford and Sir Henry Beaumont, attempted a flanking thrust with the intention of reaching Stirling Castle. The Earl of Moray brought a schiltron down to engage this body of horsemen, which it did to splendid effect, causing the badly damaged English force to retreat in disarray. This proved to be the end of that day's hostilities. The armies spent a wary night camped on either side of the Bannockburn.

The following day was Midsummer. Shortly after dawn King Robert addressed the Scots army –

"...These barons you see before you, clad in armour, are bent upon destroying us and obliterating our kingdom. No... our entire nation. They do not believe that we have the power to resist them."

He then gave the order to advance. Three schiltrons moved eastwards on the English force. Bruce led the fourth in reserve. The English and Welsh archers let loose the arrows of their longbows which rained down on the advancing schiltrons, but Scots cavalry led by Sir Robert Keith charged into the bowmen making short work of them.

Meanwhile, the English vanguard attacked the schiltron commanded by Edward Bruce, but it held doggedly, eventually getting the better of the knights who struggled to control their horses on difficult terrain.

This was the critical moment at which the Scots king directed the reserve company of Highlanders, under Angus Og MacDonald of

Islay, into the conflict. The combination of the determined advance of the schiltrons and the Highland charge proved too much for the English combatants, who began to lose ground significantly. Then it happened...

There was a further Scots reserve force which comprised several hundred common folk, untrained and poorly armed. These, interpreting the turn of events, appeared from behind the nearby Coxet Hill, in a spontaneous and ragged charge. The English, perceiving them at a distance, understandably misread the situation, taking them to be yet another formidable component of the Scots army. It was too much.

Edward of England fled, followed by his mounted nobility. Trying to follow them hundreds of English soldiers were slaughtered by pursuing Scots, or were drowned in the Bannockburn or the River Forth in their desperate flight.

King Robert the Bruce had won a victory over an English army three times as numerous, more confident and vastly better equipped than his own. Things would never be the same again. Modern historians insist that the Battle of Bannockburn did not win Scotland's independence, but to countless generations of Scots the victory of that day has been a symbol of the triumph of the nation's will to freedom. Yet it would have been impossible, perhaps unthinkable, without the earlier achievements of William Wallace.

*   *   *

Even now, in the quiet of evening, it was still uncomfortably warm. Indeed, it had been an exceptionally hot summer.

Perspiration dampened the troubled brow of Mrs Duncan Robertson as she sat by an open window in their new sandstone villa, off Knoxland Square, to the east of the town. Apart from Patricia, the maid, she was presently alone in the house. On the small table beside which she sat there were a cup of refreshing tea and the latest copy of one of the local newspapers – *Dumbarton Herald*: June 29th, 1887.

She tore herself away from a lurid piece of front page fiction – *The Temptation of Lady Ashurst!* and, turning the large pages, she observed that an outbreak of pleuro-pneumonia had been identified on a farm out in Craigendoran. There was also coverage of the recent Renton Highland Games. Mostly, though, the journal was filled with accounts of the imaginative and varied ways in which civic and individual loyalty was being expressed in this the year of Queen Victoria's Golden Jubilee. Fifty years on the throne! How the world had changed in that long time. How Dumbarton had changed.

They had been married now for seven years. Seven, if she was ruthlessly honest, disappointing and unfulfilled years. Love had not come with matrimony. Not for Hannah. A vulnerable affection, companionship, of course, security, respectability, a modest prosperity and comfort... But it had turned out to be a doll's house without a doll. Their union had not been blessed with children, and naturally the assumption, within the two families and outwith them, was that the fault lay with Hannah. Now she was thirty-one.

Duncan was, on the face of things, resigned to this, but she knew that, paradoxically, he considered it a slight on his manhood. He continued to give every appearance of loving his wife. He regularly brought her flowers and occasionally small gifts of jewellery. Sexually, he still worshipped her – regularly – but as a person he had no great interest in her – her desires, ambitions, her…depths. She possessed intellect, imagination, energy – all without any avenue of expression. He took her for granted. Almost entirely self-absorbed, he was oblivious to her frustrations, seemed not to notice her wretched boredom, the sheer lack of purpose in her life. He was faithful to her, she presumed – although Patricia, the maid, had the same red hair as herself, and with almost comparable good looks was a constant temptation to him. She, Hannah, of course, had been faithful to him. The mere thought of a wife committing adultery was absolute anathema. For a married woman to be discovered in any sort of liaison meant utter social and financial ruin. She would be regarded as no better than a prostitute. Not that she would ever dream of such a thing in any case. Yes, there were men she found attractive, stimulating. More so than Duncan, she found herself appalled to admit. She remained a very beautiful woman. There was no point in false modesty. She knew that even to think such thoughts was sinful, but…

Then there were his irritating habits. The cigars. Those horrid ginger whiskers. His habit of speaking to her like a professor… He'd got his degree, of course, and was now the editor of some boring newspaper in Glasgow. At least it had got them out of that poky little terrace by the river, with the awful noise and smell from the shipyards and the brewery. Thank goodness for the space and privacy of their little villa.

She dabbed her temples with a tiny, scented lace handkerchief and turned the page of the newspaper. Her brow wrinkled and her mouth turned down at the corners. Here it was. Inevitably there was a long and detailed account of the event. As though she hadn't heard enough of it from him.

"DUMBARTON ODDFELLOWS AT BANNOCKBURN"

"On Saturday Stirling was en fete on the occasion of the completion of improvements at the field of Bannockburn. The weather was of a delightful description, a flood of bright sunshine, although occasionally a trifle too hot, imparting a charm to the whole scene. All the early trains brought large contingents of Oddfellows, Free Gardeners, and kindered societies from the surrounding districts…"

She could bear no more of it. She folded the paper carefully and glanced at the roman numerals of the clock. He'd be home soon. Back from his wretched club. Tipsy and talkative. From the bandstand in the square she heard the sounds of children playing.

Men of the Victorian era were positively addicted to clubs – societies, fraternities, orders, associations – and Dumbarton, of course, had its share. Duncan belonged to two of them. The Loyal Dixon Lodge of Oddfellows was a "friendly society", which was to say, a charitable institution. The "Loyal" aspect was to indicate that the organisation in question was registered in accordance with legislation (commencing with the Friendly Societies Act of 1793) which showed that it was not a trade union, which in those days would have been considered disloyal, in the sense that trades unions were regarded as being contrary and injurious to the proper order of society. The "Dixon" designation related to the Dixon family who owned the town's glassworks. They were major employers and had provided three of the burgh's provosts. Such societies were of a mutual aid nature. They provided members with basic insurance against old age and sickness. They had a very pronounced social dimension, giving the participants a great sense of belonging and brotherhood. They were much given to good works for the deserving poor, public events and civic involvement.

Hannah's father belonged, of course, to the much similar Free Gardeners. Over the past few years he and Duncan had become, as Hannah put it, "thick as thieves".

The other "club" to which Duncan belonged was, inevitably, the Dumbarton Philosophical and Literary Society. Founded in 1867, the society had around one hundred members, the first president having been Mr Hugh Dickie, Duncan's old rector at Dumbarton Academy. With spacious and comfortable premises in Church Street, the club provided daily newspapers, magazines, board games and a smoking room. Although there was a lot of intellectual posing, by those, such as Duncan, who were equipped for it and disposed to it, mostly the society was social in nature.

In fact, just the previous year, Duncan had joined another organisation – the Scottish Home Rule Association, but that was a very different matter.

Anyway, it was from socialising in the Literary Society that Duncan eventually returned homeward, shortly after the sun had spectacularly but mercifully set behind the Firth of Clyde. Swinging his cane and considerably overdressed for the weather, Duncan breezed into the small villa showing all the usual signs of brandy-induced bonhomie. Hannah well knew that it was at such times Duncan was most likely to show an interest in bedroom recreation – a fact which she found frankly off-putting… not that she would care to refuse him.

His attention seemed on this occasion, however, to be elsewhere for the moment. Swiftly he found what he was looking for, lifting his copy of the *Dumbarton Herald* from the parlour table with bright-eyed anticipation. He seated himself opposite Hannah and wasted no time in locating the article which so greatly interested him (although he had already digested it thoroughly in the club). Lips pursed in an expression of serious consideration he began to scrutinise the long column of print on page two.

"Aye, here we are – improvements in connection with the flagstaff beside the Borestone... That was where they say the Bruce directed the battle from. Aye, the steel topmast featuring a battleaxe... Of course, that's a reminder of the incident when he took the head off de Bohun. Here again, the railing in the form of spears turned outward... this commemorating the famous schiltrons."

He looked up to satisfy himself that Hannah was showing proper interest.

"It's good to see Councillor Bell getting his due here in print... see, they point out that the original idea of the flagstaff came from him. That's excellent."

He read aloud –

...and the inscription on the tablet attached to the memorial bears that it was erected in 1870 by the Loyal Dixon Lodge of Oddfellows, Dumbarton, and the Royal Rock of Hope Lodge, Stirling.

"Then they quote quite a lot of his speech." –

Around the Borestone on the memorable field of Bannockburn, as well as at Dumbarton Castle, our civil freedom was won and our country's independence was secured by the valour and heroism of our forefathers…at the cost of their blood, testified their love of country, their love of freedom, and manly independence.

"I have to say, Hannah, he delivered it wonderfully well. Listen to this." –

…we love to think and dwell upon the glorious times of the noble patriot and generous king, Robert the Bruce. Who can think of Bruce and Sir William Wallace without admiring their pure patriotism, their indomitable courage, and their magnificent bravery? These men, with their devoted followers… beat down oppression, stood in the front of fearful odds, and gained a glorious inheritance for Scotland.

"No wonder he got elected, with oratory like that."

Duncan's eye ran further down the column and a frown furrowed his brow.

"Aye, here it is. It's the man Rogers. The minister I told you about…"

He looked up and caught Hannah in the act of rolling her eyes.

"I know. I know. I'm repeating myself. But bear with me. This takes a lot of coming to terms with."

He gave her a look which called out for patience and forbearing.

"I managed to speak to him afterwards. After the speeches and so on. It turns out he was, by his own account anyway, the main force behind getting the Wallace Monument built. But this is the damnable thing – It seems some years ago – fifteen years he told me – he'd written to the War Office asking their permission to take the Wallace Sword away from Dumbarton and put it in the Monument!"

Duncan was indignant.

"Well, he looked the sort of man that if you said a word to cross him, he'd burst a blood vessel, so I never told him what I thought of that! Fortunately, though, the War Office had told him that the sword had been examined by an expert in 1825 and declared fraudulent. So that, thank God, was the end of that... Or should have been."

He looked up with an expression of exasperation.

"The maddening thing was that I was longing to tell him that I could *refute* that old assessment. I could show, step by step, point by point, how yon man Meyrick had been wrong, and the sword *is* the sword of William Wallace."

Again he glanced up to see how his wife was reacting to this. She had managed to set her features in a mask of polite interest.

"It was only on the way home on the train that the penny dropped with me. Fifteen years ago would have been 1872 – the year the Keeper got the letter from the War Office telling him the sword was not to be referred to as the Wallace Sword – It must have been because this Rogers had stuck his oar in. They decided to take a hard line."

Hannah nodded dutifully and her husband carried on.

"You'll mind, Hannah, how I discovered the James the Fourth reference in the Lord High Treasurer's accounts…"

With this he rose and strode purposefully through to his study, returning in moments brandishing a well-thumbed six-page, hand-written document. At the sight of the oft-quoted "paper" Hannah braced herself.

"Aye… Here we are –

For bynding of WALLASS SWORD with cordis of silk and new hilt and plomet, new scabbard, and new belt to the said sword…

"Now, d'you remember the significance of that?"

It was, of course, a rhetorical question.

"This was done on the orders of King James the Fourth in the year 1505, eighth of December, when he was at Dumbarton Castle. *A new hilt and pommel.*"

His eyes were alight with enthusiasm.

"Meyrick concluded that the sword dated to the end of the fifteenth century. *But he did so on the basis of the features which were added in 1505 – the 'new hilt and pommel'…* Meyrick was wrong!"

Duncan excitedly waved his document in the air.

"I have here, as I've said, a step by step account of the history of the Sword of Wallace at Dumbarton Castle which near as damn it proves that it is authentic!"

His eyes burned into hers. She could have gone through each step in her sleep.

"The sword was brought to Dumbarton Castle by Sir John Menteith, the Sheriff, at the time of Wallace's capture, in 1305."

One finger pointed to the ceiling.

"James the Fourth had it repaired exactly two hundred years later."

A second finger was raised.

"From the Dennistoun Manuscript in the Advocates Library, I was able to confirm that in 1646, in the inventory made by Provost Sempill, the sword appeared, *not with all the other swords in the castle's armoury*, but on its own in the Wallace Tower – thus indicating its unique importance."

A third finger.

"That in the year 1803 it was still in Dumbarton Castle, and shown to the poet William Wordsworth as the Sword of Wallace.

Fourth finger.

"That in 1825 it was sent to the Tower of London and further interfered with, but returned to Dumbarton."

An open hand now.

"That in 1847, *despite the stated opinion of the supposed expert, Meyrick*, it was presented to Her Majesty Queen Victoria and Prince Albert as the Wallace Sword."

The index finger of the left hand was now raised.

"And that, having been repaired yet again, after being abused by some Cockney vandal, and being reverently used on various appropriate occasions, the Sword of William Wallace remains in Dumbarton Castle to this day."

He strode to the window and gazed unseeingly at the architecture of Knoxland Church across the square.

"I had wanted so much to have this paper published in order to defend, to uphold, the authenticity of this great relic, but now I fear to do so, because armed with this information yon Rogers would, no doubt, be able to persuade the War Office that the sword is genuine, and, so doing, he could very well get their permission to take it away from Dumbarton."

Duncan was a picture of frustration and exasperation. He dug deeply into a trouser pocket retrieving the calling-card which the Reverend Doctor Rogers had given him: "in case you ever have reason to contact me", and tossed it disgustedly onto the mantelpiece.

"But Duncan, would it not be better in Stirling... in the Monument? Would that not be more suitable?"

He looked at her appalled.

"You surely can't be serious? The Sword has belonged to Dumbarton for nearly six hundred years. It's one of the Burgh's proudest possessions..."

Her nostrils flared and she raised her chin defiantly.

"Well, for such a proud possession it has hardly been very well taken care of, has it?"

"What do you mean?"

"Oh come now, Duncan. You've said it yourself, often enough. Allowed to rust. Broken. Repaired. Broken again. Repaired again. Abused. Neglected... The castle isn't even secure."

Duncan hadn't expected this. He'd taken her agreement with his own point of view for granted.

"What on earth do you mean – insecure?"

"Half-a-dozen old men, cadging tips from occasional tourists? It isn't even dignified."

"I think, Hannah, you'll find the people of the town will feel differently. Why, when I spoke to the fellows in the Society about it this evening they were indignant..."

She interrupted him.

"The fellows in the Society…" Her contempt was undisguised. "How many of them have ever gone near the Sword? When was the last time any of them even stepped foot in the castle?"

"What has got into you, Hannah? You know how I feel about this. I've been fascinated with the Sword since I was a boy. Why do you want it to be taken away from our town?"

He was not so much angry now as hurt.

"I just think it would be more appropriate, Duncan, for Wallace's Sword to be kept in Wallace's Monument. I think this minister… Rogers… is quite right about that. Also, I repeat – it would surely be better looked after there."

"I see…" He spoke coldly now. "Fortunately your opinion on the matter is neither here nor there."

He turned his back on her, looked out of the window again, and the sight of Knoxland School, at an unfortunate psychological moment, made him think of children… and the lack of them. Speaking in what Hannah thought of as his 'professor's voice', he added,

"So I want to hear no more from you on the subject."

He could have bitten off his tongue. He realised at once what a pompous ass he sounded, but he could not bring himself to admit it, to apologise to her, so Hannah did not have the satisfaction of knowing that he was experiencing the humility of contrition.

That night neither of them slept well. There was no lovemaking, of course, and the oppressive heat, added to their respective mental torments, made rest impossible. Duncan agonised through the small hours over his desire to have his defence of the Sword published versus his fear of the Reverend Doctor Rogers exploiting the knowledge in order to persuade the War Office to remove the relic to Stirling.

Hannah burned with indignation. Why should he, simply because he was a man, always have the power of choice? Why should all decisions of any real importance be made by him? Her opinion being, as he had so laceratingly put it, being "neither here nor there".

From the River Clyde, a ship's horn sounded eerily in the night.

Past and Future

I have reached an age at which I am fascinated and appalled by the passage of time. The apparent acceleration of the years as one gets older, and the horror of realising the transitory nature of all things, have become a daily preoccupation. I am assured that this is common at my time of life, but I fear in my own case it borders on obsession. Why is it that events of my childhood, and twenty or thirty years ago, feel more vivid and real than the experiences of more recent years? I ask myself what is the fundamental difference between memory experience and present experience, and although I have not looked into current scientific speculation on such themes, I have a profound instinct that the past is still happening, somewhere, just around the edge of normal consciousness. For example, the site of the house in which I lived during childhood is now a busy roundabout. The road actually runs through my old bedroom. But a part of me believes that the old red sandstone house is still, in some very real sense there, and of greater substance and permanence than the busy road which makes only a shallow impression on my consciousness. All of which is, of course, the road to madness.

The point of all this is that my recollections of the past dozen or so years – which have undoubtedly been the best years of my life – are less well-stocked and recoverable than previous ones. They are available to me as a kind of mental album of snapshots.

It was 10.50pm on the night of the 31st of December in the year 1999. I had persuaded my aged mother to accompany me to a special midnight service in the old Kirk. It had been the church of her childhood, the place where she had worshipped with her mother, her father and her brother. The church in which she had been married. For one reason and another she hadn't been here for many years and I thought this visit would give her great satisfaction. Great sentimental memories, a sense of spiritual homecoming... that sort of thing.

"These pews are awfy uncomfortable. They're sore on you."

The tired old features screwed into a snooty scowl as she sniffed and looked around her, apparently unimpressed.

"When will they get started ? We came faur too early."

"We had to come early rather than late, Mother. You've no idea when these taxis are going to turn up. I had to be on the safe side."

Around us the pews were filling up and there was a buzz of expectant conversation. I was a little nervous. I had my "turn" to do. Then, just a few minutes before the service was due to start, big John Forrester came over to us.

"Willie, do you think you could give me a hand upstairs? I need someone to hold the ladders for me."

Frankly, I could have done without this, but one has to do the decent thing.

I was wearing my best dark suit for this rather special occasion, and, as John clambered up the ladders into the bell-tower, a certain amount of dislodged minor debris – dust, paint-flakes, mouse droppings – goodness knows what, fell into my hair and onto the shoulders of my suit. Being already nervous and irritable, this little added detail did not soothe. Anyway, that was John in place for his own date with destiny. He was set to ring in the Millennium.

It is very easy to forget all the irrational fears and superstitions which attended that particular event. It was thought, for example, that there would be a global computer crash. That there would be the Second Coming of Christ. That the world would end... and so on. So there was that certain tension.

Once the service got underway Mother settled a bit. I studied the Order of Service sheet with exaggerated concentration until my turn came. I stood and walked with assumed composure to the microphone at the lectern. Deliberately pausing for a long moment for effect I looked slowly around the packed church. Looked down at the Bible...

"The Lord is my shepherd..."

The minister had mentioned to me, very much in the passing, that I'd be the last person to recite the 23rd Psalm in Bonhill

Church during the second millennium. Well... there had been a church here in Bonhill since as far back as 1188 – probably earlier, in fact. It was a thought.

I reckoned I'd carried it off pretty smoothly. Apart maybe from a slight hesitation before "thy rod and thy staff", which no one would have been conscious of but myself. I paced back to my seat head modestly down-turned, heart pounding and palms sweating. It was a little thing, but I knew that my mother would have been proud. After the singing of the next hymn I leant over and quietly asked her how I'd done. In dry tones she answered –

" Aye, you were fine... apart from that bit when you got stuck."

In July of the year 2000, Alex Salmond surprised most political observers by resigning as leader of the Scottish National Party. He felt it was time for the party to have a new image under a new leader. In fact, he was fulfilling an earlier promise, that he would stay in the job for no more than ten years.

Later that year, on the 11th of October, Donald Dewar died tragically, at the age of sixty-three, as the result of a brain haemorrhage.

John Swinney was elected as the new SNP leader, and Henry McLeish became the next Labour First Minister of Scotland.

It was two days before my mother's eightieth birthday. I was standing in a jeweller's shop in Alexandria, in the process of choosing a Citizen ladies watch as a gift for her, when a man came in from the street, asking if there was a television on the premises. Apparently a plane had been deliberately crashed into one of the

World Trade Center towers in New York. A bemused assistant went into the back shop and switched on a portable TV. Sure enough, she returned to confirm that live coverage – not actually visible to customers – was on air. I confess to being mystified, at that stage, as to the man's excitement. Acts of terrorism were tragically common enough not to warrant this sort of response. By the time I returned, by bus, to Balloch and home, however, I was unfortunately in time to watch, in horrified silence, some of the heartbreaking images of the three attacks – one aircraft crashing into each tower, and another on the Pentagon. This terrorist atrocity was of a unique nature and extent, and it was to change global politics forever. With questionable speed, the US authorities announced to a stunned world that the outrage had been perpetrated by the organisation al-Qaeda, led by Osama bin Laden. Within a month the rather curious military response was the invasion and occupation, with British participation, of Afghanistan.

The 21st of September 2002 was a day of blue skies and glorious sunshine. Mary and I were married by Father Dominic Doogan in the little white 15th century chapel of St Mahew's in Cardross, overlooking the Firth of Clyde. The Reverend Ian Miller participated in the service, giving a sense of balance between our Roman Catholic and Presbyterian traditions. (Our wedding invitations bore a symbol in gold of an intertwined thistle and shamrock.) Mary looked like an angel in white, and I wore a kilt of MacGregor tartan – my "entitlement" being a great-great-grandmother of the name. We obviously have many fond memories of that perfect day – being piped out of the chapel by big Colin Lawrie, the reception in the Dumbuck Hotel, all of our guests, friends and family, but one little recollection comes to mind. As we sat in the back of the wedding car at Dalreoch traffic lights, on the way to Dumbarton Castle for the photographs, two motorcyclists, in their leathers and helmets, drew up alongside. Seeing that we were newly-weds, they raised their gauntlets in a thumbs-up gesture of good luck. It was a wee moment which we appreciated enormously and still remember fondly.

We spent the first night of our honeymoon in Ross Priory on Loch Lomondside (a wedding gift from Rev Miller), and although it was not uppermost in my mind at the time, I was told that in the room next to ours Sir Walter Scott had written part of his novel *Rob Roy*.

I had finally married, at the ripe old age of forty-nine. How I managed to get a beautiful young bride, fourteen years my junior, remains a mystery to me. I wish my father had lived to see it.

Perhaps I might be forgiven for mentioning in the passing an artistic fulfilment which brought me particular satisfaction. The Reverend Miller celebrated 25 years of ministry at Bonhill in the year 2002. He was kind enough to afford me the opportunity to mark the occasion by designing a special stained glass window for the church. My painting depicted a Resurrection theme, showing the soldiers and priests looking into the empty tomb. It was actually taken from a scene in the Franco Zeffirelli film *Jesus of Nazareth*, and was not perhaps my most skilful or imaginative work, but it was used as the basis of the circular window and the fact that it was for the church allowed me to imagine myself as the poor man's El Greco.

The 2003 election for the Scottish Parliament resulted in another ruling Labour/Lib-Dem coalition, with Jack McConnell as First Minister, but it wasn't "Old" Labour that Tony Blair and his people buried, it was *Real* Labour. His programme of "modernisation" was a euphemism for a wholehearted embrace of Thatcherism. I had a certain sympathy for Labour activists who spent their lives earnestly striving to defend the working-class against the worst evils of Capitalism, only to find themselves in a centralised party which had been reinvented to suit millionaires and the middle-class. But perhaps history's most damning verdict on Blair will be with regard to his decision, that year, to commit Britain to the war in Iraq. He has been widely criticised for misleading parliament and the country, by using Iraq's alleged "weapons of mass destruction" as the motive for military action. No such weapons of mass destruction were ever discovered and it has even been asked if Blair had knowledge of this before taking the UK into that war.

Sadly, I felt that many Labour politicians and supporters, knowing full well that their party had sold its soul for power, lashed out all the more self-righteously at their opponents. I remember asking Socialist friends how they could bring themselves to vote for Blair and his "New Labour". The first time they said they'd have to give them a chance. The second time they suggested that the party needed another term to slip in some left wing measures. I don't know how they voted the third time.

After the resignation of John Swinney, Alex Salmond, in a move which was even more unexpected than his earlier departure from the job, was re-elected to the leadership of the Scottish National Party in September of 2004. The Westminster General Election of the following year was, however, disappointing for the

Nationalists. They gained only two seats, bringing their total number of MPs to just six.

In the summer of 2006 I retired. Thirty-five years of inglorious underachievement in the Finance Department of the local council and free at last. There was a strange sense of unreality about it all. This escape I had longed for, for so many years, so easily and so unremarkably accomplished. Yes, there had been speeches and gifts, best wishes and all of that, but, essentially, I just left one Friday afternoon (just as I had left on approximately one thousand, seven hundred and fifty Friday afternoons before), except this time I wasn't coming back.

When Mary and I married we had moved into our new home – a modest wee house looking onto the River Leven. A lovely location, with fishermen, ducks and swans in constant attendance.

In a cabinet here beside me, I have a copy of the *Good News Bible For Scotland*. We use it in the manner of the old fashioned "Family Bible". On the first page, written in my own careful hand –

James Edward, Born 9ᵗʰ February 2004.
John Duncan, Born 25ᵗʰ October 2005.
Margaret Catherine, Born 12ᵗʰ January 2010.

All by the Grace of God.

It was a great joy to me that my mother lived long enough to hold her first grandchild – Jamie – in her arms. She passed away when he was just six months old.

So… as these wonderful years passed, I settled into a style of living which was very different from that of the council clerk and pub-haunting bachelor. My priorities obviously changed and although I retained an interest in political developments it was not with the same young man's passion as in decades past. In fact, I confess that at one stage I, like certain other Nationalists, began to suspect that some of the SNP politicians had settled rather too comfortably into the devolved parliament, having lost their zeal for independence. As things turned out, this was shown to be a groundless suspicion and an unworthy thought.

Just after I left the Council, an English friend and colleague, knowing of my keen interest in local history, suggested that I might consider writing articles for one of the local newspapers, explaining the history behind the area's street-names. So it came about that I began to do my *Streetwise* column for the *Lennox Herald*.

My first piece appeared on the 28th of July 2006 and it concerned Garshake Road in Dumbarton, where I had spent my working life. The second article was about Dalmonach Road in Bonhill, and the third gave the story of St Mary's Way in Dumbarton. At this stage a member of the editorial staff pointed out to me that another local historian, Mike Taylor, was already doing articles on Dumbarton, so would I in future confine my stuff to the Vale of Leven? I was more than happy to comply, but I had begun research for a piece on the Burgh's Wallace Street. Of course, that one was never published, but I found some material which fascinated me and convinced me that there was a great story here for the telling. I didn't realise it at the time, but the seed was sown then for what turned out to be this book.

At the Holyrood Election of 2007, the SNP became the largest single party, with 47 seats to Labour's 46, and Alex Salmond was elected Scotland's First Minister. Most Unionist politicians were very much against the Scottish people being given an opportunity to express a choice for independence. Accordingly, when approached with a request to join in a coalition, the Liberal Democrats refused to do so unless the SNP broke its promise to give the Scots an independence referendum. But independence *was* still the fundamental goal of the SNP, so they held to that principle and carried on as a minority government. Throughout the duration of that government, the Unionist parties combined determinedly to prevent an Independence Referendum Bill being implemented.

In recent years my life has, naturally, been revolving around the school gates, the nursery, trailing the streets with bags of shopping, and supervising the homework. I distinguish one day from another in a pleasantly banal way – Mondays: I take out the bins, Tuesdays: I buy the *Reporter* (local paper), Wednesdays: I buy the *Lennox* (other local paper), Thursdays: I get the *Doctor Who* magazine, Fridays: I buy my beer for Saturday night, Saturdays: We go to Clydebank or Braehead shopping centre with our children... In quiet moments, though, I listen to beautiful harp music, played by a lady called Lori Pappajohn, and the haunting melodies transport me to the green glens and tumbling waters of the Scotland of my ancestors.

The Westminster General Election of 2010 brought an end to thirteen years of "New Labour" government under Tony Blair and Gordon Brown. It resulted in a coalition between new Prime Minister David Cameron's Tories, and the Liberal Democrats led by Nick Clegg.

In the following year Tony Blair appeared before the Chilcot Inquiry into the Iraq War, and the RAF bombed Libya.

On the 5th of May, Scottish voters had their say in another Holyrood Election. It was a result that was never supposed to happen –

SNP: 69 seats, Labour: 37 seats, Conservative: 15 seats, Lib-Dem: 5 seats

The people of Scotland had given the Scottish National Party an overall majority to run the Scottish Parliament. I have been able to recover extracts from an email I sent to a friend at the time –

The Dumbarton result is relatively insignificant against the background of national sensation. As I write it cannot be said with any certainty that the SNP will win overall control. Should this happen it will be monumental. Over the years the Unionist Establishment has employed many devices to frustrate Scottish aspirations toward Independence. I think, for example of the "Lib-Lab Pact" and the 40% Rule which killed off the first bid for a devolved parliament, then the "Second Question", the purpose of which was to scare off voters in 1999. When the Scottish Parliament was eventually and grudgingly established a particular form of proportional representation was imposed upon it with the deliberate and cynical purpose of ensuring that no one party (specifically the SNP) could ever hold power. It would be most satisfying to overwhelm such a "precaution"...

Yes - we have come a long way from the days when we were regarded as a bunch of harmless eccentrics. Many good and unsung souls, now

sadly gone, kept the faith and toiled against apparent odds, that such a day - and an even better day - should come. We are indeed privileged...

I salute those hardy souls who, after the bitter disappointment of '79, stuck with the cause, attending meetings, fighting apparently hopeless elections, running local councils, simply keeping the faith, through the long, bleak era of Thatcher, and the uncertain years of Blair, while I, and many like me, slipped silently out of the ranks and drifted off to other interests with more immediate rewards.

No less a figure than Labour's First Minister, Jack McConnell, apparently admitted that the "Mixed Member Proportional Representation" system was chosen for the Scottish Parliament specifically to prevent the Scottish National Party from ever obtaining an overall majority. In May of 2011, then, the SNP, led by Alex Salmond, achieved the impossible... and they did so with a promise to deliver legislation for a referendum on Scottish Independence.

*   *   *

Even after being defeated at Bannockburn, the English refused to acknowledge Scottish independence. In 1320 Pope John XXII had political reasons for favouring King Edward II. Scotland, on the other hand, felt papal displeasure, being blamed for the continuing warfare with England. Accordingly, the excommunication of Robert the Bruce had not been lifted.

With the Pope and the King of England refusing to recognise the Bruce as rightful King of Scots, a Great Council was held in

Newbattle Abbey, near Edinburgh, in March of that year, to discuss a possible communication with His Holiness, the purpose of which was to seek the Pope's help in persuading Edward to accept Robert Bruce as king of an independent Scotland. The outcome of the council was that Bernard de Linton, Abbot of Arbroath and Chancellor of Scotland, penned, on the 6th of April, a letter which has come down in history to us as the *Declaration of Arbroath.*

The completed document bore the seals of eight Scots earls and numerous barons. It represented the views of "the Whole Community and the Realm of Scotland", and was primarily a reassertion of nationhood. It was addressed –

To the most Holy Father and Lord in Christ, the Lord John, by divine providence Supreme Pontiff of the Holy Roman and Universal Church...

–   and began with an account of the perceived origins of the Scottish people, going on to confirm their conversion to Christianity by none other than the brother of St Peter himself – St Andrew. The Scots had resisted all manner of invaders until King Edward I of England had exploited a moment of their weakness, when they were without a monarch. There followed a detailed description of Edward's oppressions and numerous atrocities –

But from these countless evils we have been set free, by the help of Him who though He afflicts yet heals and restores, by our most tireless prince, King and lord, the lord Robert...

— that Robert the Bruce was their rightful king in accordance
    with divine providence and their laws and customs –

*...and the due consent and assent of us all have made him our prince
and king... and by him, come what may, we mean to stand.*

Yet, it added –

*...if he should give up what he has begun, and should seek to make us
or our kingdom subject to the King of England or to the English, we
would strive at once to drive him out as our enemy and a subverter of
his own right and ours, and we would make some other man who was
able to defend us our king; for, as long as but a hundred of us remain
alive, we shall never on any conditions be subjected to English rule. It
is in truth not for glory, nor riches, nor honours that we fight, but for
freedom alone, which no honest man gives up except with his life.*

These words were revolutionary. For the first time in mediaeval
Europe here was a statement of contractual monarchy. It was no
less than an assertion of the sovereignty of the people. The king
belonged to, and could be disposed of by, his subjects. A great
step, indeed, on the long road to democracy. George Buchanan,
Scots poet and intellectual who was tutor to the young King
James VI, promoted the same political theory in the 16th century,
and had his royal pupil heeded him, much subsequent religious
warfare might have been avoided.

The Pope did not immediately respond to the Arbroath letter
quite in the manner hoped for, but the seed had been well sown.
Even though, at peace talks during the following year, the English
persisted in claiming suzerainty over the Scots, three years later, in
1324, the Holy Father did, indeed, give full recognition to Robert

I as the king of an independent Scotland.

*   *   *

It was a thoroughly miserable day, with a blizzard of driving sleet tormenting them all the way from the railway station to Stirling's town hall. Not that they could have expected anything else in the middle of November. The building had been adorned, especially for the occasion, with Saltires of St Andrew, Lions Rampant and, inevitably (however inappropriately) – Union Flags.

It was just past noon and the couple of hundred invited guests had taken their places in the main hall. Duncan and Hannah, it has to be said, were not invited guests in the manner of "those and such as those". Duncan was there in his professional capacity as the editor of his Glasgow newspaper, and Hannah, who had absolutely insisted on coming, accompanied him as his "secretary". They sat discreetly at the back of the hall.

Earlier that day – just over an hour earlier, to be precise, the Reverend Doctor Charles Rogers had rolled up to Stirling Castle in a rather impressive carriage. There he had been received with great courtesy by none other than Colonel Nightingale, Commander of the Garrison. After suitable civilities had been exchanged, the Colonel had led the Reverend gentleman, accompanied by some carefully chosen associates, to the Mess Room. At eleven-thirty, with the Sword of William Wallace lying splendidly on red velvet on a central table, Colonel Nightingale, surrounded by a company of officers and important civilian administrators, addressed his principal guest –

"Doctor Rogers, I am deputed by Major-General Lyttleton-

Annesley, commanding the forces in North Britain, to carry out the instructions of the Secretary of State for War, and His Royal Highness Commander-in-Chief, in presenting to you the sword of Sir William Wallace, the great hero, and I am proud of the honour of doing so, especially in Stirling Castle, as from its walls we look down upon the field of one of the grandest exploits of that memorable patriot..."

Rogers, now sixty-three, grey and portly, beamed at all around him and took the floor. He reminded those present that he had, some thirty-three years previously, been Chaplain to this very garrison.

"You have handed me the sword of Wallace, and so conferred upon me one of the greatest honours which any Scotsman has received since the hordes of Surrey fled from Stirling Bridge, or the Bruce was acknowledged victor at Bannockburn..."

He went on to pay tribute to some of those present, including Mr Hugh Robert Wallace of Busbie and Cloncaird who had, it transpired, been recently recognised by the Lyon King of Arms as the head of the House of Wallace, and to whom he, Rogers, would now entrust the revered relic.

The Sword had then been taken by a military escort to Stirling's burgh hall.

As Duncan sat peering over the heads of those seated in front of him, he reflected on his own complex feelings regarding these proceedings. There were, he recognised, resentment, indignation, indeed, he could go so far as to say, anger. These emotions because his cherished Sword had, as things had turned out, been taken from Dumbarton Rock, where he had been paying homage to it from earliest childhood. On the other hand, there was an undeniable satisfaction, yes, pride, that the weapon was being unequivocally and officially accepted as absolutely authentic. This, though, inevitably led on to an agony of curiosity, How had this been accomplished? How had the authorities of the War Office been persuaded to change their minds about the status of the relic? In 1825 they had pronounced it a fake. In 1872 they had repeated the verdict and gone further, by prohibiting any claim that it was the Patriot's own weapon.

There was something else which aroused his curiosity. Something about Hannah's manner and bearing. He could well understand a certain smugness, an unspoken air of triumph. This was, after all, very much her preferred outcome. They'd had many an argument about it over these past few months. Was that why she'd been so determined to come with him to the ceremony? Yes, yes, yes… but there was something more. He sensed it. Some more mysterious and profound satisfaction behind the strange expression on her face. Her face… She had never looked more beautiful. All the way from Dumbarton to Stirling on the train he'd been struck by just how lovely she looked. Those so clear blue eyes. That henna-red hair, tumbling over her fur-collared shoulders. That creamy complexion and those wonderful ruby lips… There was something…

His thoughts were, almost mercifully, interrupted by the sound of music. A choir was singing *Scots, Wha Hae,* and as they did so Duncan scribbled the names of the platform party into his journalist's notebook. (It would surely look more convincing if Hannah were doing this, instead of sitting there like a duchess) –

Provost Yellowlees, Rev Dr Rogers (Duncan observed that the minister looked even more objectionable than he'd remembered), Hugh Robert Wallace of Cloncaird Castle, Sir James Maitland, Colonel Nightingale, Rev J.P. Lang, several Stirling bailies, the Dean of Guild, Mercer, William Christie, Master of Cowane's Hospital...

The choir came to the end of their stirring rendering, and Provost Yellowlees, garbed in the full panoply of his office, got to his feet. He remarked on the inclement weather, passed on apologies for absence – including those of the Duke of Montrose – and, without further ado, as it were, introduced in the most fulsome terms the Reverend Doctor. It was his day of glory. Perhaps he was entitled to be at his most self-satisfied and vain. Only one man in the hall grudged him his triumph. That man was, of course, Duncan Robertson.

The Reverend Doctor looked around the room slowly, lingeringly, almost teasingly, savouring his moment, before he began to speak.

"This swoard is associated with a glorious history... "

He punctuated his romantic flights of patriotic zeal with almost incongruous technicalities –

"Consequent on two weldings the weapon has been reduced from its original length, but it was originally a noble blade..."

He told his listeners of how, after Wallace's betrayal and capture, the hero's weapon had been presented to the treacherous Menteith and taken to Dumbarton Castle.

"At Dumbarton the sword has for six long centuries remained as a protest against treachery and injustice, and now, from the hands of the commander at Dumbarton, it is to become a trophy in our Patriot's monument..."

Duncan glanced around to see Hannah's eyes shining with a fascination which appeared to be heightened by suspense. For, little though Duncan knew it, Rogers was coming to the point.

How, then, had the learned minister, historian and so prolific author, managed to gain the previously withheld permission of the War Office for this transfer from the rock of Dumbarton to that of the Abbey Craig? How had he managed to rehabilitate, so to speak, the Wallace Sword in the eyes of British officialdom? There were, as it happened, two main factors involved. Firstly, the political climate of 1888 was subtly different from that of 1872. At the earlier date manifestations of Scottish national feeling had been regarded in London with suspicion and hostility. By the 1880s, however, Prime Minister Gladstone had come around to being sympathetic to the introduction of some measure of Home Rule, and the office of Secretary of State for Scotland (and the Scottish Office) had been introduced in 1885. Even *the Times*, which had earlier referred to Wallace as "merest myth", eventually came around to remarking on the "deep and lasting impression" Wallace had made.

Even given this change of climate, however, in order to acquiesce to any request relating to the Wallace Sword, the War Office had needed something to get off the hook of its previous dogmatic and repeated assertion of the sword's fraudulence. That something, miraculously, as it seemed to Charles Rogers, had appeared quite out of the blue.

In the summer of '88, when he was working on two memorials – one on the Scottish family Glen, and the other on the Gourlays – he had received an anonymous letter. It consisted of several pages of script, neatly written in what, he was certain, was a lady's hand. To his astonishment he discovered that the missive contained a step by step account of the history of the Wallace Sword from the moment of its arrival at Dumbarton Castle in 1305 up to the present date. With all of this he had been intimately familiar… apart from one crucial detail. The writer had emphasized in bold capitals the episode where King James IV of Scots had given instruction for the sword to be repaired, and the adding to the weapon, in the year 1505, of a new hilt and pommel. Further highlighted was the implication that it had been by these 16th century features that Sir Samuel Meyrick *had misdated the weapon* when he had examined it in the Tower of London in 1825.

Rogers read and reread the letter several times checking the logic of the argument. He could not fault it. Now that he knew where to look, it was not long before he managed to check the provenance – the Royal Exchequer Records – of the 1505 reference. Gleefully armed with this new information he had wasted no time in writing to the War Office with a fresh request for the transfer of the sword. He was, as it transpired, pushing at an open door. The officials concerned were given the approval of the highest authorities and Rogers's request had been swiftly granted.

For many a long day the one-time Chaplain of Stirling Castle mused in vain over who might have sent him this treasure. The only clue he had was a Dumbarton postmark.

"As governor of Dumbarton, Sir John Menteith received this sword in August 1305, and two hundred years thereafter, namely, on the 8th December 1505, the accounts of the Lord High Treasurer inform us that, at the command of James IV, the sum of twenty-six shillings, equal to about thirty pounds of our present money, was paid to an armourer for... the binding of Wallas sword with cords of silk and providing it with ane new hilt and plomet..."

Duncan's jaw dropped. His head burled around to see the reaction of Hannah. Her features gave nothing away. How had Rogers found out? Duncan had thought this to be his own secret. Well... this explained a lot. He felt a sinking in his stomach. A sourness in his mouth. As Rogers went on, triumphantly to take full personal credit for this discovery and his use of it to gain the approval of the military powers for the removal of the weapon from Dumbarton, Duncan heard little of it. His mind was in a whirl of anger, frustration and sheer disbelief.

"...But now that we have got possession of the sword, we shall be careful that the weapon with which the hero was wont to 'mak great rowme' about him, will be mounted in the fashion in which he nobly grasped it, and we shall retain it as no unimportant addition to the national regalia."
The minister spoke, perhaps somewhat tongue-in-cheek, about the possible incongruity of such a weapon of war being in the hands of a man of the cloth, and went on –

"I now transfer it from my personal keeping, and place it in the hands of Mr Wallace, to whom it had belonged by inheritance had his illustrious progenitor not been plundered of it while he slept; and I ask him to hand the great blade to the Provost of Stirling, as Chairman of the Custodiers of the National Wallace Monument…"

Duncan Robertson had been right about one thing – When the people of Dumbarton found out about the removal "by stealth"of the sword from Dumbarton Rock there had been civic indignation. Letters to the local papers – poetry, even – impassioned words at meetings of the burgh's council, official attempts at recovery, of course to no avail… It was even lamented that in future, when Clyde passenger steamers were passing the Rock their bands would no longer play *Scots' Wha Hae* in salutation!

Hannah had been right about one thing, too – the Sword of William Wallace was far better in the National Monument overlooking the field of his greatest triumph, than rusting on the rock so associated with his betrayal and capture. But Duncan would never come see it that way.

They had walked in a brittle silence, heads bowed and collars held around their faces, from the railway station after the long, cold homeward journey. Cold in more ways than one. Here, to the west, the weather was less inclement. The temperature was that of a winter's evening, granted, but it was dry. The sky was cloudless and stars were visible in the heavens. Hannah had intended to wait until they were home, comfortable, warm and able to relax at last in their little villa, but she could contain herself no longer. She had to tell him. As they walked over a deserted Knoxland Square, she spoke –

"Duncan, there is something I have to tell you…"

There was, in the tone of her voice, something which arrested Duncan's attention. Her eyes had that special brightness again. She smiled gloriously.

"I'm going to have a baby."

Postscript

In the mornings I walk along the banks of the Leven. Just a few hundred yards to the north is Linnbrane, where the monks from Paisley Abbey cast their nets in the days of Wallace. Downstream, some three miles or so, just beyond Renton, is the site of the manor house where Robert the Bruce died in 1329. Almost directly across the river from my home stood the old Bonhill Kirk, the bell of which was rung in the year 1715 to warn Dumbarton Castle that Jacobite MacGregors, led by Rob Roy's nephew, Gregor of Glengyle, were raiding the parish.

From the top of one of the *Braes o' Bunnill*, I look northwards along the length of the valley. In the distance, beyond the *Rainbow Bridge*, and set off against the gold-green backcloth of *Ledrishmore*, I can see the elegant red sandstone spire of Jamestown Church. It speaks to me with a silent eloquence of my roots.

As I write, we are a matter of months away from the designated date of the referendum on Scottish Independence. It has seemed to me that such debate as there has been, over these past many months, between politicians of both sides, and newspapers, exclusively on the Unionist side, has centred almost entirely on the economic dimension – money. The future of Scotland is being balanced on the scales of "better off" and "worse off". Will independence make Scots richer or poorer? Frankly, I find this disappointing, even disgusting. I fully appreciate that money is a great consideration in Life, but where a nation's independence is concerned there are surely deeper dimensions. I wonder if the people of Ireland, or of Canada, were persuaded that they would be a few Euros or Dollars "better off" if they returned to London rule, they would give up their national independence for it? It is a rhetorical question.

I felt very strongly that there was a need for the argument for independence "from the heart" to be heard. In a sense, this book has been my way of expressing that case.

The politicians of the Scottish National Party have for many years scrupulously avoided making any reference to Scotland's historical relationship with England. It seems that any "harking back" would be considered "bad form". Not politic. As an individual, however, I feel no inhibition whatsoever about bringing to the light of day uncomfortable truths about Scotland's historical experiences with our English partners in the Union. I am no longer a member of the Scottish National Party. I allowed my membership to lapse some time ago. I speak for no political party or any organisation. The views I express in this book are entirely personal, but I would be very much surprised if they are not shared by many Scots. I know that there are positive reasons for those in the Yes Campaign to steer clear of historical controversy. It's all about the future, after all. But perhaps I can be forgiven for suggesting that any nation is defined, to a great extent, by its past, and by the nature of its relationships with other nations.

I may have missed it, but I have not heard a single Unionist politician or columnist asking these questions –

"In what way has the Union let you down? "What are your grievances?"

"Can we sit down together and mend the Union?"

Instead, almost exclusively, the anti-independence case is based on scaremongering. On a daily basis Unionist politicians and newspapers issue dire warnings about the terrible things which will befall us Scots if we are irresponsible (and ungrateful) enough to opt for independence. Those who oppose Scottish independence suggest that the Union is one of mutual respect between equal partners. Historically, this has never been the case – it is important to say so.

The Union was originally brought about by bribery and intimidation and it has had little to do with equality ever since. How could fewer than sixty Scots MPs be the equal of over five hundred English MPs ? Put simply - the larger dominates the smaller and Scotland is regarded as little more than a colony. Honestly stated, the argument of those who oppose Scottish independence is that we Scots are actually dependent on the English. Dependent on English money. Dependent on English influence. Dependent on English protection. So, from that point of view, the real "benefit" of union is dependency.

Dozens of states, large and small, gained independence from London rule during the twentieth century. To my knowledge not one has come back humbly seeking to be re-admitted to British governance. The essential factor that Unionists leave out of their reckoning is *national self-respect*. The great majority of nations prefer the dignity of self-determination.

*   *   *

William Wallace and Edward I must be judged (if we have any right to judge them at all) by the standards of their time. They were terrible standards, but we would deceive ourselves greatly if we thought that the warfare of our own age is any less diabolical. In researching and attempting to relate the story of Wallace I did not set out to romanticise him or glorify his deeds in any way. Yes – evil should be resisted and sometimes fire must be fought with fire, but as I schooled my imagination to dwell on the barbarities of man's inhumanity to man, I found the concept of political violence all the more abhorrent.

I am relieved – proud, indeed – to be able to say that, certainly within my own lifetime, the slow and dignified political progress in the direction of Scottish independence has, apart from relatively minor and isolated acts perpetrated by misguided fringe elements, been non-violent and democratic. Authentic democracy is precious beyond price. It is my heartfelt prayer that, whatever the outcome of the coming referendum, no government, no organisation, official or unofficial, and no individual, will find in it any excuse whatsoever to shed a single drop of blood.

The English are a great, indeed inspirational, people who have contributed incalculably to the world, not least through the British Empire. But the time came for a new and better relationship between the British and their former colonies. It has, without doubt, been the historical experience of their neighbours that the English have regarded themselves more as bosses than as partners. So, it might well be time for a new and better relationship between Scotland and England.

*   *   *

I always assumed that as I got older I would become more assured and confident in my opinions and attitudes, at least regarding the important things in Life. In fact, the opposite appears to be the case. In matters of faith and politics I am daily tormented by doubts. I ask myself if it is perhaps unchristian of me to support Scottish independence – to seek the end of a relationship. The answer I find is that it is perfectly possible to love one's neighbour, without letting that neighbour retain control of one's affairs. Further, I am persuaded that an independent Scotland will be able to do more good in the world than a Scotland which continues to relate to the community of nations through a London parliament.

Even so, it may be that, when confronted with my ballot paper on Referendum Day, I might have a failure of nerve. With an uncertain hand I may opt for the "devil" we have known. I am sure many will. (No, I could not live with the shame of it.) But whatever the outcome, it will be the first time in history that the Scottish people have been able to choose the nature of their relationship with the English… and that must surely be a good thing.

Notes

Much of the information which has been passed down to us about William Wallace comes from a work entitled –

"The Acts and Deeds of the Most Famous and Valiant Champion Sir William Wallace Knight of Ellerslie."

This book was written by Henry the Minstrel – otherwise known as "Blind Harry". Most modern historians believe that it was composed around 1470, but Henry himself claimed that his material came from a Latin account which had been written by John Blair, the Benedictine monk who was a close companion of Wallace. There seems to be no compelling reason to doubt this. It may also be that Henry drew on a considerable body of transmitted oral tradition which should not be automatically regarded as fictional simply because it was spoken rather than written.

*   *   *

Today's experts do not believe that the sword in the National Wallace Monument dates, *in its present form*, as far back as the

13th century. However, as we have seen, the weapon has been seriously abused over the centuries and the blade is now composed of three different parts which have been welded together. Qualified opinion concedes that one section of the blade might well date to the time of William Wallace.